Sue Howard, BA, MA, Assoc IPD, was born in London, raised in Essex, and later travelled widely. She lived, worked and studied in the USA for four years where she gained a degree in theology. Her diverse experience of business includes professional roles in training, career counselling, communications and consultancy. Most recently she was the Business Development Manager in the Management Development Unit at Cranfield School of Management in the UK, where she met with clients to determine the implementation path for organizational change strategies. She completed a Master's degree in Management Learning with Lancaster University in 2000 specializing in her dissertation on 'Spirituality and its links to learning in the workplace'. Subsequently Sue has become involved in a variety of related roles including becoming a member of the board of trustees for two national charities and a member of the management committee of MODEM. She has also published a number of articles. She currently lives in Hertfordshire with her husband and two children, and conducts her freelance interests from home.

David Welbourn, BD (Hons), AKC, DMS, an ordained minister, has devoted nearly all his ministry to the work of Industrial Mission and is currently chaplain to QinetiQ, a UK science and technology organization, and to the UK government's defence research laboratory, Dstl. Author of two published books, he has written numerous articles on 'faith and work' and served as editor of two journals devoted to the subject, the *ICF* (Industrial Christian Fellowship) *Quarterly* and the *Faith in Business Quarterly*. Since 2000 he has researched the Spirit at Work phenomenon, beginning with a sabbatical study in California, and has also been involved in the practical application of spirituality within organizations. Married with two children, David and his wife Jenny currently live in Guildford, Surrey.

In memory of Sue's father Bob White, who worked long and hard,
and helped his family see both the good and bad in organizations;
and of David's parents, Eric and Phyllis.
And with fondest love to our spouses Tony and Jenny.
But not least, we dedicate this book to our respective children,
to Tim and Amy as you grow up and into the future,
and to Simon, Rachel and her husband Andrew
at the early stages of your working lives.
May you, along with all our readers,
increasingly experience inspiration, soul-satisfaction,
and rich rewards in your life and work.

And we remember that:
'God . . . has made everything beautiful in its time.
He has also set eternity in the hearts of men; . . . there is nothing better for
men than to be happy and do good while they live. That everyone may eat
and drink, and find satisfaction in all his toil – this is the gift of God.'
(Ecclesiastes 3.10–13, NIV)

The
Spirit at Work
Phenomenon

Sue Howard

and

David Welbourn

First published in Great Britain in 2004
Azure
1 Marylebone Road
London
NW1 4DU

British Library Cataloguing-in-Publication Data
A catalogue record for this book is available from the British Library
ISBN 1-902694-29-5

1 3 5 7 9 10 8 6 4 2

Designed and typeset by Kenneth Burnley, Wirral, Cheshire
Printed by MPG Books Ltd, Bodmin, Cornwall

Contents

Appendices

Acknowledgements

So many people have contributed to the formulation of ideas for a book such as this, and the gestation process goes back a long way – to well before we had even thought of writing a book together. We wish here to show our appreciation for those who have been directly involved, or who have given us some particular encouragement along the way. But we are also grateful to those many others who have shaped our thoughts and whom, sadly, space prohibits us from mentioning.

Sue would particularly like to thank all those involved in the Master's degree in Management Learning (MAML) at Lancaster University. The students and tutors who took part in MAML 17 (you know who you are!) created a once-in-a-lifetime experience, and the inspiration found during that time freed Sue to become true to her own learning path in life. Thanks too to Angela and Nigel Kiemander for their positive encouragement.

David is grateful to the American friends he made during his sabbatical in 2000, whose dedication to the 'spirit at work movement' has been such an inspiration – most of them are referred to in these pages – and especially to Pat Sullivan both for her (and her husband John's) personal hospitality and for arranging introductions to many key people.

Both of us want to thank Alan and Di Harpham for being such great examples in living their spiritual values authentically. Thanks to Alan especially for his ongoing enthusiasm towards our creative attempts, and energy in helping promote this volume. Also thanks to Toby Thompson and Karen Szulakowska who brainstormed ideas with us, and who have helped to raise the profile of Spirit at Work; and to Pauline Weight at Cranfield School of Management, who sees the need for this subject within the MBA curriculum and who gave us her support when we needed it. David is grateful to QinetiQ both for the general support they give his chaplaincy work and also for encouraging the introduction of Spirituality at Work Conversation Groups within the organization.

Since our decision to embark on the book many others have encouraged us, especially the members of the wonderful Spirituality in the Workplace network at Douai Abbey: Georgeanne Lament, with her strong guidance and words of wisdom at the early stages; Michael Joseph, for the jewels of insight contained in his PhD thesis, and for giving us his permission to extract ideas from his labour of love; Dermot Tredget for his faithful commitment to living in line with his deepest values and principles and for sharing his path with others; and Gillian, our 'practitioner' friend, who has strengthened our conviction that spiritual values in business can make a huge difference to business success. Thank you to everyone who has read parts, or the whole, of our script and offered us both praise and suggestions for improvement. Thanks to Azure, and especially Alison Barr, for not only agreeing to publish us, but for approving the extensively additional word count!

We would also like to acknowledge the support and enthusiasm for our work that we have received from MODEM, and linked to this, the support of the wider Association of Spirit at Work community.

And we wish to thank the following publishers for their permission to quote copyright material: Macmillan and HarperCollins, for the extracts from Stephen Mitchell's translation of the *Tao Te Ching*; HarperCollins (again) and the Friends of Creation Spirituality, for passages quoted from Matthew Fox's *The Re-invention of Work*; The University of Scranton Press for substantial citations from Jerry Biberman's and Michael Whitty's symposium *Work and Spirit*; Sheed and Ward for extracts from Pat Sullivan's *Work with Meaning, Work with Joy*; and, finally, Random House Inc. for the use of verses from Rainer Maria Rilke's poem 'Live the Questions'. If we have made any errors or omissions in our efforts to trace the owners of copyright material we apologize and would ask those concerned to contact the publishers, who will ensure that full acknowledgement is made at the first opportunity.

Most of all, thanks to our families – to Tony, who has given Sue the time and space to focus in the midst of hectic family life and helped in so many ways; to Tim and Amy – you tried hard and very nearly succeeded in leaving Mummy alone in the study! And thanks to Sue's sister (and 'number one fan' as Sue likes to think of her), Christine White; as well as Sue's mum, Alma White, for looking after her so well during the most intensive moments of the writing schedule. And to David's wife Jenny for her tolerance and constant support for David both in life generally and during those family-unfriendly periods of single-mindedness, especially in the advanced stage of authorship.

PART ONE

WHY SPIRIT AT WORK NOW?

Introduction

> An invasion of armies can be resisted, but not an idea whose time has come.
>
> Victor Hugo[1]

The context

Businesses have become the most powerful and influential institutions on earth in recent years. Their impact exceeds that of nation states and more than rivals that of any government institution. In the interests of a healthy and sustainable world order it is vital that organizations understand and honour their social and planetary responsibilities. But how are they performing? Scandals such as those starkly demonstrated by Enron, WorldCom and others raise serious questions about the whole basis of business. It is clear that there are deficiencies in the 'bottom line rules all' approach. Are we approaching a crisis-point in the world of work and business? It is clearly time for a rethink.

In addition, following on from September 11th and the global war on terror, individuals are asking deeper questions about meaning and purpose in their lives, including their working lives. People increasingly want more than simply being used to maximize profits for shareholders. They long for something authentic and worthwhile. This is a time of searching for a larger, nobler vision to sustain our efforts and engage our souls.

It isn't surprising that there are calls for spirituality to have a greater place in our lives, our work and our world. Debates about how to make work more spiritually rewarding are growing in momentum. This book offers an overview of these debates, a 'roadmap' to the territory, a foundational guide to show how spirituality can make a difference to organizations, to the individuals who work in them and to the future of the world economic order.

We review why and how the Spirit at Work (SaW)[2] phenomenon – or movement, as it has come to be known – has arisen, provide an outline of the key subjects being discussed under the SaW banner, and introduce readers to some of the best representative literature, websites, networks, support structures and other resources. We also give examples of organizations seeking to reflect spiritual principles in the way they operate.

This book is for ...

. . . those who are daunted by the sheer number of books on spirituality and wonder where to start in order to get to grips with the subject. It is for people who want to 'dip their toe in the water' and find out what spirituality is all about, but also for those who are already 'into' spirituality and who want to keep abreast of what's going on.

More specifically this book is for:

- Busy executives who want to grasp the essentials of spirituality, and why and how it can inspire change and success in their businesses.
- Anyone who works for an organization who is interested in bridging the gap between what they do in their paid employment and who they really are, or aspire to be; people who wish for more from their working lives and wonder how to achieve it.
- People who are interested in developing spirituality in the workplace but are unsure about what this involves and how to go about it in an appropriate way.
- Individuals looking for a resource guide which maps the territory of the growing phenomenon of spirituality in the workplace.
- Managers, consultants and academics who want to understand what SaW is all about and why it is of value to organizations.
- Management and organizational development specialists who want to know how to introduce and implement a move towards spirituality in their workplace.
- Those who are 'secretly spiritual' and wonder how to 'come out of the closet' with what's really important to them.

It is a book to support people who want to make a difference with their life's work.

Why this particular book?

It was during a meeting at Cranfield University as fellow members of a working party preparing an MBA elective on Spirituality and Organizational Transformation that we decided this book needed to be written. In the various sessions we have run for MBA students and others at Cranfield, we have connected people together around the question of 'How to create the organizations we want to be part of' and around deeper questions such as 'What is our purpose?' We have discovered that spiritual questions are just *so* relevant to business. Indeed, we believe that for anyone who has the ambition to lead organizations in the twenty-first century there is nothing more important than to consider the guidance that spirituality offers at the individual, team, group, organizational and societal levels.

We have been greatly encouraged by the interest and enthusiasm for discussions about spirituality amongst the students at Cranfield. One student described one of our evening speaker events as 'the best thing I've done at Cranfield'; another said, 'This is the leading edge of leadership and we need more of it'. From this we deduce that there are some people with a real desire to reflect about their own spirituality and a deep need to explore what impact this might have on their working lives.

Significantly, it is our business roles which are now provoking the timeless spiritual questions that remain as poignant and relevant to us today as they have been to people throughout all ages. We are frequently faced with choices that require us to have some understanding of our identity – Who are we? What do we stand for? How do we determine meaning and purpose for ourselves? Are our lives making a difference? Are we influencing the world for good or bad? And what do we do with such questions? Do we attempt to answer them, and can they be addressed through our working lives? How can we, in the words of Mahatma Gandhi, 'be the change we want to see in the world'? Such questions are the lifeblood of the individual sense-making process, and answering them in the context of our work holds the promise of huge benefits to society as well as organizational life. This book seeks to show how these questions are being explored in debates about SaW.

Given the explosion of literature, the proliferation of websites and the sheer number of conferences, networks and seminars devoted to this subject, how do those interested in these questions embark on the SaW journey? How do they decide which books are significant, which resources, contacts and supporting networks to follow up? Whilst there are already a huge number of books on SaW, this is the first one to draw together in a single volume all the central aspects of workplace spirituality. It is also significant in being UK based, whereas the majority of books thus far are American in origin.

Our intention is to produce a helpful and easy access point, by providing a little knowledge of all the main parts, so that readers can gain a 'helicopter' view of the whole subject area, while at the same time offering guidance on what to read, where to go, whom to contact and so on if one wants to pursue a particular area in greater depth. We believe this book provides a balanced overview of the many links spirituality makes in our personal and business life. Such an overview is, we feel, much needed.

Stories

The SaW story is a story of many parts. It is made up of the personal stories of all the individuals who have identified with the ideals of the SaW movement. There are many people in the UK and throughout the world who, having uncovered their own sense of spirituality, are working explicitly with spirituality in organizations. We share some of their stories, having specially selected those which illuminate moments, or journeys, of self-discovery or organizational breakthrough. We hope that at least some of these may connect with our readers' own stories and by so doing help them to identify and articulate their own truths, and encourage them to find their own pathways towards authenticity.

In particular, we feature the continuing story of Gillian, Organization Development Manager in a large, privately owned global organization.

Gillian epitomizes just the sort of person we are writing this book for. In April 2001 David was contacted by Gillian, who had been asked to spend five hours per month researching spirituality on behalf of her company. They were keen to discover the advantages to their organization of taking SaW seriously. David showed Gillian twenty or so books from his library whereupon she exclaimed, aghast, 'How can I possibly get to grips with all that?' She was of course referring to a mere fraction of the material available.

In order to help the 'Gillians' of this world get started we track Gillian's progress as she seeks both to develop her personal spirituality and, in her organizational role, to encourage her globally branded business to operate in accordance with spiritual principles. Her journey clearly demonstrates the questions that living congruently creates, and provides encouragement to those who might wish to embark on a similar journey. It offers insights into the processes involved, and the ultimate benefit to the business of encouraging spirituality within its culture. We shall be hearing from Gillian a few pages on.

More about ourselves

To begin the process of telling stories we wish to offer you a glimpse into our own journeys:

Sue's story

Prompted by questions about myself and my place in the world, alongside larger questions about why the world is the way that it is, I have become progressively braver in my journey towards living my own life in harmony with core spiritual truths that I hold dear. I am becoming more authentic and on my way I have discovered that many more people than I would have dared imagine hold deep yearnings for their spiritual lives to be central to their daily walk in this world. These yearnings are so often hidden, buried because we are fearful of others' opinions. But they are a powerful driving force in us, and as such influence society and organizations implicitly. I have wondered many times why we are so reluctant to talk about spiritual things more openly. However, more recently it is clear that these yearnings are 'coming out of the closet' as more and more people are wanting to explore the nature of their spirituality and its relationship to work explicitly.

As Business Development Manager in the Management Development Unit at Cranfield School of Management, I have met development professionals and senior figures in a wide range of organizations. I have been privy to much 'behind the scenes' information about organizational life during wave after wave of change initiatives and development programmes. In meetings I have explored different organizational development issues in varying degrees of depth. And I have felt the anxieties and emotions of working with change consultants during times of uncertainty. The need to develop leaders who can be confident and inspire others runs close to the top of the pile of change agents' wish list. Just what are the ingredients that create a good leader? This was a question that we have often sought to address at Cranfield.

Exploring the multitude of approaches to management development in order to respond to clients' needs appropriately expanded my comprehension of the differing perspectives that abound in this field and simultaneously raised a lot of questions for me. During this time I embarked upon a Master's degree in Management Learning with Lancaster University in the hope that I would be able to unravel some of the complexity of the terrain of organizational and management learning.

I found this whole experience deeply stimulating and challenging. The joy of learning with others and from others about learning itself was both stretching and delightful. But juggling 'me' as a learner, business development manager, organizational employee, wife and mother created even more questions about identity and role. Lots of the thoughts I have had about learning during this time will resurface and be developed further in this book. Suffice it to say, my post-graduate degree has left me with the belief that learning is one of the most fundamentally important qualities of being human.

Exploring the territory of learning through papers on learning itself, development, management development, and dialogue gave me confidence to make the subject of my dissertation 'Spirituality and its Links to Learning in the Workplace'.[3] Here for the first time I was able to bring together things of concern to the 'real me', my spiritual life and the questions it raised, and connect this part of me to the world of work. One of the key findings from my research and extensive reading was that there is very often a gap between who we are, our 'being', and what we do, our 'doing'. Spirituality seeks to bridge this gap and that is why it is so challenging and so important for us all.

Exploring the territory of spirituality has put me into contact with many who have arrived at the conclusion that our spirituality is important to our work. These include groups such as MODEM; the Ridley Hall Foundation (who publish *Faith in Business Quarterly*); the Spirituality in the Workplace network; management education institutions such as Roffey Park, Surrey University, Bath University and of course Cranfield and Lancaster University contacts; a range of web resources; and finally, numerous individuals, many organizational consultants and development practitioners – all of whom have been inspiring and supportive. (See Chapter 15 for details.)

An unexpected outcome of the research I undertook with a group of management development specialists was that some expressed a wish to continue to meet in order to create further opportunities to develop and explore ideas with managers and academics. We have met regularly since I finished my dissertation (September 2000) and so far our joint involvement has led to the publication of a number of articles, the design of a course for MBA students, a series of evening speakers at Cranfield, lectures at Imperial College London, Roffey Park Institute in Sussex and Nottingham University, workshops, conference papers and of course this book. We have also become involved in a broader international network of business leaders interested in this field and have come to see that the SaW movement is genuinely a global phenomenon.

David's story

Like Sue I have often thought of my journey as a spiritual pilgrimage. The part of it that relates to this book began more than 30 years ago when I made the decision to abandon the normal career path of an Anglican clergyman, ministry within the parish, and join the small band of rebels called industrial chaplains. We have had a somewhat uneasy relationship with our sponsoring churches and have often felt marginalized. While the business world has welcomed us and we have made many friends, we have not got as far as we would wish in fulfilling our main role – that of articulating the relevance of spiritual values for business life. The main problem has been dearth of common conceptual ground.

But things are beginning to change. Our task is considerably easier now that spirituality is on business's own agenda: it is now business books, not just books on ethics or theology, which are highlighting and promoting all the values and many of the concepts we are committed to. Nor is this interest confined to academia; it is also to be found in the workaday world, in the companies we visit. So SaW is proving something of a godsend.

My direct involvement in SaW dates from the latter part of 1999. Like most industrial chaplains I have had a strong interest in the Mission, Vision and Value statements of business organizations, and in how they are lived out. So I was bound to turn my attention to SaW. At that time, however, I knew very little about it and decided to devote some forthcoming sabbatical leave to investigating it further.

By Spring 2000 I was preparing in earnest for the sabbatical which would be taken the following autumn. By then I had read a few books on SaW and written a couple of articles on the subject in *Faith in Business Quarterly* (FiBQ), a British faith-and-work journal of which I was then a co-editor. In the summer of that year I was shown by Alan Harpham, a fellow-member of MODEM, a draft of Sue's dissertation 'Spirituality and its Links to Learning in the Workplace' and noted with surprise that she quoted extensively from one of my FiBQ articles. I got in touch with Sue to announce that I was just about to go to California on sabbatical and would, on the strength of our shared interest, send her a copy of my sabbatical report.[4] This led to Sue subsequently inviting me to join the working party preparing the Cranfield.

Another millennium-year initiative was to co-found, with Father Dermot Tredget of Douai Abbey, the Spirituality in the Workplace Network, starting with those whom we both knew were interested or involved with SaW and operating in the South East of England.

During 2001 I produced a five-page summary of my 67-page sabbatical report as a further article for FiBQ and in June that year participated in the Ridley Hall Foundation's Conference on Spirituality in the Workplace in Cambridge. My research for a lecture I gave at this conference marked a further significant development in my study of SaW.

At the end of my sabbatical I returned to the companies I serve as chaplain, keen to share with managers and staff my sabbatical experiences, but wondering what – if anything – they would make of the SaW concept. One company's Christian Fellowship group gave me an opportunity to 'test the waters' by setting up an open meeting and inviting me to speak. I came along expecting to address a small group of six or eight people, but to my surprise and delight found that over 30 had turned up! During subsequent months I discovered that many senior people in the organization were interested in SaW. I eventually plucked up courage to request of the Chief Executive an opportunity to address all the senior managers at a forthcoming Extended Leadership Team Conference. After taking soundings among a few close colleagues he consented. In the end it was just a fringe meeting I got to address (as it happened, on the fateful date of 11 September 2001), but that was a good start. This led to an invitation to make a similar presentation the following month at the company's Human Resources Conference. Towards the end of the year, I was encouraged to set up Spirituality at Work Conversation Groups for anyone interested to attend 45-minute lunchtime gatherings to explore their own and the company's spiritual values. Some 50 people signed up for these, and at the time of writing two groups are still meeting. Similar conversations were started in another company I visit. (More will be said about Spirituality at Work Conversation Groups later on.) My interest in the practical realities of spirituality in the workplace is deepening each day, and this book is our attempt to synthesize what Sue and I have learned over the last few years.

A footprint along the way

While feeling very upbeat about what we are engaged in, there is a sense in which writing this book feels a very rash undertaking on our part. True, we have drawn on the knowledge and insights of many fellow travellers, but our own ability, qualifications and time (we both have day jobs) are limited. We share the sentiments of Ken Wilber who introduced one of his books in this way: 'This book is a brief overview of a Theory of Everything'. Fittingly he then went on to admit, 'All such attempts, of course, are marked by the many ways in which they [. . .] fall short, drive specialists insane, and generally fail their stated aim of holistic embrace [. . .] The task is inherently undoable.' How true this is bound to be when the subject is spirit, which is by nature mysterious, unpredictable and indescribable. Nevertheless, prompted (we believe) by that same spirit[5] we decided to 'have a go'. We believe in the SaW cause and want to do our bit to promote it, although we hasten to add that we are learners, simply feeling our way forward.

We now hear our first word from Gillian. She writes:

As an Organization Development practitioner, one of my roles is to ensure that we, as a business, are abreast of, and ideally driving, leading-edge thinking about organization effectiveness. My journey into spirituality in the workplace began in the autumn of 2001 when my line manager requested that I follow up on some support we had offered to an institution organizing its first international conference on Organization Spirituality. In truth, I wasn't quite sure what 'Organization Spirituality' meant, so before I attended the first conference steering team meeting I thought I had better investigate!

It wasn't as difficult as I had imagined to track down some information. The *Financial Times*, in the wake of September 11th, had printed two articles on the subject – 'Souls Restored in the Workplace' and 'A Reconnection with Core Values'. Listed there was a whole range of companies, spanning various industries, talking about their interest in spirituality at work including UBS Warburg, ServiceMaster and Kingfisher. From there I began to read books such as Alan Briskin's *The Stirring of Soul in the Workplace*, and meet with key thinkers on the subject referenced in the articles.

Like a neural network, the contact I initiated with one person or organization seemed to form connections with the next and so on until it seemed that, with now heightened awareness, everywhere I looked there was some mention of spirituality in the workplace. But by this point it was more than just intellectual curiosity. I had met with something that had prompted a change in what I perceived as the very purpose of business. I hadn't been expecting that.

I had been impacted by the idea that profit could be regarded as a *result* and not the *purpose* of an organization. The notion that a business could see itself in broader terms than simply making money – and not just the not-for-profit organizations – was a revelation. Indeed, I began to see that business, as surely the most powerful force in society today, had an obligation to its broader stakeholders. As I came across more and more businesses that were talking about the 'triple bottom line' (see Chapter 11), I began to wonder what this could mean for our organization.

I decided to start conversations within my business on the subject of spirituality. What emerged, in every single case, was one of two distinct responses. One was a look of suspicion, quickly turning to unease, when the colleague imagined my approach was all about religion and proselytizing; the other was what I can only describe as a 'soul connection', with the conversation moving quickly and animatedly to deeper things. I loved this second type of conversation but was troubled by the first and realized that, if I were to be able to research further and have a forum to present my findings, I would need a mandate from senior management.

With much thought I decided to approach the European head of HR and take him through what I had come across so far and present a project plan for the next phase. I was specifically requesting his personal support and sponsorship for my work. He quizzed me at length and we energetically debated a number of key issues, at the end of which he agreed to my proposal but requested that, instead of me supplying him with regular updates, we should go on the journey together. Although I was pleased to have his support, I wondered how on earth we could go on a journey together when I had neither a destination nor a roadmap.

Plan of the book

In the first part, Chapters 1 and 2 set out the factors which have led to the emergence of SaW. Part 2 explores the personal dimension of SaW. First we examine the thorny question of defining spirituality (Chapter 3), concluding that, while no single definition can be agreed, there is a widely held view that the terrain of SaW includes four sets of connections – to self, to others, to nature and to higher power. These connections form the subject matter of Chapters 4 to 7, in which we show how aspects of our personal spiritual journeys are being illuminated by new (for the West) insights about psychology, nature and fundamental reality. We next, in Chapter 8, explore whether and how the world's religions can help us on the journey. While in the course of the earlier chapters much is said about working life, it is in Part 3 that we explore the organizational dimension of SaW more fully. In Chapters 9 to 12 we apply the four connections to work organizations using the themes of leadership, learning, corporate social responsibility and organizational transformation, and Chapter 13 gives examples of organizations that are attempting to operate by spiritual principles. In the final part, Chapter 14 gives an overview of the progress of SaW to date and a prognosis of its significance for the future. The last chapter lists some of the main resources that are available to readers wanting to become more involved in SaW.

1

Global Issues and Workplace Sensibilities

The challenges in our society and our businesses are so profound, so fundamental, so universal, that they must [. . .] be resolved at the level of the human spirit.

Laura Hauser[1]

The present chapter touches on the main global issues and developments that have paved the way for SaW. These include:

- technological advances and their limitations;
- stakeholder capitalism and corporate social responsibility;
- feminism and the green/environmental movements;
- recent financial scandals leading to concern about business ethics;
- September 11th;
- the oil price hike, triumphant capitalism and globalization.

Also there are aspects of current and recent workplace experience which are leading people to ask deep questions about working life, indeed about life generally, and thus preparing the ground for SaW. We focus on four:

- working life experienced as an affront to the human spirit;
- disenchantment with the material, the search for meaning and the inner quest;
- the search for soul satisfaction at work;
- 'baby-boomers' in the boardroom.

We take a brief look at each of these items.

Technological advances and their limitations

In the nineteenth and twentieth centuries many people hoped that technology would solve most of the world's problems. This clearly hasn't happened, despite the tremendous gains technology has brought. So it would seem that more than technology is needed. A more serious intent on the part of our politicians to tackle major world problems such as poverty, inequality and environmental pollution (seen in acid rain, global warming and the greenhouse effect, destruction of rain forests, toxic waste etc.) is one vital ingredient. The real answer, many would now say, is the inspiration and guidance that can come only from a spiritual vision.

In general, technology is perceived as both a blessing and a curse. For example, new biotechnologies have the potential to cure disease but carry the risk of releasing into the environment new gene forms whose impact is wholly unknown. It will soon be possible to prolong human life, perhaps one day almost indefinitely, but would that be a good thing? And what of the prospect of designer babies? Technology raises as well as solves problems.

Much technological development, though informed by the best of motives, has had unintended consequences. Improving standards of health care, for instance, have increased life expectancy and diminished infant mortality but have also caused the world's population to increase to a point where millions are balanced on a knife-edge between survival and extinction. The development of pesticides and fertilizers, intended to increase crop yields to sustain this expanding population, has led to the pollution of the world's water – one of our most precious resources.

Technology has brought about enormous improvements to the material side of life, at least to most of us in the West. It has opened up material possibilities beyond the wildest dreams of previous generations. But technology has largely become 'technologism' – a term signifying the turning of technology into a sort of religion. Technologism stands for technology developed for its own sake, irrespective of the effects it might have on people or the planet. A related idea is 'technological determinism' – the theory which says that if something *can* be produced it *will* be, provided somebody can make money out of it.

So there are two ways in which technological advances have paved the way for SaW. The first is the failure of technology to remedy our ills, leading to the quest for a more fundamental solution to the world's problems. The second is the perceived need for an ethical and spiritual underpinning to guide technological development along appropriate paths.

Stakeholder capitalism and corporate social responsibility

In recent years in Britain, thanks largely to the work of the Centre for Tomorrow's Company, Business in the Community, SustainAbility and the like (see Chapter 15), there has been a growing criticism of the view that the sole, or even primary, purpose of a business is to make profits for its shareholders (and there have been parallel developments in the United States and other countries). The latter, though a very important group, are now regarded as just one of many stakeholders for whom the company must have regard – the others being employees, suppliers, customers, the community in whose area the business is located, wider society, the planet and future generations.

Tomorrow's Company have devoted much thought to the updating of company law to reflect these wider stakeholder concerns. At the moment companies are legally obliged to have regard only to the interests of shareholders. This is all part of the current debate about corporate governance, and Tomorrow's Company in the UK, like Ralph Nader and the Center for Responsive Law in the United States, are at the forefront of that debate.

Hand in hand with the stakeholder movement has been an increased emphasis on the need for businesses to be more socially responsible. Distinctly *passé* now seem the sentiments of economist Milton Friedman, who declared in the mid-1980s that there was no such thing as corporate social responsibility.[2]

The change of climate has been so marked that European industrialists have now got together to campaign for Corporate Social Responsibility, declaring the year 2005 as 'CSR Year'. We would point those interested in following the progress of CSR to an article that appeared in the January 2003 issue of *Management Today* by Stephen Cook, entitled 'Who Cares Wins'. We shall be referring to that article again in Chapter 11, where we shall speak further about stakeholder capitalism and CSR. By that stage of the book we hope to have made it clear that the success of both these related movements depends on the attainment of a high degree of spiritual awareness. At the moment we simply note their part in paving the way for a more spiritual approach to business and economics – i.e. one based on concern for all others who are affected by our business activities.

Feminism and the green/environmental movements

The feminist or women's liberation movement (in its various forms) has drawn attention to the shortcomings of the macho-male view of life and work and pointed out the need to adopt a 'softer' approach. Thus it has been suggested that we counterbalance the 'hard' values of rationalism, analysis and hard-headedness with the more spiritual values of intuition, synthesis and compassion.

The green (or environmental or ecological) movement has reminded us of the need to regard nature as not just a utilitarian resource for us human beings to plunder at will for our own ends but as something over which we must exercise responsible stewardship, both for its own sake and in order to pass on a safe and resource-rich environment to future generations. This too would require a more spiritual approach to economic life than the one typically adopted now, as we shall see more clearly later on.

The fact that the word 'sustainability' is on the lips not just of environmental futurists but also of traditional politicians and, increasingly, business people (e.g. in reference to the 'triple bottom line' – see Chapter 11) is an indication of the green movement's success in getting its message across.

The word 'ecofeminism' has been coined to indicate the linkage between, and often common membership of, these two movements. The alarming forecasts of groups like the Club of Rome (who were among the first to point out, way back in the 1970s, the strain we were putting on our planet by our unsustainable level of economic growth) alerted us all to the environmental impact of our industrial activities and general way of life in the West. Such groups gave an added impetus to the message of the ecofeminists.

The ecofeminists' background influence on, and in many cases actual involvement in, SaW is very significant. Similarly with the feminist movement as a whole. As we shall note when considering the new paradigm in the next chapter, it is the intuitive, feeling, caring, right-brain, more typically female approach to life that SaW promotes. This is by way of counterbalancing the more masculine approach which, though not without its valuable aspects, has become over-dominant in the world of work.

Recent financial scandals leading to concern about business ethics

The recent corporate misdemeanours have caused many to question the values and indeed the ongoing viability of the present way of doing business. In consequence a better, more spiritual, way is being sought – even if some of those searching would not call it that. Key to the current crisis in many people's eyes is the dominance of the financial bottom line. It is the placing of this above all other considerations which has led to these corporate scandals. Evidently some will go to any lengths in order to present their finances in a favourable light. Many regard such behaviour as the almost inevitable result of the way the current capitalist system operates, and there is clearly a need to address anew the whole question of business ethics and corporate governance. This sort of behaviour may also be seen as a form of addiction, a species of evil which we shall be discussing in Chapter 7.

Significant interest on the part of corporate Britain in business ethics dates roughly from the establishment of the Institute of Business Ethics. The IBE was spawned by the Christian (formerly the Catholic) Association of Business Executives some twenty years ago. Other influences were the Human Relations school of management science, and such groups as the Industrial Society[3] and the Grubb Institute (both also of Christian foundation). It has become the practice for leading businesses to formulate codes of ethics or statements of company philosophy, nowadays more commonly known as Mission, Vision and Value statements. This trend has certainly helped to pave the way for SaW.

September 11th

The events of 9/11, and the ways they have been reacted to, have taught us many things. One obvious lesson is the danger we are all in from religious fanatics, and the need to recognize and confront the great evil there is in our world. But many in the SaW movement are highly critical of the particular political response made, and of the particular style of the 'global war on terrorism'. Terrorism has been identified by our national leaders as something that has to be 'fixed': you go for it, and you eliminate it. Too little thought has been given to the deeper causes of terrorism and to what might have led people to engage in such acts of desperation. Nor has it seriously been asked why terrorism is so strongly supported by certain sections of the Arab world; or why the West in general and the United States of America in particular are seen as 'the great Satan'. If such questions had been faced, a very different response might have been made. The war on terrorism might have taken the form of a war on want – the want of those in the Third World (which is significantly Muslim) who cannot break out of the cycle of poverty and debt that they have largely been plunged into by the way the current global economic system works – the system presided over by us and operated to our advantage. In short, we should have tackled both terrorism and the causes of terrorism.

But there have also been positive aspects of 9/11. One was the great outpouring of sympathy and compassion for the victims, and for the United States in its hour of grief. This illustrates the best in human nature. So do the feats of courage and heroism shown by the people directly caught up in the tragedy. Margaret Wheatley reports the words of one of the World Trade Center survivors: 'We didn't save ourselves. We tried to save each other.'[4] Pat Sullivan tells how 'people who once never found a moment to pray or do community service suddenly found hours or days for both [. . .] Donna Reifsnider, a journalist who worked for the *Bowie Blade News* in Maryland, says that no one on the paper ever wants to have to cover an event so painful or to work so intensely as they did in the weeks after September 11. But they all want to maintain the new gifts that the crisis pulled out of them and their community.'[5]

9/11 has prompted many people to examine what their true values in life are. A Lutheran Evangelical minister from Chicago paid David a visit in early 2002. He desired to learn about how corporate chaplaincy works in the UK, because business organizations in his area were suddenly wanting corporate chaplains to 'come in and help them discover the meaning of life' as he put it.

That awful event then has made people more open to spiritual values and insights. Not only has it revealed how dangerous it is when groups and nations operate on the basis of pseudo-spiritual values – and we have seen this both in the actions of the terrorists and in the reactions of our own politicians; it has also caused us to ask ourselves deep questions about the values we live by, including at work.

The oil price hike, triumphant capitalism and globalization

We group these three items together because they have all led, directly or indirectly, to a deterioration in people's working conditions. The quad-rupling of the cost of oil in 1973/74 by the oil producing countries led to a severe economic downturn in which survival became the name of the game for business corporations. The route to success, it was thought, lay in severe cost cutting, combined with super-efficiency, which led to great pressure being put on working people to achieve as much as possible with as little as possible. Coupled with that was the growing threat of unem-ployment.

The fall of the Soviet Union and its satellites was taken by many in the West as proof of the inherent superiority of capitalism over every other conceivable economic system. There was talk of capitalism being 'the only game in town'. This served to discourage any further internal scrutiny of capitalism and coincided with the adoption of a more *laissez-faire* type of economic practice, as championed by economists such as Milton Friedman and their political disciples. The result was that in the 1980s and 1990s economic values came to eclipse human values, and the negative impact on the quality of working life has been all too apparent. Another factor was the decreased power of the trade unions.

Globalization, or the trend whereby business became increasingly international, and internationally competitive, only served to increase the pressures. The tendency of firms to relocate to countries where labour was cheap and fiscal and environmental restraints on business were minimal left comparatively high wage workers in the West increasingly vulnerable. Organizations still located in the developed world were 're-engineered' to become even more efficient.

Working life experienced as an affront to the human spirit

All these factors have served to make working life harder and more stressful for people, prompting questions like: Is all this sweat and stress worth the effort? Is my work any longer something to which I want to devote so much of my life? Am I prepared to tolerate such an unbalanced life, working virtually all the hours God sends and having so little time to devote to family and leisure? Am I willing to take such risks with my health and sanity? Am I serving any worthwhile purpose in making so many sacrifices? Am I too much a slave of a system that is draining me and no longer offering me any rewards except material ones? And what sense of commitment do I have left when even those rewards can be snatched away at the drop of a hat through my being declared redundant? What loyalty do I feel when my company can offer me no guarantee of job security? And recently there has appeared an additional worry – the possibility of firms being increasingly unable to provide adequate occupational pensions. In short, the quality of people's working lives has taken a turn for the worse and led to our feeling that there must be a better way. The whole basis of our working life and indeed of our life generally needs rethinking. This raises deeply spiritual questions.

Let's take a quick look at how a few SaW writers have reacted to this situation. First, Laura Hauser on the current work scene and the spiritual crisis it engenders:

> Reengineering, downsizing, and mergers – the cost-cutting profit-making strategies of the 1980s and 1990s – are taking fierce tolls on organizations. More and more, employee morale is depleted [. . .] The spiritual crisis begins for the formerly effective employees who now feel less competent, less appreciated, and less connected to meaningful work and relationships.[6]

She also notes how the widespread changes have led to:

- staff reductions, with remaining employees left with huge workloads;
- managers and staff feeling devalued and discouraged;
- people being drained of their energy and feeling psychologically empty;
- people feeling distanced from their work and the organization;
- leaders becoming so preoccupied with survival that they ignore the needs of people.

Hauser's remarks appear in *The New Bottom Line*, a collection of essays edited by John Renesch and Bill DeFoore. Other essayists in that volume add to the grim picture. Michael Scott Rankin sees in people today 'a sated, self-conscious, listless despair'.[7] Barry Heermann believes

> We have lost our relationship with spirit. This is at the heart of breakdowns in many areas of modern life [. . .] Many organization workers are unconscious of the spirit that moves in their lives, leaving them with an inner longing and feeling of emptiness, leading them to a kind of 'busyness' that produces little. This emptiness is at such a level that we have been dubbed the 'Prozac' nation after the 'miracle' drug that replaces the lost spirit.[8]

Tanis Helliwell writes in similar vein. 'Our souls are starving,' she says. 'Everywhere I go, I sense a chronic low grade depression in people, a soul sickness . . . These are all symptoms of unhappiness that people feel when their lives and work are not in keeping with their soul's purpose.'[9]

According to King, Biberman, Robbins and Nicol, the interest in SaW has occurred 'as a direct result of societal insecurity'. Many people they surveyed mentioned 'that the world was becoming more "messed up" (e.g. increasingly rapid rate of change, increased information and technology overload, loss of family life and community, general loss of security)'.[10]

The editorial of a recent special issue of the *Journal of Managerial Psychology* has this to say about the current work scene:

> So many individuals' experience of corporations is one of a blind pursuit of shareholder value through cost cutting, thus creating tensions between an ever greater reduction of the workforce and a need to complete large volumes of work. Such tensions result in a deep mistrust of corporations generating emotions such as fear, frustration, anger, isolation, alienation and feelings of being an expendable object in the pursuit of profit maximisation [. . .] Such experiences in turn create a hunger for a deeper meaning of life, a need for finding an anchor and a desire for greater integration of the spiritual and work identities.[11]

As many of the foregoing paragraphs imply, a significant issue for many is *work–life balance*, or rather lack of it. A study carried out in 2002 by the UK's Department of Trade and Industry and *Management Today* magazine found the number of people working more than 60 hours a week in the UK had increased over the preceding two years. In 2002, about one in six was working more than 60 hours per week, compared with one in eight in 2000. And the number of women working those hours had doubled: from one in 16 to one in eight. This was despite the introduction of the European Union's Working Time Directive. The study also found that one in five men had visited their doctor complaining of stress; and that more than 70 per cent of workers who were highly stressed belonged to organizations that didn't offer flexible working patterns. A recent issue of *Personnel Today* reported that stress is costing British firms £1.24bn a year.

Disenchantment with the material, the search for meaning and the inner quest

Even those fortunate enough to remain winners have begun to feel something is wrong or missing in their lives. The latter decades of the twentieth century were characterized by a growing dissatisfaction with materialism. People, especially in the United States, had for the most part done pretty well in material terms but many were finding that material abundance alone left them unfulfilled. Materialism had in some way disconnected them from their true selves. This resulted in the quest for more interior forms of satisfaction. In terms of Maslow's famous Hierarchy of Needs,[12] people's lower order needs had in general been met; they were now focusing on the higher, more spiritual needs.

One prominent inner need, highlighted by many writers (e.g. Zohar and Marshall[13]), was for meaning and purpose in life. People who 'had it all' wanted to know what their lives were now 'for'. It was to meet this sort of need that many found solace and support in the New Age movement, which claimed to cater for the deep needs of body, mind and spirit. They turned to those religions, or quasi-religions, which looked inwards to the depths of the human personality. To many it was the Eastern religions like Buddhism and Hinduism that seemed best to fit the bill. Western religion was reckoned (partly erroneously we have to say – see later) to be less amenable to the idea that the divine is found within.

We say no more at this juncture about the New Age and Eastern religions, because they will feature later on, but we do need to note here their background importance in paving the way for SaW.

The search for soul satisfaction at work

We find people today, more perhaps than ever before, bringing their deep needs and spiritual aspirations to their workplaces, as the following stories illustrate.

The tale is told by Danah Zohar of a senior manager who complained:

'When I am home for the weekend with my family, we go for walks in the country. We talk to each other, we meet with our friends. I love my children. I care about nature. But when I go to work on Monday morning, I am expected to leave all that outside the door.

My job is about making money'. Yet this man's actual job is in the human resources division of his company. He feels he can't give all of himself to his job.[14]

Zohar also tells of a secretary who explained how if one of her children became ill, her boss didn't want to know.

'I had certain hours I had to be in and a job I had to do, and he didn't care what was going on at home. I hated him and I hated the job and I did just what I was required to do and no more'. [Now this woman works as a secretary in another division of the same company.] 'My new boss is completely different. He always smiles in the morning and asks how I am. He asks after the husband and the kids. When one of the kids is sick, he tells me not to come in to work. I adore him and will do anything for him'. Now she puts in extra hours, does things outside her job description, and has volunteered for a training course to become a conference organizer. She works with her whole person, and both she and the job are growing.[15]

The documented and anecdotal evidence that people wish to function as whole people at work is vast. A colleague of ours in the Douai Abbey-based Spirituality in the Workplace Network, Karen, tells the story of how she decided she wanted more out of life than the 'privilege' of just making money for the shareholders of the company of which she was Managing Director. So she resigned and became a personal and corporate development coach. She now earns a fraction of her previous salary but she's happier.

In her book *Turning to One Another*, Margaret Wheatley notes some important features of truly meaningful work. She writes:

Working for something beyond ourselves teaches us about the human spirit [...] When we serve others [...] we gain energy. People who volunteer for a community or service project often arrive straight from work, exhausted. But after several hours of meaningful volunteer work, they go home energized. In disaster relief efforts, people work without rest for days, gaining energy from the work of saving others [cf. 9/11]. Work that serves the common good doesn't take away our energy. Instead, energy pours into our bodies through our open hearts and generous spirits.

Most people describe working for the common good as memorable, and contrast this with their day-to-day work.[16]

She goes on to wonder why we have such low expectations of our normal work.

Here is a story about the Hewlett-Packard company; David heard Margaret Wheatley (again) tell this story at a seminar evening he attended in Oakland, California while on sabbatical in autumn 2000. It shows how important it is for organizational goals to be aligned with the personal goal of 'making a difference in the world'.

> The Hewlett-Packard management wished to gain their employees' commitment to their Mission Statement, and set up focus groups for the purpose. The Mission Statement was worded: 'We will be the best R&D lab in the world'. One woman employee said she got no energy from being the best in the world. 'But,' she went on, 'if the statement had said, "The best for the world", that would have made all the difference!' That caught everyone's attention. The Mission Statement was adapted accordingly. A poster was designed around the new statement, showing doors of a laboratory opening up to a picture of the globe. There were 150,000 requests for this poster.[17]

Thomas Moore in *Care of the Soul* suggests that at job interviews candidates try to find out 'the soul values' of the particular firm. They might ask such questions as, 'What is the spirit in this workplace? Will I be treated as a person here? Is there a feeling of community? Do people love their work? Is what we are doing and producing worthy of my commitment and long hours? Are there any moral problems in the job or the workplace making things detrimental to people or the earth, taking excessive profits or contributing to racial and sexist oppression?' He adds the comment, 'It is not possible to care for the soul while violating or disregarding one's own moral sensibility.'[18]

'Baby-boomers' in the boardroom

A key enabling factor if there is to be any real move towards spirituality in the world of work is the attitude of business leaders. One influential and quite numerous group of leaders who might give us cause for hope are the baby-boomers. 'As the Baby Boomers [those born in the 1940s] reach mid-life', writes Kay Gilley, 'efforts to make the world a better place have moved from the streets of the 1960s to the boardrooms in the 1990s.'[19] King, Biberman, Robbins and Nicol have found in the course of their research that 'these "boomers" are increasingly questioning the meaning of their work, with the consequent search for work that will enable them to integrate their personal values within their work in the organization'.[20] Catherine McGeachy refers to the special interest taken in SaW by people in powerful decision-making jobs – the 'babyboomers [. . .] seeking meaning in life'.[21]

There is one more major background feature to mention – the New Paradigm. But that deserves a whole chapter to itself. And to understand the significance of the New Paradigm we need to set it within a wider cultural context.

2

Disconnection and Reconnection: The New Paradigm

We have lost our relationship with spirit.

Barry Heermann[1]

The science of today is new and thus offers us a radically new cultural understanding. This applies to our corporations as much as to our societal and personal lives.

Danah Zohar[2]

The short answer to the question 'Why SaW now?', is that at the beginning of the twenty-first century so many of us feel 'disconnected', and we are looking for answers. We saw in Chapter 1 how this is being expressed in relation to life at work. As David Whyte puts it, 'This split between our work life and that part of our soul life forced underground seems to be at the root of much of our current unhappiness.'[3] Soul life forced underground is a phrase which well sums up our cultural history of the last 200 years.

Modernism and post-modernism

The scientific mind-set of the nineteenth and twentieth centuries – part of a set of ideas referred to as *modernism* – cast doubt on the very existence of soul and spirit. Fortunately this modernist-era, 'old paradigm' science, as those in the SaW movement call it, is being gradually replaced by what is termed 'the new paradigm'.

It was Thomas Kuhn in his 1962 book *The Structure of Scientific Revolutions*[4] who popularized the idea that we bring to our reading of reality what he calls a 'paradigm'. A paradigm is an interpretation, a particular 'take' on 'life, the universe and everything' (to quote Douglas Adams' *The Hitchhiker's Guide to the Galaxy*). It is a mind-set, a worldview, a particular way of looking at reality. The history of science shows, says Kuhn, that paradigms are modified – a paradigm shift occurs – when an existing paradigm cannot encompass new questions that scientists wish to put to reality, or when a new discovery puts into question existing assumptions. An example of a paradigm shift is when people came to accept that the earth moved round the sun rather than the other way round, when one minute the earth was the centre of everything and the next it was just a tiny planet somewhere within the vastness of space.

It is now widely agreed that how we perceive things is significantly affected by the particular ways our minds have been shaped – by the accumulated experience of thousands of years of human evolution, and also by our particular cultural beliefs and social norms. We have been programmed, in other words, to see things in certain ways rather than in other possible ways.

Many examples have been given to illustrate this. One is showing a picture of a human being to primitive people who have never previously experienced a two-dimensional representation of a three-dimensional object – and finding they simply don't recognize it as a picture of a human being. Another example is people living in the Middle Ages not seeing the curvature of the earth when they went to the sea shore, because according to their paradigm the earth was flat. In short, we do not perceive things out there just as they are. We *interpret* them.

Some post-modernist thinkers have taken the idea of interpretation to extremes, arguing that reality is not just coloured by our interpretations but entirely created by them. There is no reality, they say, 'beneath' our interpretations. Furthermore, if everything is a matter of interpretation through paradigms, could it not be claimed that one interpretation is as good as any other? In this way these thinkers sought to attack the objective reality of science. Kuhn himself strongly resisted drawing such a conclusion. He pointed out that science could never make progress if one interpretation was as good as any other. An interpretation can be a good or a bad interpretation. A good one is one which enables an adequate working relationship with the universe, and for that to be possible the paradigm has to have a purchase on 'how things actually are'.

Given that old-paradigm science was able to generate the industrial and technological revolutions of modern times, there was clearly a sense in which it had – and has – a very good purchase on how the universe works. It was only when Einstein and others came to ask questions that couldn't be satisfactorily answered by Newtonian mechanistic science that the latter's limitations became apparent.

Before we contrast the old and new paradigms in detail, let us spend a moment looking at the effects of old-paradigm thinking on human life. We have already noted its propensity to force soul and spirit underground. How did this happen?

The scientific paradigm adopted in the nineteenth century and which persisted for most of the twentieth century and is still in a sense mainline, was based on a decision going back to the seventeenth century which said: We'll rely on reason and on our five senses to tell us about the world. We'll take nothing on trust. We'll take nothing from any established authority or tradition. We'll regard as firm truth only what can be established by scientific experiment based on observation of how physical things work – and physical things are the only things that can be 'picked up' by our physical senses. All else we'll regard as myth or superstition or, at best, as matters of little importance.

That is, admittedly, a summary of scientism (as this view has been called) in its extreme form. Perhaps comparatively few have gone quite as far as that. And those who have done so as scientists have clearly operated by other assumptions in their personal and family lives. But, officially at any rate, out of the window went all the 'truths' of art and religion, even the concept of there being a human mind behind the physical brain. Mental life, aesthetic life, spirituality, free will, meaning, purpose – all were banished from the realm of the 'really' real, or made matters of personal taste.

Not everyone was prepared to settle for the removal of the things that made human life warm, meaningful and interesting from the realm of real knowledge. There was bound to be a backlash. It occurred in the form of a whole series of developments that come under the umbrella of what is called *post-modernism*.

The contribution of Ken Wilber

If you were to attend a SaW conference, or have a consultant who works with spiritual ideas visit your company or lead an external training session, the chances are that you would hear references to 'regaining a sense of oneness with nature', or 'tuning in to a higher mode of consciousness'. These ideas stem, respectively, from Romanticism and Idealism. If you are interested you can read more about these and other post-modernist movements in Ken Wilber's book *The Marriage of Sense and Soul*.[5]

As well as being a guide through the labyrinths of modernism and post-modernism, Wilber's book also makes a scientific case for accepting as real the knowledge that comes to us via our minds and souls. Wilber does this by demonstrating that the same scientific procedures may be applied as those used to establish the truths of empirical science (the knowledge that comes via the senses and their extensions – scientific instruments like telescopes and microscopes). This is how it works in relation to knowledge about spiritual realities: if you want to know what the mystics know, set up the appropriate experiment (viz. meditate), study the data (the knowledge that comes through meditation), and check out your conclusions with those competent to judge in that particular field of investigation. By this means, says Wilber, we are able to build up a full-spectrum science that covers knowledge that comes from the senses, knowledge that comes via the mind, and knowledge that comes via the soul and spirit. We then arrive at the holistic view of reality represented in Figure 1.

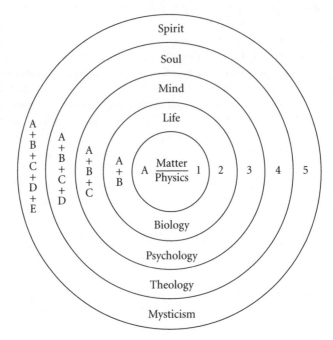

Figure 1: The Great Nest of Being[6]

Wilber here shows which branches of science – and yes, he includes theology and mysticism as branches of science! – study which aspects of reality. The diagram also illustrates a key principle in Wilber's system, that of 'transcend and include'. Each branch of science is based on and develops further the subject matter of the branch below it. Physics is the ground-floor science and studies physical matter; biology includes matter but also transcends it by studying life, and so on.

If we think of each ring of the diagram – 1, 2, 3, 4, 5 – as emerging one after another in time like the rings of a tree trunk, then we have a simple outline of Wilber's theory of the unfolding of spirit or evolution of con-sciousness – his 'brief history of everything' (to cite the title of his best-known book).[7] Progress is made from one level to the next through transcending and including the state previously reached.

We need to say just one more thing about Wilber's theory. Like the Idealists in whose tradition he stands, he regards spirit as the reality underpinning everything. This turns completely on its head the materialistic worldview that we moderns have grown up with. Even those of us who have a place for spirit within our mental map find the Idealist picture a strange one. This is because we tend (as a result of the way we have been taught about evolution) to think of the spiritual as emerging out of the material: spirit is what matter at its most evolved best somehow gives birth to. Idealism reverses this by making spirit the basic reality and regarding the material as what spirit becomes, but only temporarily; the material being but a phase of a journey that begins and ends with spirit.

On this point readers might find it helpful to read Peter Russell's *From Science to God*.[8] He is a leading-edge new scientist who, like the Idealists and Wilber, makes spirit the primary reality – only he prefers the term consciousness, as do many in the SaW movement.

While we might find Idealism hard to accept, we can see that at least it presents a holistic view of reality, covering the totality of things from subatomic particles 'in the basement', through atoms, molecules, cells, organisms, etc., to the loftiest realms of spirit 'up in the attic'. (Actually, the uppermost reaches of Wilber's philosophy take us right up through the roof, as we shall see in Chapters 4 and 7.)

Readers might be wondering why we have focused our attention so much on Ken Wilber. It is because for many people in the SaW movement Wilber is something of a hero. He figures often in the SaW literature and is frequently referred to in SaW conferences and discussions. It would be too much to claim that he is the resident philosopher of SaW, and such a thought would certainly surprise Wilber himself. But he is certainly very influential. We recommend readers who have the time to take a look at the two books by Wilber we have mentioned in this chapter. A secure grasp of the ideas he presents helps us get a proper fix on the SaW movement and its place within the changing culture of our times.

It is a more holistic view like Wilber's (not necessarily identical in detail but compatible with it) that is found in the new paradigm. Our aim now will be, first, to outline the new paradigm in science, where it has largely been 'invented'. Then we shall enter more into 'home' territory as far as this book is concerned and chart how new paradigm thinking has been taken up by management scientists.

The new paradigm in science

As we have noted, paradigms can change; a paradigm shift can occur. A massive paradigm shift has taken place within the last few decades. In fact it started in the first decades of the twentieth century, the earliest seeds being sown by Albert Einstein in physics and Carl Jung in psychology.

The main contrasts between the old and new paradigms in science are shown in Table 1.

Table 1

OLD PARADIGM *Universe as a machine*	NEW PARADIGM *Universe as an organism*
Solid individual bits bumping about like billiard balls	Nodes of energy, related to all other nodes of energy, in an interdependent web of being
Atomistic view	Holistic/systems view
Predictable	Unpredictable, except at macro level; otherwise, novelty
Blind, purposeless, life an accident	A directional, creative unfolding, life-producing by design
Not inherently mysterious	Inherently mysterious
Describable	Indescribable; models and metaphors only
Physical laws the basis of everything	Different laws apply at different levels Theologians can contribute
e.g. psychology is about automatic responses to external stimuli	Freedom of response
Materialist/anti-spiritual	Material and spiritual aspects affirmed
Science a 'matter of fact' discipline	Scientist as mystic Awe and wonder

The basic models of the universe employed in the old and new paradigms respectively are machine and organism. In the old view the stuff of the universe is solid individual bits bumping about like billiard balls, whereas the new conception is of nodes of energy, related to all other nodes of energy in an interdependent web of being. So we have, on the one hand, an 'atomistic' view of reality, on the other a 'holistic' or 'systems' view.

With the new paradigm, gone is the notion that the universe is fundamentally predictable. The philosopher Laplace reckoned that if we knew the position, speed and direction of travel of every atom in the universe, we could predict precisely where each atom would be at any point in the future. The end of the universe, in other words, was in its beginning. In that sort of scheme the only role for God was to set things going. This is the 'celestial watchmaker' view of God, technically called 'deism', as opposed to 'theism' in which God is held to be in continuing interaction with the created order.

The newer view is that while there is predictability at the macro level (how otherwise could we have landed people on the Moon?) at the level of subatomic particles there is a fundamental unpredictability. Things can go a number of different possible ways. At the very basic level there is even, apparently, complete randomness.

The universe at all levels produces novelty. Instead of the idea that cosmic and terrestrial evolution is blind and purposeless and that life is an accident, the new paradigm envisages a directional, creative unfolding of a universe that is life-producing by design – one in which life will establish itself wherever and however it can.

In the old view the universe was not inherently mysterious, whereas the new understanding recognizes a profound mystery at the heart of things. The universe, it is now admitted, can't really be described; it can only be referred to by using models and metaphors. The best that can be hoped for is that our models and metaphors will give us a working relationship with the universe.

By the 1980s those at the leading edges of the various scientific disciplines were taking the new paradigm into their systems. A growing common commitment to this new way of thinking meant people in the different disciplines were more ready to welcome each others' insights. No single discipline believed that it alone defined 'the truth'. No longer was it being asserted, for example, that physics was the basic science in terms of which the whole natural world – physical, biological and sociological – would one day be 'explained'. Under the old paradigm it was thought that even at a high level of reality like the biological, life was about quasi-automatic responses to external stimuli – i.e. the mechanical model was applied. The new-paradigm thinkers, however, saw the need to develop different models and metaphors for each particular level – physicists using concepts appropriate to their level, and similarly biologists, psychologists, sociologists and so on. It was conceded by some that even theologians can contribute valid insights to the overall picture of reality.

It is interesting to note that a mystical attitude to life is now often being reflected in the scientific community. Certainly the most creative and ground-breaking scientists approach the realities they study in a spirit of awe and reverence. More perhaps than ever before, scientists find themselves astounded by the elegance and beauty of the universe. Scientists are becoming more like mystics. Previously science was considered a cold, emotion-free, matter-of-fact discipline.

It will be apparent that the new paradigm is much more sympathetic to religion and spirituality than the old. (For example, in *The Tao of Physics*,[9] Fritjof Capra finds close parallels between modern science and Eastern philosophy.) That is why we claim the new paradigm as a major enabling factor behind the emergence of SaW.

However, we must add that not all present-day scientists subscribe to the new paradigm. But this state of affairs is typical at times of paradigm shift. New paradigms are accepted gradually and, at first, piecemeal. Some people go on resisting the new concepts for quite a long time. A tiny minority may go on resisting them for ever! This sort of thing happens in all disciplines.

Examples of new-paradigm scientists are Paul Davies in physics, Rupert Sheldrake in biology and Stanislav Grof in psychology. We briefly note their respective contributions.

In *God and the New Physics*[10] Davies argues, on the basis of the astounding mathematical elegance of the universe, for the existence of a Cosmic Mind, although he cannot quite see his way to affirming a transcendent Creator. He comes closer to the latter idea in his later volume *The Mind of God*[11] which closes with a remarkable section on mysticism. Davies is quite prepared to see the latter as a valid, indeed indispensable, path to truth. He introduces the concepts of the new science in general in *The Matter Myth*,[12] co-authored with John Gribbin.

The British biologist Sheldrake is even more upfront regarding religion. His book *The Rebirth of Nature*[13] actually contains sections on prayer and the Trinity. His greatest claim to fame rests on his remarkable theory about 'morphic fields' and 'morphic resonance'. He believes that every atom, cell or organism etc. is held in a 'field' which ensures the continuation of its general shape. An evolutionary advance happens when an element of novelty arises and is passed on via the field to other beings of the same type. Thus, for example, if a rat in a laboratory learns a new trick, the ability to learn that trick is (without any physical contact taking place) passed on to other rats in other laboratories all around the world, so that they themselves are now able to learn the trick more easily. These theories were first aired in *A New Science of Life*[14] and were restated, with more empirical back-up, in *The Presence of the Past*.[15]

Taking many of his cues from Carl Jung, Grof is one of the pioneers of a new branch of psychology called transpersonal psychology. His book *Psychology of the Future*[16] sums up his life's work in this field. He claims, on the basis of much evidence, that in 'holotropic' states – the word means 'tending towards wholeness' – induced by psychedelic drugs[17] or by meditation or other spiritual techniques, people experience higher levels of consciousness or spiritual awareness. Grof claims that some people's experience in such states even provides evidence for the reality of past lives (reincarnation). Such views, not surprisingly, have sparked off much controversy. Many have claimed that there are alternative ways of interpreting the evidence.

It is clear that there are people in many branches of science who are really 'pushing the envelope', but the sort of radical questioning that is going on is typical at a time of paradigm shift. Those wishing to read more on the new paradigm are recommended the following:

* Fritjof Capra, *The Turning Point*
* Danah Zohar, *Rewiring the Corporate Brain*, and
* Stephen Covey, *The 7 Habits of Highly Effective People*, pages 23 to 45.

The new paradigm in management science

We now look at the impact of the new paradigm on the thinking of those scientists closest to the world of work, the management scientists. The table below sets out how the two paradigms were being compared by a pioneering group of writers in the earliest days of the SaW movement. Each of them was a contributor to John Adams' book *Transforming Work*,[18] written in the early 1980s. We compiled the table from the first few chapters of that volume. Many of the points are already familiar but there are some interesting additions.

Management science and organizational development theory were once dominated by the thinking of Frederick W. Taylor, who in true old-paradigm fashion saw organizations in thoroughly mechanistic terms. If the 'machine' wasn't functioning properly, his advice was: find the part that wasn't working and mend or replace it.

Working life under the old paradigm has been well documented by Alan Briskin in the large central part of *The Stirring of Soul in the Workplace*.[19] Briskin shows how the way work has typically been organized since the Industrial Revolution has all but squeezed out of existence the soul-ful aspects of work. He is especially critical of 'Scientific Management', the theories of which have dominated work organizations since the 1930s. Even the later Human Relations movement, he believes, offered little respite, for the principles of scientific management remained basically unchanged.

Table 2

Old paradigm	New paradigm
1 Cartesian/reductionist/mechanistic view of reality	1 Holistic/ecological/systemic view of reality
2 The world regarded as divisible, separate, simple and finite	2 The world regarded as a complex, interconnected, infinite, ecological-social-psychological-economic system
3 Monochrome view of reality with same kind of laws applying throughout	3 Different laws apply at different levels of reality
4 The world is to be manipulated and controlled	4 The world is to be surrendered to and enjoyed
5 Emphasis on form and function	5 Emphasis on energy and flow
6 Reason is the only reliable guide	6 We need intuition as well as reason
7 Change thought to happen in a mechanical, linear sequence, and regarded as predictable	7 Change conceived as having multiple causes, as being subtle and unpredictable
8 Events and situations classified and their outcomes controlled through the application of known laws	8 Each situation or event is unique and its outcome is not controllable simply by applying general laws
9 Human attitudes and feelings can be disregarded	9 Confidence, expectation and love are critical aspects of causality
10 True knowledge is disinterested, dispassionate	10 All knowledge is 'interested knowledge'
11 People regarded simply as employees	11 People treated as multi-dimensional beings with a life outside the organization
12 Fulfilment is sought from material rewards alone	12 Fulfilment is sought through the opportunity to pursue lofty (even cosmic) objectives in line with people's deepest spiritual values
13 People are brought into line through rules and regulations	13 Alignment is achieved through commitment to a common vision
14 The leader controls the whole show	14 The leader's role is to inspire and teach
15 Problems are solved from the top	15 Problems are solved participatively with staff at all levels making their contribution
16 Management is a science	16 Management is a performing art

The new-paradigm thinking sees organizations as highly complex systems, as wholes that are greater than the sum of their parts. Each organization moreover is different from any other organization. Not surprising then that the old-paradigm approach of many a consultant has been found wanting. Many business leaders can no doubt think of occasions when a management consultant came to their firm, analysed what was going on there, related it to one of the many predetermined model-categories he or she had, and prescribed accordingly. This contrasts with the new-paradigm approach that regards every organization and situation as unique, and refuses to prescribe a set answer, because there is none. The pretence that there is has led to the common failure of management consultants to provide lasting solutions to organizational problems.

It is apparent from the table above, as from the one about the old and new paradigms in science, that the new paradigm represents a new openness to the things of the spirit. It shows how the different views of reality represented by spirituality and science can come together to form a single, holistic worldview. It also suggests how business goals may be reconciled to a wide range of personal goals. For to the extent that the business world takes human and spiritual values more fully into its system, people will increasingly recognize the goals, structures and methods of the workplace as compatible with, not at odds with, their own deepest values.

Adams' book discusses in connection with the new paradigm a new movement of the mid-1980s called Organizational Transformation (OT). This was a development out of and beyond Organizational Development (OD), which latter is well known in the business world both sides of the Atlantic. OT, we are told, works from a clearly articulated set of humanistic values. Unlike OD, which is about form and function, OT focuses on energy and flow. Whereas OD is about organizations 'moving furniture around the floor' OT encourages them to 'move their furniture to a new floor, both for their own good and the good of the planet'. OT emphasizes human empowerment, which involves creating the conditions for people to achieve their full potential. 'In order to tap the true human potential [...] we must focus more on individual well-being [...] and on encouraging the development of the spiritual self [...]' The hope is that we will each contribute in our own way to creating 'a world that works for everyone'.[20]

Adams and colleagues comment on the failure of traditional, old-paradigm management science. Peter Vaill, for instance, notes that the 'facts and methods' approach of behavioural science 'simply [does] not facilitate liberation'. The new paradigm, on the other hand, brings 'new substantive discoveries about man [...] [and] a refreshing, even thrilling new interest in ethics, morality, and the spiritual nature of man'. The 'facts and methods of modern behavioral science don't deal with the things that matter to more and more people in their active roles today. Ethics matter. Feelings matter. Community matters. The human spirit matters more and more.' Vaill describes the OT movement as 'a profound impulse towards a developed alternative [to the] old paradigm which says that "knowledge" and "truth" are learned and expressed through the verbal, linear-logical window alone' and dismisses 'everything else as "style" and as such too unique for scientific laws to encompass'. Vaill sees spirituality as a crucial element in 'the developed alternative'.[21] These snippets from Adams *et al* give a fair indication of how management science in the mid-1980s was beginning to take on board the new paradigm.

The background or 'enabling' features mentioned in these first two chapters have cumulatively brought about the advent of SaW. But what is SaW? And in particular what is signified by the 'S' in SaW, and by the related 's' words, soul and spirit? We must now turn to the task of defining spirituality.

PART TWO

MAPPING THE TERRAIN: THE PERSONAL JOURNEY

3

What is Spirituality?

> Spirituality is a life-filled path, a spirit-filled way of living [. . .]
> A path is the way itself and every moment on it is a holy moment;
> a sacred seeing goes on there.
>
> Matthew Fox[1]

Spirituality helps us in our struggle to determine who we are (our *being*) and how to live our lives in this world (our *doing*). It combines our basic philosophy towards life, our vision and our values, with our conduct and practice. Spirituality encompasses our ability to tap into our deepest resources, that part of ourselves which is unseen and mysterious, to develop our fullest potential. It also sets alive our web of relationships as we look outward in order to make meaningful connections and help others achieve their fullest potential. Both this inward and outward journey give us the opportunity to discover and articulate our personal meaning and purpose in life. On the way we are able to learn about love, joy, peace, creative fulfilment and how to live expectantly with a sense of vitality and abundance. But we also encounter suffering, moral ambiguity and personal fear. It is our spirituality, providing as it does a deeper identity, which guides us as we chart our way through life's paradoxes.

And yet, when spirituality is discussed people frequently ask, 'What *is* spirituality?' We therefore need to begin by exploring how spirituality is defined, and understood, in SaW circles.

Some insights

Since people of all faiths and none participate in the SaW movement, bringing their diverse conceptions, it is virtually impossible to devise a definition of spirituality to which a majority of people would subscribe. In fact, there are almost as many definitions of spirituality as there are people writing about it.

Definitions seem to centre around three areas:

- the basic feeling of being connected with one's complete self, others and the entire universe;
- underlying principles, e.g. virtues, ethics, values, emotions, wisdom, and intuition;
- the relationship between a personal inner experience and its (positive) manifestations in outer behaviours, principles and practices.

We wish to share a selection of insights from writers in the field, which reveal their views of what spirituality is for them:

Business writer Peter Block:
'Spirituality is the process of living out a set of deeply held personal values, of honoring forces or a presence greater than ourselves. It expresses our desire to find meaning in, and to treat as an offering, what we do.'[2]

J. Turner:
'Spiritual needs are fulfilled by recognition and acceptance of individual responsibility for the common good, by understanding the interconnectedness of life and by serving humanity and the planet.'[3]

From André Delbecq:
'[Spirituality is about] each person's journey in faith to discover their true self in union with the transcendent.' (This statement by Delbecq, and those by John Renesch and Alan Briskin below, were made in private conversations with David during the course of his sabbatical study.[4])

John Renesch is opposed to hard and fast models of spirituality:
'There can't be a spirituality model that people go through and come out spiritual at the other end. Spirituality is in each person.'

Alan Briskin provides three pointers:
1 Spirituality is associated with mystery, so it can't be defined by language, which points to definite things. The 'language' of spirituality allows projection onto it.
2 Spirituality is about an internal experience of life, a movement towards a different understanding, a point of interaction with a larger story.
3 Spirituality is the grasping of a larger unity, as historically found in the mystical tradition. (We talk more about the mystical tradition in Chapters 6 to 8.)

Russ Moxley sees it differently:

> When I use the word *spirit*, I am not talking about being religious or about accepting and following the beliefs of a particular religion. I am not even talking about spirit as always achieving an elevated state of mind or being through prayer or meditation – as important as these may be [. . .] For me being spiritual is about being *fully human*, about integrating all the energies that are part of us. It is about connecting to that life force that defines us and connects us.[5]

Harrison Owen:
'Man in his essence is Spirit, and the forms and structures of our existence are only momentary manifestations of that Spirit [. . .] Whatever Spirit is or may become, it is initially "that which underlies all that I am or we are".'[6]

Dermot Tredget, a Benedictine monk who runs courses on spirituality in the workplace (see Chapter 15), summarizes some of the common ideas associated with spirituality. It involves:
*   growth;
*   becoming a person in the fullest sense;
*   conversion and *metanoia* (metanoia meaning a fundamental shift in mind in which individuals come to see themselves as capable of creating the world they truly want rather than reacting to circumstances beyond their control);
*   relationships (vertical and horizontal);
*   attitudes, beliefs and practices;
*   the intellect, emotions and soul.[7]

Philip Sheldrake suggests that spirituality has four central characteristics:
*   non-exclusivity – open to all; found in all faith traditions;
*   soundly theologically based but not dogmatic or prescriptive;
*   not about defining perfection but looking at human growth in the context of a living relationship with the Absolute;
*   seeking integration of all aspects of human life/experience, not just the interior life.[8]

Turner surmises:
'The spiritual life is, at root, a matter of seeing – it is all of life seen from a certain perspective. As with love, however, spirituality is multi-dimensional and some of its meaning is inevitably lost when we attempt to capture it in a few words.'[9]

After surveying numerous definitions, Michael Joseph (a member of our Spirituality in the Workplace network (see Chapter 15) whose doctoral research we draw upon shortly), recognizes: 'Perhaps one thing writers in this paradigmatic field agree on is that spirituality is difficult to define!'[10]

It is perplexing that spirituality is such a nebulous concept and that definition of it is so elusive. Having such a wide diversity of meanings attached to a term does create difficulties, particularly in an organizational context. Yet the paradox is that definitions of terms are not as important as actually recognizing the territory and debating meanings together. In fact the importance in exploring the diversity of meaning people associate with their spirituality is part of the spiritual process itself, part of the journey of pursuing wholeness in community.

Certainly our experience in working with a variety of groups has been that many individuals express how valuable it is for them to engage openly in discussions about spirituality. As Ó Murchú states: 'The spiritual story itself is much more powerful and coherent than any text-book definition or description of spirituality.'[11] We each have our own experience and understanding of how our spirituality is being worked out and that's what the spirit at work phenomenon is striving to cater for.

Gillian's story

The importance of open discussions has indeed been a huge learning for me on the journey. It has been a valuable insight that the most significant connections seem to be born less out of agreeing on a set of values or principles, but rather from the *exploration* of meaning and difference in what people deem to be important. An example of this in practice is a tool we offer globally to our employees to enable these conversations – an 'engagement map'. On it there are the values and principles which the corporation holds dear, and participants are invited to discuss together how they experience these values being lived out by themselves and others on a daily basis. Meaning, importance and application are debated, and even if there is not one consolidated view at the end of the discussion, the value of simply having conversations about what is important is seen as highly beneficial.

The terrain of spirituality

Let's explore the territory we are in a bit more. SaW claims that spirituality is an integral dimension of human beings. Many believe that we are made up of body (physical), mind (sometimes intellect/mental and emotions/emotional) and spirit (spiritual), but how do we create distinctions between these terms? It is becoming clearer that mind and spirit at least are very closely integrated and interconnected; that, in fact, they cannot be separated or fragmented as they affect each other. In debates about spirituality it is suggested that our identity is formed holistically, that things of the 'spirit' cannot be separated out from our mind and emotions. There is also research to suggest that our physical well-being is connected to our spiritual/mental well-being. To fragment concepts is, as we have seen, to adopt a reductionist, old-paradigm approach. In the light of such conclusions (and the new paradigm) we should rethink our frames of reference and look at things more holistically.

Rowan warns against the tendency to go for 'one-two-three-infinity' definitions of spirituality, where we say 'there is a body and its sensations (one), the emotions and feeling and desires (two), the intellect and its thoughts (three), and everything else is a sort of mystical oneness called spirituality (infinity)'.[12]

Rather our physical/emotional/intellectual/spiritual make-up is deeply interwoven, as Maslow recognized when he stated, 'Man's inherent design or inner nature seems to be not only his anatomy and physiology, but also his most basic needs, yearnings and psychological capacity. This inner nature is usually not obvious and easily seen, but is rather hidden.'[13] In the simplest terms the 'hidden yearning' within us is an indicator of our spirituality. Our spirituality is a subject for deep contemplation. It includes our will, how we choose and decide; our heart, the manifestation of complex attitudes; and the influential yet controversial spirit which, many believe, is in its essence both transcendent and immanent. ('Immanent' refers to that which we encounter inside ourselves and the world; the word literally means 'remaining within'.)

In his doctoral thesis, Michael Joseph begins to draw a significant conclusion: 'I [have] an increasing sense of conviction [. . .] that the spiritual dimension is unlike the other three (intellectual, emotional and physical) – not just a co-equal component but in some way playing a more fundamental role, interacting with the other mind-body components in a subtle and complex way which defies simple explication'.[14]

Soul and spirit

In SaW literature, the terms soul and spirit appear frequently. Sometimes they are used interchangeably, sometimes they are distinguished from one another. Perhaps clarification about these terms will aid our understanding.

Some, especially those influenced by the Swiss psychologist Carl Jung, locate soul at the core of the human struggle between the most corrupt passions and the loftiest ideals. They understand it to be full of contradictory urges and a multiplicity of drives, instincts and emotions that at times oppose reason and virtue. 'In each of us there is [. . .] the capacity for courage, personal insight and compassion as well as the ability to act with timidity, distorted perception and malice.'[15] Our struggles are, in fact, part of the universal struggle that goes on all over the world – the age-old struggle between good (beauty and truth) and evil. Whyte agrees that the soul represents a struggle, for 'the path the soul takes to fulfill its destiny seems troublesomely unique' and the 'vast hidden [. . .] underworld of the soul'[16] houses both positive and negative aspects of our lives (as we show more fully in the next chapter). We cannot treat it lightly or expect that by unveiling it in working life we will see only positive energy.

Thomas Moore, highly respected author of *Care of the Soul*, explores this area in depth and distinguishes soul from spirit. He complains of a comparative lack of attention given to the former in this age of 'runaway spirituality', when many fail to note the humble, but vitally necessary, lessons which the soul teaches.[17]

Carl Jung explored the struggle of opposites throughout his life. He believed that in each one of us there is a struggle between the conscious intention to be good and the unconscious suppressed motives. He called the unconscious aspect the *shadow*. In the past psychology has ignored or denied the existence of the soul as a substantive entity, referring instead to the self in terms of behavioural consciousness (not as a being that is conscious). But more recently the field of transpersonal psychology has emerged, and this explores the links between psychology and spirituality in more depth.

Our spirituality encompasses the struggle of soul, but 'spirit' itself is often thought of as an essence which seems to lift us above and beyond the struggle. Briskin talks of spirit as being something distinct from soul, something which suggests 'a transcendence of the mundane, a capacity to see far off into other worlds and into other dimensions'.[18] Spirit is something that links us indefinably to the very essence of life. Wilber in his diagram 'The Great Nest of Being', which we looked at in the previous chapter, regards spirit as something wider and, in terms of spiritual development, deeper than soul.

The Greek word for spirit is *pneuma*, meaning wind, which blows, and, by extension, implies the breath of life. It is the unseen, invisible, immaterial yet powerful force, which breathes life into us, enlivens us, gives energy to us. Spirit helps to define the true, real, unique self that is us and confirms our individuality. It also enables us to recognize that there is something sacred at the core of all existence. Spirit is seen as something which is 'more than' and 'outside' ourselves. But the word is also used to refer to an aspect of ourselves, as in the term 'the human spirit'.

Some clarity is provided by research undertaken by members of MODEM (see Chapter 15). They use the terminology 'little "s" and big

"S"'. In one sense spirit with a little 's', the human spirit that is part of our being, can be discussed somewhat separately from the big 'S', e.g. God or other transcendent entity. Sue conducted additional research into this matter with a group of management developers, one of whom commented that 'the big "S" inspires people to be on the search, but the small "s" is the bit that we all have opportunity to work with'.[19]

Whilst soul and spirit are difficult concepts to define, understand and agree upon, the plea of those interested in SaW is that their importance should not be overlooked. Soul and spirit have to do with the way human beings belong to the world, engage in work and live in human community. Fundamentally, the soul and/or spirit are about 'preserving a desire to live a life a man or woman can truly call their own'. Taking our spiritual identity seriously means recognizing the 'palpable presence of some sacred otherness in our labours, whatever language we may use for that otherness: God, the universe, destiny, life or love'.[20]

Spirituality, God and religion

Scott Peck agrees that whilst our spirituality includes our attempts to be in harmony with the unseen order of things, the unseen order is actually and actively attempting to be in harmony with us.[21] This would suggest that the spirit we are discussing is alive and is in relationship with us, and implies the concept of a living spiritual being, e.g. God.

While some reject the idea of God, for many people deep exploration of their spirituality naturally takes place within the context of their belief in God. Such people are usually also led to explore the ultimate questions of humanity – Who am I, and why am I here? And this brings them into the sphere of religion, where such questions are systematically explored.

It is thought-provoking to find that many influential thinkers and writers conclude their lives with a belief in God's existence. For example, Jung said that he knew God existed and believed that the metaphysical was an integral part of human individuality. Over the entrance to his home he had placed a Latin sign which translated into English reads 'Invoked or not invoked, God is present'.[22] Similarly Moxley describes spirit as being always present. 'Whoever you are, wherever you are, whatever you are doing [. . .] spirit is present. It may be outside your conscious awareness but it is present.'[23]

Whatever our personal view of God, it is important to note how the concept of spirituality aligns to the idea that there is an unseen order of things behind the veil of materialism. It is the common conviction of all in the SaW movement that there is a spiritual reality which offers a unifying oneness and that such a notion can change our perspective on the fragmentation we experience in our lives and in society. We have seen that one can connect to the always present 'spirit' without labelling it as God, or one can attest to it as God and develop understanding from there.

Gibbons clarifies to some extent the different types of spirituality that are put forward in our post-modern culture and raised in SaW literature:

- *Religious*: more theistic, trust in God who will provide direction and support. Our spiritual needs are met through God. Includes worship and prayer. Emphasizes salvation.
- *Secular*: more humanistic, a faith in the universality of the human spirit that binds people to other human beings and to the Earth and that instils within them a compassion for their fellow humans and for the world that is motivational and sustaining. Human effort is important and personal growth/therapy is a route to the sacred expressed aesthetically. Spirit and soul are areas that need cultivation. Emphasizes self-actualization.
- *Mystical*: more transcendent, union with the divine provides spiritual strength and aids right living. We are all part of the universe and connected to every other living thing. Includes meditation and prayer. Emphasizes enlightenment.[24]

Much of the language of spirituality has its roots in religious traditions and philosophies. This is recognized by Gibbons who is critical of the current trend to map spirituality in psychological and secular terms. He argues that we should take the link with religion into account in formulating the content of spirituality. In Chapter 8 we explore more fully the connections of spirituality to a religious foundation.

Our outlook is made up of a mish-mash of ideas that we collect from our society, culture, family and belief systems. To understand who we are we need to unpick our particular inheritance. This is a personal task which no one else can complete for us. But exploring ourselves at this depth, bringing our sense of our self into the light, is what discussing spirituality permits.

Spirituality, work and organizations

While some SaW authors regard God or the Divine as a fundamental component of spirituality, the current use of the term 'spirit at work' is most often not associated with any specific religious tradition.

But before we leave the subject of religion, we note a danger that can arise from the presence of people of different faith traditions in our workplaces, each expressing their spirituality in diverse ways. This can cause tension and division, especially if people do not understand the essential values and beliefs inherent in others' faith systems. On the other hand the diversity of religious pathways can become a cause for deepening our understanding of others. Such understanding is essential if we are to work together successfully. We can be enriched by learning more about the values that others hold. But we also suggest that the awakening to spirituality at work is provoking a challenge to world religions too.

What is important to note here is that our sense of our own spiritual existence persistently expresses itself, whatever our current beliefs about it. And what SaW posits is that workplaces and organizations can benefit if they begin to acknowledge and work with the deeper level of values and beliefs that we hold collectively.

We have noted throughout this chapter how central are concepts of spirituality, religious or otherwise, to the core of a person's identity, their *being*, and to the creative application of their energies in life, their *doing*. It is fairly straightforward for us to understand how our physical, mental and emotional energies are used at work, but we are not so clear that it takes spiritual energy. 'Once we realize that it is spirit that defines our self at the deepest levels of our being – that spirit enables us to offer our whole selves to the activity of leadership, to connect to others richly and rewardingly, and to give us deep sources of meaning – then we begin to understand [. . .] its importance in work'.[25]

What we can glean from the movement towards spirituality is that whatever one's underlying belief system, everyone has a spiritual life, just as they have an unconscious, whether they acknowledge it or not. That many may ignore, actively deny or vigorously flee from the unseen order doesn't mean they are not spiritual beings; it only means they are trying to avoid, or are unaware of, the fact. Or perhaps, as Lips-Wiersma and Mills argue, spirituality is already present in work but people are reluctant to express this spiritual dimension because they judge the work environment to be less than welcoming and safe.[26] The emergence of SaW represents a turning point in our long history of denial, for alongside those who flee from the spiritual are many who have embraced spirituality. We are at different points in our spiritual journey and recognizing this is a key to understanding the struggles we engage in daily.

We are beginning to recognize this and that is why the spirituality debate is not only emerging but becoming central to leading-edge thinking in organizations. It is important that we discuss spiritual realities openly. If spirit is everywhere already, we are inescapably affected by it. By recognizing and labelling spirit we give ourselves the chance to work more purposively with it. By denying its existence we deprive ourselves of its energizing power. The value to organizations of understanding and working with the spiritual dimension is that, 'they will be able to harness the "whole person" and the immense spiritual energy that is at the core of everything'.[27] We look in more detail at how spirituality is an essential element of leadership in Chapter 9; and at the role of spirit in transforming organizations in Chapter 12.

We want to emphasize again that we are at a turning point in organizational life. There is still 'an overall perception that spirituality is a risky topic to raise and discuss within an organizational setting and that individuals self-censure their spiritual values, beliefs and attitudes'.[28] And yet, as researchers Mitroff and Denton have found, many people wish that they could express their spirituality.[29] This is the tension that SaW is getting to grips with.

Gillian's story

'Recognizing' and working 'purposively' with spirit are indeed emerging traits of many leading-edge businesses in my experience. 'Labelling' them as such can still create a disconnect with much of the business community who may regard it as 'fluffy' or 'wishy-washy' and wonder what the benefit to the bottom line might be. I have found that the language employed when describing this phenomenon can significantly affect the quality of conversation. I may choose to talk about the 'corporate spirit', the values and principles of the business, what really matters to people or even refer to specific values of trust, integrity, authenticity and care of fellow employees. Linking these notions and employee fulfilment to the bottom line is more likely to attract the attention of the more sceptical senior manager.

A model for discussing spirituality

Throughout this chapter we have recognized the difficulty in defining spirituality. One way of moving forward, so that we can begin to work with spirituality in a business setting, is to consider the general terrain spirituality occupies. We conclude this chapter by suggesting a particular way of mapping the territory. For this, we are indebted to Michael Joseph whose story indicates how he arrived at the perspective of 'spirituality as four sets of connections'.

Michael Joseph's story

In an article he wrote for the British journal *Faith in Business*,[30] Michael tells the story of how he arrived at what he describes below as four dimensions of spirituality, or spirituality as four sets of connections. He asked two groups of people to brainstorm answers to the question, When you think about spirituality, what comes to mind?

The first group were those active, now or in the past, in the professions. Here is the list of words and phrases they came up with:

Non-judgement – quiet, peace – purpose – mystical being – being connected as you choose to – conscience, values, inner guidance – totally unselfish giving of yourself – link to Divine source – intangible yet concrete – links to outside myself but also part of me – mutual – controversial – precious – connectedness – harmony – common-purpose – energy – beauty – scary – high order – unselfish – beliefs – wholeness – compassion – mystical – being – sacred – love – goodness – misunderstood – vitality – pan-fraternal – deep within.

Michael's second group consisted of those in training for workplace counselling. Here are their suggestions:

Religion – death and dying – saintliness – life after death – harmony – connection with the unknown – 'The Other' (more than this world) – mediums – heightened awareness – refinement – joining together – elements: earth, air, water, fire – lessons/karma – being who we are – separateness – soul – intimacy – search for peace – God – other-worldliness – inward (religion) – healing – simplicity – integrity – oneness – way of being – planes, depth – calm tranquillity – spirit and soul – person centred – higher learning – onward progress.

The typically wide disparity of these answers taxed Michael as a researcher. He began to ask whether it was possible to link these different words and phrases, and if so, how? Gradually he came to the view that there are four dimensions of spirituality – which he categorized as

- connection with God, or the Divine or a higher power;
- connection with others;
- connection with and awareness of self;
- connection with nature and the environment.

Applying this view, he says, 'it becomes possible to understand and often to reconcile quite different expressions of what spirituality might be about. For example, using some of the words listed earlier we can see where they might fit.'

Under 'connection with God or a higher power' he lists: link to Divine source etc; higher order; sacred; more than this world; other worldliness; God; spirit and soul.

Under 'connection with others': totally unselfish giving of yourself; compassion; mutual; intimacy; common purpose; harmony; pan-fraternal; joining together; person centred.

Under 'connection with nature': beauty; elements: earth, air, fire, water.

Under 'connection with self': purpose; to be connected as you choose; being who we are; wholeness; beliefs; separateness; intimacy; integrity; way of being; inward.

What Michael's story suggests is that, while it is virtually impossible to define spirituality in any neat or commonly acceptable way, it is possible to indicate, using the model of the 'four sets of connections', the general territory it covers. In fact, we find many SaW writers following, with varying degrees of explicitness, the four-fold categorization that occurred to Michael. We have quoted snippets from Russ Moxley earlier, but want to offer here, as a kind of summing up, his full (and we feel inspiring) flow of thought:

Spirit is the unseen force that breathes life into us, enlivens us, gives energy to us. Spirit is the 'other' – the life force – that weaves through and permeates all of our experiences.

Spirit works within us. It helps define the true, real, unique self that is us. It confirms our individuality. It works within us to nudge us toward [. . .] our 'hidden wholeness'. We are who we are because of spirit.

Spirit also works between and among us. It connects us to every-thing that exists. It is because of the work of spirit that we experience deep communion with others, experience ourselves as part of something much larger, experience connectedness to all of life [. . .]

Spirit is always present, and it is everywhere present. Whoever you are, wherever you are, whatever you are doing [. . .] spirit is present. It may be outside your conscious awareness, but it is present. It is present in the places we work and in our leadership activities, whether we notice it or not. It is not something that has to be developed or formed. It needs to be *un*covered, not discovered. Uncovering spirit does not require that we develop a new set of skills or abilities so much as learn to reconnect to it. It is part of each of us, not just the special few [. . .] We each experience it, at least sometimes, in our life and our work.

Just as we can mask our feelings or deny our behavior, so too we can suppress spirit. We can cover it up. Our busyness, our need to please others, our quest for status and our yearning for approval, our attempts to maintain a front can all cover and constrain spirit [. . .] Our need is to be in touch with spirit, to acknowledge its importance, and to engage in behaviors – including leadership behaviors – that liberate and elevate it.[31]

We have chosen to use the four connections as our starting point for exploring the terrain of spirituality more deeply, though the following is our preferred order for discussing them:

- Connection with self.
- Connection with others.
- Connection with nature.
- Connection with higher power.

These themes form the content of the next four chapters.

We think this approach will help to amplify one of the most workable definitions of spirituality we have come across, which is provided by Mitroff and Denton. They define spirituality as: 'the basic feeling of being connected with one's complete self, others, and the entire universe. If a single word best captures the meaning of spirituality and the vital role that it plays in people's lives, that word is "interconnectedness".'[32]

4

Connecting with Self

The glory of God is a person fully alive.

Irenaeus[1]

Go into yourself and see how deep the place is from which your life flows.

Rainer Maria Rilke[2]

How we understand ourselves is central to everything that goes on in life. A well-known maxim states, 'The unexamined life is not worth living'. We can adapt this and talk about the unexamined self. SaW writers consistently point out that there is far more to the self than most people, at least in the modern West, imagine there is.

Self-examination is essential for anyone embarking on the spiritual journey. The latter has been described as a 'quest to unite one's inner and outer world, to provide meaning and purpose to one's life. The search, and consequent realization, provides an individual with a sense of alignment and order – a spiritual cohesiveness which instills a sense of rightness and well-being.'[3] This chapter explores a variety of ways our inner world can be examined.

Authenticity

Many of us live at the level of the mundane. We keep busy working through our 'to do' lists, rushing around concerning ourselves with paying the mortgage, keeping up in the material stakes, hoping for progress in our career. Our busyness, and the busyness that goes on all around us, prevents us from facing up to the more radical and frightening prospect of a life that challenges us at a deeper level. 'In our frenzy to get something for ourselves, we have lost ourselves. We have doomed ourselves to a sullen, dull sort of life, full of the things we acquire and empty of any deeper happiness.'[4] Perhaps we know there could be more, but we don't know how to find it or incorporate it into our lives.

As self-conscious human beings we are able to ask questions like: Who am I? Who is the real me, you, us? What is most important to us? What is my purpose? Are we satisfied with who we are becoming? And with what we are doing? Our personal and spiritual development begins when we start asking such questions.

We are unique in having free will and the ability to make choices. To a large extent who we are or what we do is a result of the choices we have made in life. If we want to be authentic we must first truly know what is most important to us, and then choose to speak this aloud and make it real in the outer world.[5] If we are not pleased with who we are, we can choose to change. How we change is subject to our own particular developmental journey. And in the making of this journey the spiritual realm is increasingly seen as of central significance and importance.

We don't get very far along the spiritual path before we discover how much bigger the self is than we previously supposed. Many SaW writers distinguish between the narrow 'ego self' and the greater Self that we have it in us to become, and in a sense already are. Even old-paradigm neurologists have recognized that we typically use only 10 per cent of our potential brain power. It is also reckoned that we manifest only 30 per cent of our latent creativity. Indeed, studies comparing the creativity of young children with that of adults indicate that we have lost most of the creativity we once had.[6] The quest for authenticity is about recovering lost ground as well as opening up further possibilities.

Jung's contribution and influence

We in the West have the psychologists largely to thank for opening up new vistas of the self. It was Sigmund Freud who discovered that we have an *unconscious* mind capable of influencing our conscious behaviour. The awareness of the unconscious has led to psychodynamic therapy (or psychoanalytic psychotherapy as it is sometimes called) – a general term for therapeutic approaches which try to help people to bring their true feelings to the surface so that they can experience and understand them. Psychotherapy literally means 'to nurse the soul', deriving its name from the ancient Greeks and their understanding of human nature and the psyche. In therapy sessions a client is encouraged to embark on a journey of self-discovery and to explore the links between their own feelings, thoughts, beliefs and life events such as relationships and work.

Freud's successor and, later, rival, Carl Jung, expanded our horizons by revealing the spiritual dimensions of the self. It was Jung who invented the term Self, with a capital 'S', to denote the deeper reality in which the ego-self, or self with a small 's', is grounded. His ideas planted the seed for the emergence of transpersonal psychology, which recognizes a psychological reality beyond the individual personality and includes the study of spiritual experiences. (We talk more about this in Chapter 7.)

Jung also posited the notion of a *collective unconscious* containing archetypal material common to all humanity. His studies of dreams and of world mythology revealed a set of characters and situations that recur across cultures and throughout history. For example, the Greek goddess Demeter, the Hindu Parvari and the ancient Egyptian Isis all represent the ideal, or *archetype*, of fertile womanhood, which Jung called 'the Mother'. Another archetype, much referred to in SaW literature especially in relation to leadership, is 'the Hero'.[7] Hercules faced with his twelve labours is a clear invocation of the hero archetype. Wherever there is a challenge to be overcome, the hero is involved.

The recent popularity of *Lord of the Rings* and *Harry Potter* gives an indication of how readily we identify with archetypes. Writers like Moore[8] argue that 'care of the soul' requires a sensitivity to the symbolic and metaphoric life. In particular, Moore expounds the different 'voices of the soul' vying for our attention by relating them to the archetypal images of the Greek and Roman gods and goddesses in classical mythology.[9]

A key idea in Jung's psychology is *individuation*. The process of individuation is about realizing one's aims and aspirations and reconciling inner conflicts in the search for wholeness and fulfilment. For Jung, individuation is as much a spiritual as a psychological quest. Jungian therapy aims to bring about a series of psychological transformations by accessing and analysing both the personal and collective unconscious. Clients are encouraged to measure their progress towards individuation by checking for the appearance of particular archetypes in their dreams.

In their exposition of Jung's theory of individuation, King and Nicol[10] point out that individuals, in order to realize their specific purpose, must connect with their unique Self. The Self is superior to the ego and, when properly connected with, is experienced as the centre of the personality. The Self is at the same time grounded in the collective unconscious and 'situated' at the very heart of reality.

The *shadow* is another important Jungian concept. The shadow represents all those things about us that we don't wish to face and have banished to our unconscious. We come up with defences to protect us from knowing about these painful areas, but often these defences do us more harm than good. This is especially true when we realize that not all the content of our shadow is evil. For example, our spontaneity and childlike exuberance may have been repressed because our expressing them got us into trouble with adults. There is a similar explanation for our diminished creativity. (Peppers and Briskin reproduce an amusing quotation from Robert Bly about an invisible bag that we carry around with us into which we have stuffed aspects of our disapproved-of selves.[11])

Perhaps the best-known element of Jung's thought is his characterization of individuals as either *extrovert* or *introvert*. Jung's insights about the need to hold opposites in balance led him to develop his theory of psychological types, and these concepts are at the heart of Jung's pioneering work on classifying personality where he identified further sets of polarities. For example, one person might be more of a 'thinker' than a 'feeler', while another might be a 'senser' rather than an 'intuitive'. Such models, as developed by Myers and Briggs,[12] have become important in the world of work in such areas as job/career choice, recruitment and training.

The influence of Jung in SaW is immense. For those who wish to study him further, a good, short outline of Jung's teaching is provided by Anthony Storr.[13] More leisured souls are referred to Jung's biography by Ronald Hayman.[14] A marvellous introduction to Jungian archetypes and myths is Carol Pearson's *The Hero Within: Six Archetypes We Live By*.[15] Many SaW writers are themselves modern-day exponents of Jung and his successors. Two we have already mentioned are Cheryl Peppers and Alan Briskin. Their book *Bringing Your Soul to Work*[16] is highly recommended to anyone wanting to begin work on their shadow side. It's full of practical exercises and examples from working life, and serves as a good starting point for exploring this complex area.

From darkness to light

The process of growing towards greater consciousness includes the realization of our own darkness and a desire to move towards light. This is no easy task. 'Anyone who talks glibly about integrating the shadow, as if you could chum up to shadow the way you learn a foreign language, doesn't know the darkness that always qualifies shadow.'[17]

The word 'darkness' can sometimes carry sinister meaning: the darkness of evil. Scott Peck points out, 'Carl Jung helped us [. . .] understand the unconscious, ascribing evil to our refusal to meet the shadow [. . .] Note that Jung ascribed human evil not to the shadow itself but to the refusal to meet this shadow. Those people who are evil are not just passively unconscious or ignorant; they will go far out of their way to remain ignorant or unconscious. Evil, like Love or God or Truth, is too large to submit to any single adequate definition. But one of the better definitions for evil is that it is "militant ignorance".'[18] We return to the subject of evil in Chapters 7 and 11.

Facing our shadow means confronting some difficult home truths. We all have vulnerabilities in our character. As Whyte says, 'Perhaps the parent of all these vulnerabilities is [. . .] the deep physical shame that we are not enough, will never be enough and can never measure up.'[19] The journey to soul recovery often begins in this very lonely place of self-assessment. To find the 'real path' we may have to go off the path we are on now, or even lose our way completely. In the course of this difficult journey there awakens in us an element of self-doubt, which Whyte describes as 'that part of the soul that is able to taste the bitter in life as well as the sweet. It is open to a side of life that a sunny disposition must ignore in order to carry on smiling. It is less interested in pretence and more aware of the suffering entailed in daily living. It is realistic about the balance of suffering and happiness.'[20] This journey may happen more than once in our lives, and some refer to it as 'the dark night of the soul'. (More on this in Chapter 7.)

And yet, the word darkness doesn't have to carry a sinister connotation. Shadow elements are not always negative; we have a dark shadow and a light shadow. There is another part of us about which we may be equally unaware: our greatness. We deny and repress much of our goodness, light, our gifts and spirit. We give away our power to gurus, teachers and idols, just as much as we project our darkness onto our enemies. Root aspects of our personality are being mismanaged, misunderstood or mislabelled and this means we are losing out on vitality and treasure in our lives, with the result that our potential is never realized. Just as important as knowing our limitations is knowing our gifts, talents and abilities, and becoming free so that we can shine.

Nelson Mandela spoke of this when, at his inauguration as President of South Africa, he read the following inspirational statement from Marianne Williamson:

> Our deepest fear is not that we are inadequate. Our deepest fear is that we are powerful beyond measure. It is our light not our darkness that most frightens us. We ask ourselves, who am I to be brilliant, gorgeous, talented, fabulous? Actually, who are you not to be? You are a child of God. Your playing small does *not* serve the world. There's nothing enlightened about shrinking so that other people won't feel insecure around you. We are all meant to shine as children do. We were born to make manifest the glory of God that is within us. It's not just in some of us; it's in everyone. And as we let our own light shine, we unconsciously give other people permission to do the same. As we're liberated from our own fear, our presence automatically liberates others.[21]

Our complex inner world is a 'continual interplay of the mystery of who we have been and who we are seeking to be', say Peppers and Briskin.[22] We see that it is by reflecting on our own inner depths that we may embark on a journey of spiritual growth. The process of searching for light to illuminate the shadow seems to take us along many paths and is repeated continuously throughout our development towards maturity.

In the previous chapter, we showed how spirituality can be explored from a secular, religious or mystical perspective. We can use this reference point of differing perspectives when we examine the self. The mystical perhaps offers the most helpful insights here. For his appreciation of the importance of living from our deep centre, Jung was much indebted to the thirteenth-century scholar, preacher and spiritual director Meister Eckhart. Cyprian Smith provides a modern-day interpretation of Eckhart and reveals some deep truths about the journey into self. For example, 'We identify ourselves with what we do, with the role we believe we are called to play in society'.[23] Eckhart insisted that these roles can be illusory, they are not the true 'us'. Our real identity is deeper than this; our Self has potential to make manifest the 'glory of God within us'.

Smith suggests that instead of trying to understand the world from the outside, we find that the answers lie within ourselves. Instead of being tyrannized continually by our thoughts and emotions conjured up by the multiplicity of selves, reacting to external stimuli and conditioning, we need to penetrate to the true Permanent Self or the Ground of the Soul – that which is most inward and secret in us. This Self, the centre of our being, is sometimes labelled as 'God within us'. We need to learn to live and act from that centre. Many testify that this centring process is only made possible by our communion with the transcendent. So we see how it is that reflections about who we are at the core of our being will gradually kindle the divine spark within us. Only divine light can fully illuminate shadow.

These concepts about Self help us to understand more clearly the issues we have with self-belief, and self-limiting beliefs. Our beliefs about our core identity and worth are so vital to the creation of a healthy self-esteem and self-respect.

Paradox

Psychologists show that we make spiritual progress at the level of soul when we become aware of and confront the contradictions contained in our shadow. These contradictions help us to become aware of paradox in ourselves. Williams talks of 'our own inner opposites – within each of us is the sinner and the saint, the love and the greed, the cynic and the believer'.[24] Organizations, being full of people, are acknowledged to be full of paradox, and the personal/professional split is one example of the creative tension that makes up our life. Williams suggests that to 'live fully requires us to acknowledge and embrace these paradoxes'.[25] Contemplation of paradoxes helps us to understand who we are. Smith says that paradox is the way to open the 'wisdom eye'.[26]

We can see paradox in ourselves when our unconscious desires and aspirations are the very opposite of what we are consciously trying to achieve. We may think we are working for peace, justice and the good of others when in fact we are seeking power, domination and the subjection of others to our own selfish ends. Actions which are good in themselves, if done for ungrounded and uncentred motives, can result in harm. To draw from the Bible: 'For I do not do the good I want, but the evil I do not want is what I do.'[27] So even if we do examine our motives we are left grappling with paradox. What can we do?

Morgan suggests that the tension of opposites lies 'at the basis of all change'.[28] Embracing paradox brings the human intellect to an awareness of its own limitations and thus opens it up to the possibility of a higher kind of knowing. Eckhart's view is that the key to this mystery is attitude; it's not so much what we do, but how and why we do these things, having an attitude of relaxed openness, detachment and receptivity. To expound his views for just a little longer, he puts forward that the way to the Ground of the Soul is detachment. Detachment that is attained by stripping away our images and projections and operating from a place of stillness and unconditional love. This is why so many believe this can only be achieved when this centring process is based on a union with the grace of God. (We explore the connection to a higher power more fully in Chapter 7.) St Ignatius said that before we can become divine, we must become fully human. Perhaps the paradox is that to be fully human means to find the divinity at our core. Certainly this is an idea Wilber seems in tune with.

Wilber's 'levels' or stages of spiritual growth

We have seen that our spiritual journey takes us from the ego-self, or immediately presenting self, through the labyrinthine paths of the shadow self with its paradoxes, conflicts and contradictions, and out into the light of the Self which is the very centre of our being and of all reality.

Jung saw the journey as something we make in stages. He divided our life into two main stages, holding that in the first half of life we develop our ego, and in the second half we explore the more holistic Self. There are numerous other theories about our human development and many of them recognize and appreciate the spiritual dimension in our growth. Space only permits us to skim over that of Ken Wilber, and we have picked him because he is currently so influential.

However, we want to add a word of caution. While it is possible to talk of levels or stages, there are some who question whether human development advances in a stage-like manner at all. The alternative thought is that an individual's praxis and unfolding towards maturity is much more to do with the capacity for reflective judgement. We need to bear in mind that development doesn't necessarily take place in a linear way, but is rather dialectical and contextual. However, adult development does seem to emerge as distinctive to that of the formative early years of life. But it is not a straightforward process, more a continuous spiralling, switchback, rollercoaster ride! As Thomas Moore says, it may not even be quite correct to speak of the soul's path. 'It's more a meandering and a wandering.'[29]

In his *A Brief History of Everything*[30] Wilber discusses the various levels of spiritual awareness. Ranging from being a baby to mature adulthood, these levels progress through realizing our biological and emotional separateness (levels 1 and 2), being concerned about ourselves and our own rights (level 3), then on to recognizing the rights of others, particularly our own family, team, school, community, nation (level 4).

A crucial developmental moment is at level 5 ('formal reflexive') when, typically as young adults, we learn to criticize our own thoughts and habits and become willing to consider those not of our own kin, nationality or faith. This is the 'change the world' phase often associated with idealistic teenagers – the time when we begin to question the norms and rules of our culture and start asking 'what if' questions. We here move to a self which truly thinks for itself and is able to look critically at the system in which it finds itself.

As we progress to more mature adulthood (level 6, 'vision logic') we consolidate our worldview. We have more of a global consciousness. We become more consistent and serious about serving the world and taking responsibility for its well-being. Wilber talks about an 'observing self' that is beginning to transcend both the mind and body. This means the self can step outside any particular perspective. According to John Rowan (a transpersonal psychologist who supports Wilber's views), this stage represents at one time 'the end of the process of individual development within the confines, so to speak, of one's own skin; and the beginning of the process of transpersonal development'.[31] The quest for meaning and purpose figures largely at this stage.

Wilber portrays three levels beyond this stage which are more transcendent. At level 7 ('psychic') there is consolidation of the sense of a higher self. At this level a person may from time to time lose the sense of being a separate self and feel unity with an aspect of, or indeed the whole of, nature (on which point, see further Chapter 6). This is the stage at which 'we acquire psychic sensitivities or abilities'.[32] We are now beginning to move out of 'consensus reality'; much of the taken-for-granted aspects of the world are now radically questioned, in particular the boundaries which divide us from the world in general and other people in particular do not seem important.[33]

Level 8 ('subtle') is a stage of heightened spiritual consciousness, including bliss, deep love and compassion for all. It is the beginning phase of union with Deity, and visions of Deity as your own culture perceives the divine are experienced. Here the higher self truly comes into its own. Says Rowan, 'one may speak of inspiration at this level, meaning actual messages coming from a higher or deeper source'.[34] Rowan cites Heron[35] who refers to 'the great reversal' that happens at this stage, where the self-assertion that characterized all previous stages gives way to surrender. Most people can probably accept that development is feasible to these levels.

The next two levels seem to be rarely, if ever, achieved! On reaching level 9 ('causal'), one gains a sense of being 'drenched in the fullness of Being',[36] and of freedom and release, of transcending time, space, movement and any object or subject. There is a compassion at this stage which is different from, and deeper than, anything which one had earlier. People here speak of formless consciousness, boundless radiance, coalescence of human and divine.

The final level ('non-dual') is where 'you step off the ladder altogether. You are no longer in here looking at the world out there. You are the Kosmos. The very divine sparkles in every sight and sound, and you are simply that.'[37] Rowan summarizes this stage as: 'The ultimate. Unity. Emptiness. Nothing and all things.'[38]

The importance of these levels is emphasized by Rowan. He says that 'each of the Wilber steps requires a move to a new definition of self [. . .] it affects the whole person in a radical way'.[39] Wilber's model also proposes that we have to negotiate each developmental step sequentially. We can't jump stages. At each stage we can be hampered by our past, but we can also have glimpses of future levels of spiritual attainment. These are called 'peak', or alternatively 'peek', experiences. The transitions to each higher level can be difficult to negotiate, as we shall see in Chapter 7.

As most of us (including the authors) haven't yet experienced the upper levels, except perhaps for the occasional glimpses, much of the latter part of the above summary will have to be taken on trust. But what Wilber and Rowan seem to agree upon is that we humans are drawn to such levels of transcendence that we may enter the very realm of the divine!

Other perspectives on exploring self

For reasons of completeness we want to highlight a few other ideas in relation to self. We do not have the space to dwell on the many routes to personal development that abound, but hope that this chapter will inspire you to pursue a route that is interesting and relevant to you.

IQ, EQ and SQ

The notion of differing forms of intelligence has been highlighted by Gardner's work.[40] He argues that we have multiple intelligences, including types that are object-related, object-free and personal. These range across logical-mathematical, visual-spatial, kinaesthetic, verbal-linguistic, musical, interpersonal and intrapersonal, and (recently included) naturalist. The inter/intra personal intelligences seem to correlate most easily to the spiritual and psychological, but arguably our spirituality impacts on all the intelligences, as do our emotions.

The concept of the mind as made up of intellect and heart (emotions) has been popularly highlighted by Daniel Goleman in his book *Emotional Intelligence*.[41] He suggests that our 'EQ' (as emotional intelligence has subsequently been dubbed) might matter more than our IQ. We are not just rational but also emotional beings, and must recognize our own feelings (personal awareness) and those of others (social awareness) for motivating ourselves, and for managing emotions in ourselves and in our relationships.[42] EQ is a multi-faceted construct and is aligned with the concept of competencies. One who has higher EQ has certain competencies another person might not have. Such competencies can help a person to achieve greater success at work. Notwithstanding the social importance of using our emotions in constructive rather than destructive ways, it is questionable whether the emotions are not actually part of a deeper psycho-spiritual reality. 'There are great parallels between the awareness and skill competencies of EI and the behavioral, attitude, and personality results of spirituality,' argue Tischler, Biberman and McKeage.[43] This suggests that to enhance our emotional capabilities we really need to develop our spirituality more.

The concept of EQ has proved very popular, and it was not long before SQ or Spiritual Intelligence appeared.[44] Whilst a number of authors speak of our spirituality as an intelligence, including Emmons,[45] Levin[46] and McGeachy,[47] SQ is most frequently associated with Zohar and Marshall.[48]

Quantum physicist Danah Zohar and her husband Ian Marshall define SQ as the highest intelligence. With our SQ we 'address and solve problems of meaning and value [...] [and] place our actions and lives in a wider, richer, meaning-giving context'.[49] Building on the 'vocational types' mapwork of J. F. Holland[50] and the Jung/Myers–Briggs 'psychological types', they produce a model for working with the spiritual dimension which they call the 'the Lotus of the Self'. The outer parts of the lotus petals represent six vocational and personality types. Deeper into the petals we have the unconscious part of the self, deeper still the collective unconscious and its archetypes, and at the centre the core of the self, 'from which we draw energy and the potential to transform'.[51]

Emmons, writing in the discipline of psychology of religion, also argues that spirituality meets Gardner's criteria for an intelligence. He suggests five core abilities that define spiritual intelligence:[52]

- The capacity for transcendence.
- The ability to enter into heightened spiritual states of consciousness.
- The ability to invest everyday activities, events and relationships with a sense of the sacred.
- The ability to utilize spiritual resources to solve problems in living.
- The capacity to engage in virtuous behaviours or to be virtuous (to show forgiveness, to express gratitude, to be humble, to display compassion).

Working with the body (breathing, relaxation, massage, reflexology etc) is yet another way of connecting with self and aids the process of feeling fully alive. This can be linked to techniques such as yoga and Tai-Chi. One writer, Michal Levin, who describes herself as an 'intuitive', bases her work on the seven chakras, a model which sees spiritual intelligence and development as the discovery and release of various energy levels, each of which is associated with a different spot along the body's central axis. The chakras – base, sacral, solar plexus, heart, throat, brow or third eye and crown – correspond quite closely to Wilber's levels.

Vocation and calling

Zohar and Marshall connect living from the centre with the theme of vocation. For them, vocation is about discovering our unique path in life based on our particular skills, talents and gifts: 'Each of us must "sing our song." We must all, through our own deepest resources and through the use of our spiritual intelligence, access the deepest layer of our true selves and bring up from that source the unique "music" that each human being has the potential to contribute.'[53]

This idea of a calling is embellished by Joseph Jaworski, who says there is something outside of us that is nurturing us along: 'The call to adventure [. . .] comes in many ways, both subtle and explicit. It is the call to become what we were meant to become, the call to achieve our vital design [. . .] If we have truly committed to follow our dream, we will find that a powerful force exists beyond ourselves and our conscious will, a force that helps us along the way, nurturing our quest and transformation.'[54]

The idea of service is sometimes linked with vocation. The two come together where the heart's desire meets the world's greatest needs. The trick is to find the need that speaks to your heart and connects to your gifts. A good book which makes this link is John Adair's *How to Find Your Vocation: A Guide to Discovering the Work you Love.*[55]

Exploring our gifts, strengths and talents can inform our sense of vocation and guide us in making a career choice. Research shows that people perform better when they shape their work and their lives around their strengths. Gallup use this approach with many businesses. They say that our talents/strengths are unique and enduring. But how do we discover what they are? Essentially, it comes down to assessing ourselves in a fairly straightforward way:

- What do we really enjoy doing?
- What energizes us?
- What do we really treasure?
- What do we do well?
- When do we operate at our best?

To recognize our talents we need to look for:

- what's spontaneous and in line with our temperament – what things we prefer and do automatically and easily;
- yearnings and interests – what we simply must do;
- what is learned quickly, our aptitude – we learn rapidly in areas where we have a talent;
- the things we just love to do – e.g. meeting people, design, organizing etc.

Neuro Linguistic Programming is a widely used approach for personal development. It is based on the study of exceptional talent and an exploration of the conscious and unconscious processes that combine to enable people to achieve positive outcomes. NLP incorporates a variety of elements and includes spirituality as a primary aspect of our core make-up. A good guide to NLP is Sue Knight's book *NLP at Work.*[56]

There are many different ways in which we can investigate who we are, what we love doing and what we are good at. Pursuing answers to these quandaries helps us gain confidence to become more fully ourselves.

We would like at this point to refer you to a couple of books which elaborate on this area in more depth:

- Nick Williams' *The Work We were Born to Do.*[57] Williams emphasizes the centrality of following your inner call if you want to achieve real success in your work. 'Perhaps one of the most significant and important elements of the work we were born to do is learning to listen to ourselves and our intuitions again, discovering what we really want in our heart.'[58] His book provides a host of inspirational ideas as to how we can discover who we are and uncover our life's path.

- Marcus Buckingham and Don Clifton's *Now Discover your Strengths*.[59] This book is based on a Gallup study of over two million people who have excelled in their careers. It offers a web-based interactive component that allows readers to complete a questionnaire developed by the Gallup Organization and instantly discover their own top five inborn talents. These can help you in your own development, and your success in work. The book shows how organizations inhibit the talents of their people, and need to change.

Self-sacrifice and selflessness

To conclude this chapter we want to highlight a major paradox offered by many wisdom traditions – that of losing our life in order to find our life. This is a concept that only really makes sense if we do have a belief in a higher power, as it involves surrender and letting go, trusting in something bigger than ourselves. As we have seen, there are many different ways of understanding self (and space prohibits us from examining other views of the self, for example the Buddhist conception of 'no-self') but ultimately we believe that we cannot fully understand self without also exploring our relationship to others and higher power. Wheatley says, 'We see the world through who we are. All living beings create themselves and then use that "self" to filter new information and co-create their worlds [. . .] It is very important to note that in all life the self is not a selfish individual. "Self" includes awareness of those others it must relate to as part of its system.'[60] There is a profound relationship between individual activity and the whole. The happiness we seek sometimes comes from giving it away to others, or sacrificing ourselves for a higher cause out of devotion to a higher power. We find our own destiny by yielding to the design of the universe, which is speaking through the design of our own person.

Martin Buber talks about discovering the 'grand will' as opposed to our 'puny, unfree wills [. . .] The free man is he who wills without arbitrary self-will [. . .] He must sacrifice his puny, unfree will, that is controlled by things and instincts, to his grand will, which quits defined for destined being.'[61] Jaworski takes 'grand will' as a synonym for what the implicate order[62] is wanting to do through us. To respond to such promptings means acquiring an inner power that enables us to achieve great things with our lives.

5

Connecting with Others

We obviously cannot confront this tangled world alone [...] It takes no great insight to realize that we have no choice but to think together, ponder together, in groups and communities. The question is how to do this. How to come together and think and hear each other in order to touch, or be touched by, the intelligence we need.

Jacob Needleman[1]

SaW literature sees life as a transformative process. Transformation is essentially the movement by which our lives as individuals reach fulfilment. If spirit is the life force which stirs each one of us towards change, then there are many ways in which it can manifest its presence. Not only within us, but between and among us and in communities. As Peter Reason says, 'We actively participate in the cosmos, and it is through this active participation that we meet what is Other.'[2]

Transformation does not happen in isolation – becoming a complete person is not something we can do entirely by ourselves. As Martin Buber put it, an 'I' becomes fully an 'I' only in meaningful dialogue with a 'thou'. 'Quite simply [. . .] transformation exists as a possibility *only* in the context of *the love of another* who becomes "thou" to me, even as I am "thou" to him or her, a dearly beloved brother or sister to whom I may acceptably reveal my powerlessness, even as I am challenged to go beyond it.'[3] Moxley agrees that we relate to the other as a '"thou", relating out of deep respect and honoring who the other is as an individual'.[4] That is, there is a true turning to one another, and a full appreciation of another not as an object on a social function, but as a genuine being.

More broadly, wholeness and healing in our world require us to participate in the human community in ways that 'contribute to the flourishing of individual persons, the flourishing of human community, and the flourishing of the biosphere (environment) of which we are a part'.[5] We need each other in order to grow, develop and live a life which has meaning. At the same time we need to express our own individuality, about which Wheatley says, 'As paradoxical as it is, our unique expressions are the only source of light we have to see each other. We need the light from each unique jewel in order to illuminate our oneness.'[6]

But how many of us feel we are close to achieving such rich quality in our interactions? What can we do to make a difference in our relationships with others?

We are in contact with others all the time – partners, spouses, children, family, friends, neighbours, colleagues, professionals, staff, customers, teams, communities, church members, officials etc. And there are a whole host of ways in which people can come together to share and learn from each other. What SaW suggests is that our exchanges with one another should gravitate towards being mutually beneficial partnerships. We should be learning to create relationships which are reciprocal, providing both support and challenge to both, or all, parties.

Much of SaW's contribution is devoted to creating a desire for us to inquire together, listen to, and learn from and with each other, and many authors offer instructive examples of how we can begin to work together in deeper and more creative ways. This chapter provides an introduction to some of the thinking behind this.

Our inner work is vital

Since our own wholeness is tied up with the wholeness of others, it is important to continue to work on becoming whole ourselves so that we can help others to do the same. In a ground-breaking book called *Centered on the Edge*,[7] which details outcomes of a focused inquiry into groups who have experienced spirit at work, some powerful insights are offered. The book portrays research into the collective experiences of people working with and within groups, and the findings are outlined in the form of

- patterns (similar themes, organizational elements and dynamics which seemed to emerge repeatedly within research interviews);
- principles (categorized into elements of the experience, significance of gathering and practices for preparing and opening); and
- metaphors (the metaphoric ways people used to describe their experiences).

The most intriguing aspect of this work is that it tries to represent some of the feeling of spirit in its presentation of ideas.

The book deals with some difficult questions. For example, Hurley seeks to work out how to accomplish something specific in relation to a particular company, organization or community by drawing on spiritual wisdom. His stance highlights that we need to reconcile our personal and professional paths. The personal 'interest in how we open to deeper, more essential sources of wisdom and love, [. . .] in how we bring the truth of our personal realities into dynamic, creative harmony with the truths of others'. And the professional 'interest in how we integrate what we discover – who we become – with the work of transforming the systems and structures of our organizations, institutions and communities'.[8] The challenge is *how* to make ourselves open, and available, to expressing spiritual truths in our practical, everyday lives in such a way that helps to transform the systems and structures of the organizations, institutions and communities around us for the better.

This is an important point, which exposes a central difficulty in moving forward with spirituality. Even if we are personally alive to a spiritual life, how can we use our fledgeling wisdom to build worthwhile relationships and make a difference in the wider world?

On the constructive side, we know that working with others can create great energy. Our interactions with others show us more of who we are, and our working collectively enables us to achieve more than we ever could on our own, and can bring out the very best in us. But on the destructive side, 'group think' can lead people towards irresponsible action and scapegoating. In the previous chapter we looked at the notion of the 'shadow' self. This idea is pertinent to the current chapter because our shadow is something we often project onto others. We find in others what we hide in ourselves, blaming them for how we feel. The shadow side of our personalities can play out in groups leading to 'group shadow'.[9] This complex dynamic is an unseen aspect active in many workplace relationships.

To understand and make allowances for the shadow side of others, we cannot help but re-emphasize the importance of attending to our own inner life. The purpose of doing all this shadow work is to see that the beliefs we hold about ourselves are ego-self concepts, beliefs that we use to block awareness of our own divine nature and to shut out ideas which may challenge us deeply. Freedom means being responsible and giving up blame, trusting and acting out of spiritual wisdom rather than believing what others tell us to be true.

The key to treating others appropriately is to regard them as 'legitimate human beings', to use Senge's phrase. 'When we actually begin to accept one another as legitimate human beings, it's truly amazing. Perhaps this is what love means. Virtually all the world's religions have, in one way or another, recognized the power of love, this quality of seeing one another as legitimate human beings.'[10] The sense of the golden rule common to many spiritual paths, of 'loving your neighbour as yourself', becomes clearer. The more we understand our own individual consciousness the more we will be able to 'love' others as they work through their own inner dilemmas.

Dealing with power and politics

SaW suggests it is only through the process of working with ourselves at a more profound spiritual level that we can develop the necessary freedom and trust to release our personal truth into a more public domain. This release of truth can begin to strip away at the roles we hide behind, and the games we play, all of our pretences, and lets us move to a deeper form of shared meaning. As Needleman says, 'In our present culture [...] the main need is for a form that can enable human beings to share their perception and attention and, through that sharing, to become a conduit for the appearance of spiritual intelligence.'[11]

Hurley suggests that exchange at this level of depth is essential if we are to 'think through all the hard issues around power, resource flows and function in the organization'.[12] He thereby introduces one of the key difficulties that block our attempts to be trusting and truthful – the inappropriate ideas we have about power. Our reaction to dealing with power reveals a lot about us and affects how we treat and engage with others. On an individual basis, we may construe that we have less or more power. In an organizational setting this is manifested as organizational politics. As Williams puts it, 'Work becomes the battleground for competing for the apparent scarce resources of power, money, privilege, approval, good jobs, security and victory – the things our ego tells us are the source of our happiness.'[13] Work becomes a major source of our identity and we are scared to make ourselves vulnerable. But the greatest rewards – of joy, creativity, integrity, authenticity, love, peace – are not externally derived but spring from within ourselves. They cannot be won by game playing. Rather they are chosen by us when we see through the façade we have created or gone along with.

One of the key factors in understanding how we appreciate and use power is to explore whether we operate from a basis of fear or love. SaW suggests that we need to be able to move beyond our individual and personal limitations, our fears, if we are to reach for our fullest capabilities and live out our values and purposes, live a life of love, in practical ways. Williams, referring to the task of working with our shadow to reclaim power, says 'we reclaim our power by joining with those we are projecting on to or judging, seeing through to the divine core in our self and the others, knowing that we all come from the same source'.[14]

Whilst this chapter does not have space to elaborate on power or on politics in any real depth, we do suggest that developing an awareness of our spirituality enables us to better understand these areas, and this is a significant step forward. If spirituality consists of something in us, something outside of us and the collective effect of these in any given context, then we are able to look more accurately into what is going on when we interact with others.

We must acknowledge that we live in a world in which people possess varying degrees of power. Sharing Hurley's thoughts again:

> There are tremendous forces at work in the world not guided by the kind of values that you and I share. Those forces command enormous resources and enormous organizational and institutional power. The continuing centralization of power and resources that's taking place in the corporate world especially should be of tremendous concern to us all [...] At one level, what's needed is rigorous truth-telling about the realities in the world, the choices we face, and the paths we have available to us [...] But at the same time [...] we need to cultivate enormous compassion [...] Most people want to do the right thing [...] [and] of course the 'right thing' means very different things for different people, and that is precisely what we need processes to work with.[15]

These inequalities require us to overcome our deficiencies and not to turn away from confronting reality – in ourselves and in the world. Compassion is the choice to soften our heart as we realize our common human tendencies. The truth may be that all of us are caught up in this struggle of hide and seek. We live with our insecurities, doubts and fears, but deep down long for integrity, authenticity and love in our world. But we all have the power to spread love and kindness if we choose to.

To co-create the climate that we need for mutual support and growth we must each recognize the power structures that abound and learn to engage in them authentically; that is take up our legitimate personal power individually and in group settings. We need to 'speak our voice,'[16] engage in courageous speech and reveal what is true for us. Challenging consensual reality might make us feel vulnerable, but it can lead to healing and growth. It may not seem like the easy option at the time, but in the long run such challenges produce the results that we yearn for – peace and harmony in our relationships, and change in the way the future is constructed.

David Bohm's contribution

Our work in this world involves reconciling a host of dualities into 'a greater whole that transcends and enfolds them [...] This occurs through our listening to the call towards something [. . .] more whole.'[17] The understanding that we can resolve differences by seeing through them to a greater wholeness is a recurring theme that many in SaW promote. In fact, it is ultimately through serving wholeness, the unifying oneness of the universe, that we are able to leverage the infinite power of 'collective intelligence' and 'spiritual wisdom'.[18]

At this point, in order to explain all this from a more scientific perspective, it is essential to highlight the work of David Bohm, a Professor of Theoretical Physics. He was a significant contributor to 'new science' and thereby to SaW ideology. Whilst most people reading this book will not be physicists, Bohm's insights are important because he related his understanding of quantum physics and physical reality to human consciousness. He described his life's scientific and philosophical work as being about 'understanding the nature of reality in general and of consciousness in particular as a coherent whole, which is never static or complete, but which is an unending process of movement and unfoldment'.[19] It is no easy task to summarize Bohm's thoughts, but we attempt to highlight some key concepts since they provoke us to consider our worldview. As we shall be seeing shortly, they also illuminate the whole subject of our relationships with each other.

He suggests that theories about the way the world works are nothing more than ever-changing forms of insight, giving shape and form to experience. It is therefore crucial to understand that thought is a form of insight, a way of looking, rather than a true copy of reality as it is. Failure to realize this leads to division in thought and ultimately confusion of mind.

As a physicist, Bohm understands the universe to be an 'unbroken whole' yet argues that humans apprehend it in a fragmented way. The idea of fragmentation is critical for Bohm. Each human being has been fragmented into separate and conflicting compartments according to differing desires, ambitions, psychological characteristics, loyalties etc. He proposes that the widespread and pervasive distinctions between people (race, nation, profession etc.), which prevent humankind from working together for the common good, originate in the thought that things are inherently divided, disconnected and 'broken up' into smaller, constituent parts. Each part is considered to be essentially independent and self-existent. When people think of themselves this way, they will inevitably tend to defend the needs of their own ego against those of others. We need to see through the separateness and fragmentation in our societies, our opinions and assumptions, to something deeper, the unity where we are both one and many. Bohm believes that a 'proper world view' (his phrase) is essential for harmony in the individual and in society as a whole.

What determines that this world is one unbroken whole is the reality

Bohm calls the 'implicate order'. It is the implicate order which enfolds within itself everything in existence, every object, thought or event, wherever it is in time or in space. Each one can only be defined in terms of its relationship to everything else. At the most fundamental level of reality, physical systems consist of patterns of dynamic energy that criss-cross and 'interfere' in a pattern of unbroken wholeness. Isaacs summarizes the implicate order as 'the idea that underlying the physical universe is a sea of energy that "unfolds" into the visible, explicate world that we see around us [. . .] and then folds back up again'.[20] Each quantum 'bit' has a particle-like aspect, an aspect that can be measured, but it also has a wave-like aspect, vibrations of further potentiality. The future possibilities, and even the future identity of each bit, are internally bound up with the possibilities and identities of all the others. Bohm uses the metaphor of a hologram where each part contains information of the whole object. No one bit can be abstracted out and viewed on its own without loss and distortion.[21]

If we can understand this, we can see how our relationships with others are more significant than perhaps we realized. Bohm said:

> Yourself is actually the whole of mankind. That's the idea of implicate order – that everything is enfolded in everything [. . .] If you reach deeply into yourself, you are reaching into the very essence of mankind. When you do this, you will be led into the generating depth of consciousness that is common to the whole of mankind and that has the whole of mankind enfolded in it. The individual's ability to be sensitive to that becomes the key to the change of mankind. We are all connected.[22]

This insight means that not only is it vital to appreciate our own consciousness and what it reveals to us, but also to realize the value of every person's intuition and understanding.

Bohm's discoveries about the universe led him to explore the notion of *dialogue* as a way to develop our understanding of ourselves, others and the collective whole. He recognized that dialogue can help a group to pool their rational and intuitive insights, and so arrive at something greater than any one individual might arrive at on their own. The concept of dialogue is obviously very important for the work context, so let's move on to explore it more fully.

Dialogue and collaborative inquiry

Dialogue comes from the Greek word *dialogos* and means 'through the word'. The implication being that through the word we arrive at shared meaning. In essence, dialogue is a flow of meaning – a living experience of inquiry within and between people, a conversation in which people think together in relationship. Many writers and thinkers (Argyris, Schon, Scott Peck, Senge, Mezirow, Freire, Bohm, Isaacs, Dixon) support the idea that dialogue is important if we are to develop ourselves, our organizations and societies purposively. The separation that many of us feel between who we are as people and what we do as practical professionals is bridged when we learn to think and talk together.

To understand ourselves and others we must continue to be able to reframe our understanding of our 'self in the world' and our 'self in relation to the system'. The value of dialogue is that it puts us in touch with the many 'co-existing, colliding, overlapping worlds. In so far as any organization encompasses and exists within a myriad of (often ambiguous) "worlds", the ability to understand, move and translate between them is fundamental to the task of the manager.'[23] Isaacs sums up the area succinctly: 'The theory of dialogue suggests that breakdowns in the effectiveness of teams and organizations are reflective of a broader crisis in the nature of how human beings perceive the world [. . .] If fragmentation is a condition of our times, then dialogue is one tentatively proven strategy for stepping back from the way of thinking that fragmentation produces.'[24]

Isaacs makes powerful claims for this process: 'We can learn to kindle and sustain a new conversational spirit that has the power to penetrate and dissolve some of our most intractable and difficult problems.'[25] When we work together in groups or in teams we can begin to recognize that no one person has all the answers. We have to be willing to listen, curious about the diversity of experiences and ideas, even willing to be disturbed and challenged by those who think differently than we do.[26]

The power of dialogue lies in the ability of people to suspend their assumptions, to refrain from imposing their views on others and to avoid suppressing or holding back what they think. People are both the recipients of tacit assumptions and the creators of them. Implicit in the willingness to suspend these assumptions is a sense of confidence; that if your deepest beliefs are worthwhile, they'll withstand inquiry from others, and if they're not, you'll be strong enough, and open enough, to reconsider them. Dialogue requires that we take responsibility for thinking, not merely reacting, and lifts us to a more conscious state. It involves a deeper kind of listening, asking questions and inquiring together. It requires an attitude of curiosity rather than wanting to prove who is right. It also exposes the contradictions between what we say and what we do. When we hear and respect others' contributions, then we begin to unlock something of immense value. Our own assumptions, and any contradictions in our thinking, become available for all (ourselves included) to question and explore. The act of observing thought changes it. We rediscover the joy of thinking together. We learn to be fully present in the moment with one another.

Gillian's story

Dialogue offers the opportunity to enrich the whole as well as the individual parts, which is why we as an organization have looked into how it can help realize our business goals. In recent years we ran a series of Leadership Workshops to which a large number of our managers in the UK were invited. We wanted to explore together what we could do to better capture the energy and contributions of all our employees in order to become both a strong, successful business and a great place to work. The series of workshops was part of a programme which had the clear intention of transforming the business. Although this eventually extended across the whole of our European business, it also paid attention to the needs of the individual parts.

In developing these workshops, we believe that one of the levers on which we needed to focus to transform the business was leadership, and we developed a three-day agenda in which our people could begin to explore it.

The first afternoon was a chance for all participants to share how they felt about the organization. There would always typically be a mixture of both positive and negative comments. The interesting pattern which emerged from the negative comments was that they came from groups (of sometimes quite senior managers) who felt 'done unto'. They felt it was 'them out there' (never defined) who were making life difficult for them as they sought to do their jobs well. We then spent the next two days exploring together how, as individuals, we were responding to business issues, how we could choose to take *personal responsibility* for tackling problems and how to use our own thinking to shape the future organization.

Once individuals had begun to take increased personal responsibility for the business, we could then begin to work in partnership with one another to develop jointly our ability to lead. This gave us the opportunity for both personal and organizational growth. Dialogue was critical in fostering a positive outcome. Challenge balanced with support encouraged individuals to begin to see their own role and possibilities in a different light and, as a result, we began to see groups within the business start to work together in a different and much more powerful way.

In order to be successful it's important to have both support and challenge from others who can both sustain the effort and offer alternative perspectives. We need to be both autonomous and collaborative in achieving better relationships.

Such a participation in the formation of our shared world is vital:

> Participation [. . .] honours the basic right of people to have a say in forms of decision making [. . .] Institutions need to enhance human association by an appropriate balance of the principles of hierarchy, collaboration and autonomy: deciding for others, with others and for oneself. Authentic hierarchy provides appropriate direction by those with greater vision, skill and experience – and is always concerned with transforming relationships so that those in relatively subordinate positions move toward greater skills in collaborative and autonomous action (Torbert, 1991). Collaboration roots the individual within a community of peers, offering basic support and the creative and corrective feedback of other views and possibilities (Randall and Southgate, 1980). Autonomy expresses the self-creating and self-transfiguring potential of the person (Heron, 1992).[27]

Nancy Dixon writes about the emancipatory aspects of dialogue, outlining Freire's approach.[28] Freire used dialogue to help free the oppressed in Brazil; he taught critical thinking as a non-violent approach to revolutionary change. He saw dialogue as the means to reconceptualize the world, as it is through 'dialogue, the process of communicating, challenging and affirming meaning, that the world is transformed'. Dialogue is not simply a technique but a relationship, part of the historical process of human beings becoming more human, more aware and more conscious. Dialogue is not just talk, but involves connecting and interacting in a way that is truer and more open. Those who come to it must come to it with humility, love, faith and hope – characteristics that exemplify a relational, spiritual, perspective. Freire said 'love is at the same time the foundation of dialogue and dialogue itself'.[29]

Too many of us have lost the ability to relate in any depth. We often see conversation as the ability to trade information or win points. Our misunderstandings of each other dry up our creativity. Isaacs reminds us that dialogue involves the language and voice of meaning, feelings and power. He relates this to the ancient Greeks' view of the values to pursue in human society – the true, the beautiful and the good. At the end of the day, dialogue is about finding ways to take action. Our ability to know ourselves, each other and the world more deeply will translate into action in service of the world.

If we can really communicate then we will have fellowship, participation, friendship, love and growth. The early Christians used the word *koinonia*, the root of which means 'to participate'. Today the word is usually applied to the fellowship enjoyed by Christians with one another. But originally it meant participation in the whole of reality; fellowship, if you like, with the entire universe. Such a concept lies at the heart of dialogue.

Dialogue brings people to a new way of perceiving any issue that may be of concern to them. Even though the dialogue process is sometimes a scary and difficult journey into the unknown, it may not be as fearsome as it sounds. As Scott Peck said, 'If you let a group experience its differences, it will actually come together rather than fall apart.'[30] Experience proves that groups and organizations find they can transcend the abilities of individual members and become something far more than the sum of their parts.

We strongly recommend that readers who want to understand dialogue more fully read either William Isaacs' book or Nancy Dixon's, details of which are given in the reference section. These books contain a variety of practical methodologies for engaging people in dialogue in the workplace.

Contributing to others' well-being through love and service

We mentioned love and service in the preceding section. These are fundamentally spiritual concepts, which are linked together excellently in a book by Dorothy Marcic, *Leading with the Wisdom of Love*.[31]

What makes much work truly meaningful is the contribution it makes to our own life, the lives of those we work with and the lives of others that we touch. At the everyday human level, we can acknowledge that our lives are part of human community. Because of this it is virtually impossible for our lives not to have an impact on thousands of other lives. 'If we only ever truly learned fully to love one person, our ability to love all of humanity would increase enormously. In big and small ways everything we do touches the lives of all we come into contact with.'[32] Ultimately, the core offering of spirituality is to help us discover love as the central motivation which then guides our interactions with others. Our work becomes love made visible. Our contribution of our talents and gifts in service to the common good teaches us about spirit.

The idea of service to others is central. Instead of asking 'What's in it for me?' we should ask 'How can I help?' Cicero wrote, 'In nothing do men more nearly approach the gods than in doing good for their fellow men.'[33] God, by any name, is the spirit of giving. When we truly give we can experience our own divine nature, and that which is the essence of God is available through us to give and to share. Our contribution can be the way to find the divine in ourselves and others.

Concluding thoughts

While there are many strands of thought that could be included in a chapter on others, we have focused on the value of people finding shared meaning and wholeness through dialogue because this is central to transformation and change and to being able to live in harmony with others. This is based on a foundational premise of love and service as we turn to one another by opening our hearts, and engage more fully in our own and others' lives by truly listening.

Historically, as Wheatley points out,[34] social change often occurs because a small group of people come together and start talking about the things they really care about. Such exchanges among people, if dialogical, allow even risky areas like power and politics to be surfaced. When a group of individuals begins to change, even if they are only an informal, unofficial group, then organizations they operate in begin to change. The group begins to have an impact.

Individually, we must bring ourselves to the point of opening up and sharing at deeper levels. But taking such risks on behalf of the common good is a part of our life's purpose. And when we can engage with others who are willing to do the same we open our world to new possibilities.

6

Connecting with Nature

We can come home again – and participate in our world in a richer, more responsible and more poignantly beautiful way than ever before.

Joanna Macy[1]

In August 2002 the *Church Times* newspaper (UK) carried an article by Claire Foster entitled 'Going Green is a Spiritual Issue'. It described how ever-increasing human activity is putting the planet's well-being seriously at risk, and how the rich are benefiting from the poor. It called for a change of attitude from governments and those who elect them. 'Greed, which dictated so many of our human choices during the 20th century, has to be transformed into generosity and compassion. The transformation is first spiritual, then material.'

The transformation is indeed spiritual. A sad illustration of what happens when people with inadequate spiritual awareness are confronted with the global environment crisis was the Earth Summit on Sustainable Development held in Johannesburg in September 2002.[2] The failure to agree targets and the unwillingness of some political leaders even to attend the event, were indicative of a 'what's in it for my country?' approach. Political leaders, intent on being re-elected back home, were unwilling – even though in some cases their personal values inclined them to be more cooperative – to commit an electorate who were on average only at the 'all rights and little responsibility', or Wilber level 4, stage of spiritual development.[3]

The May/June 2003 meeting of the G8 leaders in Evian, France, provided further evidence of the unwillingness of Western leaders to make good even their own limited promises to tackle global issues. Our leaders, and we ourselves, need to be transformed from our present spiritual state of being able to acknowledge our environmental responsibilities only in our better moments to a state whereby we are motivated by a consistent, deep and passionate concern to get things done. This transformation can only happen through a vast increase in our spiritual awareness, at least up to Wilber level 6 – the level at which we become 'cosmically aware'.

Towards a spirituality of nature

Robin Skynner and John Cleese[4] tell us what being 'cosmically aware' is all about. It means having a sense of being 'plugged in', of being 'involved in the whole cosmic set-up, connected with it in a harmonious and pleasurable way'. It is not really a question of seeing anything new, rather 'you are just realising there's more significance in what you've been seeing all the time'. They add, 'But of course that will mean nothing to someone who is seeing the same facts, but not the pattern, the significance of the whole.'

They illustrate this with the well-known story of the blind men and the elephant (each exploring by touch one part of the elephant but none experiencing the whole animal), who are helped by a sighted person to discover the whole picture.

For some, discovery of 'the whole', or of our deep connection with nature, comes in the form of a dramatic revelation which can only be called mystical. We can illustrate this with two stories. The first is found in Joseph Jaworski's *Synchronicity*.[5] Jaworski recalls a vivid experience:

Joe Jaworski's story
I got up early in the morning to fish in a stream [. . .] As I walked along, suddenly in front of me a beautiful ermine popped out of the deep snow. She couldn't have been more than ten feet from me. All at once she appeared with her almost black eyes looking directly into mine. I stopped in my tracks. She sat there staring at me, moving not a whisker or a muscle. It seemed as if we looked into one another's eyes for several minutes [. . .] She turned to go but stopped, turned round again, and took another long look at me [. . .] Then she began. She jumped into the air and did a huge flip, and then looked into my eyes again, as if to say, 'What did you think about that?' She did this same trick for me three or four times, each time cocking her head to the side and looking at me as if to ask for my approval. I stood there, held transfixed. Then I began smiling and cocking my head in the same direction as hers. This went on for the longest time. There together, I felt at one with that ermine.

Jaworski speaks of this as 'a transcendence of boundaries [. . .] – a loss of boundaries with part of the natural world [. . .] I was drawn into a relation with the ermine, and she was not an "other" to me [. . .] This began to prepare me at a deeper level to recognize the impermanence and transparency of boundaries in all other aspects of my existence.'[6]

A similar experience, reported by Matthew Fox, was that of astronaut Rusty Schweikert on one of the lunar Apollo projects as he gazed in wonder at Planet Earth. He recalls his perception, on a mission in 1969, of 'a shining gem against a totally black sky'. Realizing that everything he cherished was on that gem – his family and land, music and human history with its folly and its grandeur, he was so overcome that he wanted to 'hug and kiss that gem like a mother does her first-born child'. Schweikert was but one of many astronauts to report such a mystical experience. On his return to earth he wandered round in a stupor for six months asking, 'Why did God do this to me?'[7]

Perhaps not many of us would count ourselves nature mystics, but possibly all of us could claim at least to have found spiritual refreshment in nature – whether as gardeners, or enjoyers of country rambles, or admirers of seascapes or sunsets. It could be that we are more than admirers. Perhaps a glorious sunset has literally taken our breath away! That's not far short of nature mysticism.

Nature is alive!

Rupert Sheldrake strongly believes that a sense of oneness with nature is not confined to a few saints, sages and visionaries, but is in fact quite common. He reckons that most of us experience it, at least in special moments. But when we return to our habitual everyday lives we have a strong temptation to dismiss the idea as merely subjective. Sheldrake believes we should resist this temptation.[8]

He speaks of the tension between his experience of nature as an individual and the view of nature held by the orthodox scientific tradition in which he was trained. Like many people he privately delighted in the beauty of nature and experienced her (note the pronoun) as alive and purposive. But as he advanced in his studies he was taught that direct, intuitive experience of plants and animals was emotional and unscientific.[9] He was expected to adopt the assumptions of the mechanistic scientist, or technocrat or economist or developer that, at least during working hours, nature is inanimate and neuter, that 'nothing natural has a life, purpose or value of its own; natural resources are there to be developed, and their only value is the one placed on them by market forces or official planners'.[10]

Recent developments in science, however, are helping to bridge the gap between the romantic in us and the scientist in us.[11] Sheldrake writes:

The mechanistic world view is being progressively transcended. Nature is coming to life again within scientific theory. And as this process gathers momentum, it becomes increasingly difficult to justify the denial of the life of nature. For if the cosmos is more like a developing organism than a machine running down [. . .] if nature is organic, spontaneous, creative, then why go on believing that everything is mechanical and inanimate?[12]

Sheldrake says we need to choose between the view that nature is inanimate, in which case 'the experience of a mystical connection with [it] must be illusory', and the view that nature really is alive, which means that 'such experience of a living connection may be just what it seems to be'.[13] Thus 'it is important to recognize the reality of our own direct experiences of nature in the wilderness, in the countryside, in forests, on mountains, by the sea, or wherever we have felt ourselves to be in connection with the greater living world'.[14] When we have achieved this sense of connection, cherishing and caring for our natural environment is something we shall wish to do as a matter of course.

Our attaining a sense of connectedness with nature is not just good for nature but also good for us. Many have found that being present in nature has the effect of reducing stress, or restoring energy, or even of sorting out specific problems.

Gillian's story
My own understanding of this increased dramatically earlier this year as I experienced the renewing power of nature for myself. I was attending a one-day external workshop that happened to be held in the grounds of Kew Gardens in London. I had got up early in the morning to make the journey from my home north of London to Kew, enduring busy trains, sticky tubes and a slow-moving taxi. I arrived, just minutes before the start of the workshop, hot and somewhat bothered. Upon entering the room, I was surprised to find not many of the other forty participants were there, and I was handed a small piece of paper which read, 'Take 15 minutes to go out into the garden and be still, drinking in sights, sounds and smells'. Oh the relief of stillness! Impressed by the perspicacity of the workshop leaders, I enjoyed fifteen minutes of space in nature which was just what I needed to blow the cobwebs of the journey away and centre myself, ready to learn.

There is much evidence to support the view that connecting with nature is good for our general health. Matthew Fox refers to Patrick Petrone's *The Greening of Medicare*, a book which 'suggests that the possibility of effecting change in one's state of well-being derives from [. . .] one's relationship with the environment'.[15] Citing the evidence of Petrone and many others, Fox concludes that much disease occurs because the 'wholeness of a healthy environment is being destroyed. As Earth's health goes, so goes our own. In no way, then, can our efforts at health be separated from the health of all the other species on this planet and indeed of the planet itself.'[16]

Gaia and world soul

The idea that nature is in some sense alive has been expressed in James Lovelock's 'Gaia hypothesis'. Lovelock and others have conceived of the earth as one interlocking symbiotic system, as a kind of super-organism. Lovelock's books[17] contain fascinating examples that illustrate his theory. Two of the more striking are the way the earth has regulated its atmospheric temperature, even though the sun has become increasingly hot, so that life can continue to flourish; and the way a progressive build up of salt continually washed down from the mountains has been locked away in lagoons, so that the sea's salinity doesn't increase beyond a level that is safe for marine life.

While Lovelock himself claimed to have no interest in real or imaginary spiritual dimensions of his theory, by introducing the term 'Gaia' as an appropriate label for it, he thereby gave the environmental movement a spiritual/religious dimension. For Gaia was the name of the Earth Mother in ancient Greek mythology. Some have used the Gaia theory as a cue for reviving Goddess worship as a substitute for the devotion to a male God which they see as being a major contributory cause of the environmental crisis. (Those who wish to go further into the rediscovery of the Goddess and associated subjects will find a helpfully balanced discussion in Ruether[18] and in Wilber.[19])

The Gaia hypothesis is strengthened by the understanding that our world has a 'soul'. The idea of the world soul, and of our own souls as part of it, is commonplace in the mystical tradition. These were ideas that Jung took seriously. Thomas Moore tells us that 'In his book *Psychology and Religion: East and West*, Jung says [. . .] "The soul is for the most part outside the body".'[20] He acknowledges that this will appear an astonishing claim to most moderns, taught as we are to believe that the soul is contained in the mind and is purely subjective. But here we are challenged to see that 'the mystery we glimpse when we look deeply into ourselves is part of a larger soul, the soul of the world'.[21]

Moore draws out the ecological implication of this: 'Care of the world is a tending to the soul that resides in nature as well as in human beings.'[22] This insight modifies our understanding of ecology: 'Speaking from the point of view of soul, ecology is not earth science, it is *home* science; it has to do with cultivating a sense of home wherever we are, in whatever context. The things of the world are part of our home environment, and so a soulful ecology is rooted in the feeling that this world is our home and that our responsibility to it comes not from obligation or logic but from true affection.'[23]

Were we to realize that the larger part of our own soul lies in the world, then activity in the world, namely our work, would itself be seen as 'soulful' activity, and therefore as 'a truly important aspect of our lives, not only for its literal product but also as a way of caring for the soul'.[24]

A new creation story

The views about nature that we have been discussing in this chapter have huge implications for our work. If we continue to espouse the old Newtonian view of nature as a lifeless machine, it is likely that our work will feel lifeless and mechanical. Worldview and work-view go together. E. F. Schumacher says that to 'continue to teach that the human being is *nothing but* the outcome of a mindless, meaningless process of evolution, a process of "selection" for survival, that is to say, the outcome of nothing but *utilitarianism*' is to 'come to a *utilitarian* idea of work: that work is *nothing but* a more or less unpleasant necessity, and the less there is of it the better'.[25]

The idea of this world as living, as Gaia, and even more the concept of the world soul, provide a worldview that leads us to a more vital, joyful and meaningful conception of the daily round. So does the 'new creation story' of which Fox, Swimme and Berry and others speak. It is a story that 'tells of the sacredness of the cosmos (and) can displace the utilitarianism of a mindless cosmology and help to reinstate an exciting and vigorous philosophy of work'.[26]

When we think 'creation story' our minds probably go to the Book of Genesis in the Bible. Most of us today think of that account of cosmic origins – and indeed of all pre-scientific accounts – as myth. But SaW writers are pointing out for us the real function of myths, irrespective of their literal factual truth. Stephens and Isen state: 'Myth is the story we tell to explain the nature of reality [. . .] Myths become our touchstones as to what is "real", and what is "important".'[27] Harrison Owen says, 'Myths are the stories of a group's culture that describe its beginning, continuance, and ultimate goals'; adding that 'to the extent that you know the story and it is – or becomes – your story, you are a member of the group [. . .] Each time the story is told, it challenges the group to become the dream.'[28]

A creation story is a sort of 'catch-all' myth which provides for a group, nation or civilization its sense of identity and indeed its whole *raison d'être*. Good accounts of how creation myths have functioned in the past are to be found in Sheldrake[29] and Ruether.[30] Both expound the Babylonian and Judaeo-Christian creation stories, with Ruether adding the Ancient Greek one. Sheldrake's coverage extends to what might be called the 'Newtonian' machine-world creation story, but which falls short of also being a myth because of its reductionism. Ruether devotes a chapter[31] to asking whether science has a creation myth and concludes that new science is gradually evolving one.

We are challenged today to find a new creation story, both 'in the light of the wounded earth' and because 'our souls are very large', says Matthew Fox. 'That is why we need a cosmology large enough to contain them.' 'Because we lack a cosmology – an experience of the whole – our lives have become fractured and broken, as have our hearts. We have lost a sense of community, and our efforts at work seem at best self-serving.'[32] Swimme and Berry[33] sum up the situation thus: 'In the modern period, we are without a comprehensive story of the universe [. . .] Thus we have at the present time a distorted mode of human presence upon the Earth.' Fox gets to the root of the problem: 'At bottom, the issue is one of spirituality, which is always about "all our relations", as the Lakota people pray.'[34]

The Newtonian nature story is not comprehensive; it does not provide us with meaning and purpose. It simply 'objectifies' nature, sets us over against the natural world, regards the world merely as something we use and exploit. It does not connect. 'A parts mentality fits the Newtonian paradigm, but it belies the truth of *interdependence*.'[35]

'A new creation story is essential for our species [. . .] A common origin story lends meaning to our work and to our being in the world.' Fortunately we have such a story – today's creation story from new science. But, Fox reminds us, 'this is also the teaching of our mystical traditions.'[36] 'Today science is rediscovering the mysteriousness of the universe and is generating a new creation story. This new cosmology reinforces the awareness of the one work of the universe and our relation to it. It is this new creation story, say some, that will provide us with the mythology to move our civilization.'[37] It is also a story 'that can unite us all, just as creation stories always have united human communities from as far back as we know'.[38]

A brief summary of this awesome story is given in Appendix 1 at the end of the book. A slightly longer account is provided by Rosemary Ruether.[39] Those who desire to read a whole book about it are recommended Swimme and Berry's *The Universe Story*.[40] The most recent phase of the story, the period during which we the human species have been causing environmental mayhem, is chillingly recounted in Ruether.[41]

The Great Work of the universe and our work

Fox's *The Reinvention of Work* makes constant reference to 'the work' of the universe. 'All creatures in the universe have work – the galaxies and stars, trees and dolphins, grass and mountain goats, forests and clouds, chickens and elephants – all are working.'[42] And it is all the same kind of work: 'There is only one work going on in the universe – the "Great Work" of creation itself – the work of creation unfolding, the work of evolution or creativity in our universe. The poet Rilke[43] speaks of '"the great work" and the gap we feel in our work lives, cut off as we are from the Great Work.' The Rilke passage which Fox refers to says: 'For somewhere there is an ancient enmity between our daily life and the great work. Help me, in saying it, to understand it.'[44]

The enmity in question is this: that human work normally aspires to less than helping co-create the universe. Worse still, we can actually work *against* the great work. 'When humans cut themselves off from the greater work of the universe, our work worlds become very small.'[45] The enmity aspect is well brought out in this quotation from the *Tao Te Ching*:

> When [humanity] interferes with the Tao[46]
> the sky becomes filthy,
> the earth becomes depleted,
> the equilibrium crumbles,
> creatures become extinct. [47]

(What an amazingly apt comment about what human work is currently doing to the planet from this sixth-century BCE[48] writing!)

Fox claims that 'work is about a role we play in the unfolding drama of the universe'.[49] He suggests we each ask about our own work: 'What role does my work have me play in the Great Work and in the work of my community and my species at this time in history?[50] But before we can even ask that question, we need to change the whole way we look at the world: 'If we think we live in an interconnected universe, an organism unfolding the one Great Work of a trillion galaxies, all of it in motion and expanding, then we will start living in such a world as well. And our work will change accordingly.'[51] Therefore 'we dare not miss the truly radical and creative moment in which we live – one in which we are being asked to redefine work itself'.[52]

Whether or not we adopt the new view of work, what we do inevitably impinges on the universe in one way or another. In the words of the twelfth-century nun and mystic Hildegard of Bingen, 'Whatever humanity does with its deeds in the right hand or the left hand permeates the universe.'[53] Human work's effect on the universe is never a neutral one.

Fox refers to the work we do in the world as our 'outer work'. Before we can do our outer work properly we need first to do some 'inner work'. This inner work 'is the work the universe is asking of us – work on our own selves, our own species. Why is this so pressing? Because we are the problem; we are the ones who are destroying our own habitat and that of other species by our blindness, greed, envy, violence, and rapaciousness.'[54] Thus 'the environmental crisis [. . .] furnishes us with an opportunity and a responsibility to ask deeper questions of work'.[55]

What difference does adopting the new view of work make? Obviously a huge difference to the universe itself. But also a huge difference to the quality of our work lives. First, we gain a new sense of joy in our work – a joy which stems from knowing that we are serving an infinitely wider purpose than we could ever otherwise imagine. Often cited in the SaW literature are these memorable words of George Bernard Shaw: 'This is the true joy in life; being used for a purpose recognized by yourself as a mighty one.'

Another outcome is a marvellous sense of freedom and exhilaration. Says the Hindu scripture the *Bhagavad Gita*:[56] 'I will teach you the truth of pure work, and this truth will make you free.' Other wonderful quotes from the *Gita* mention other blessings of authentic work – deliverance from vain hopes and selfish thoughts, inner peace and fullness of joy.[57] Another passage mentions how seeing our work as part of the total work of the universe saves us from self-centred delusion and the mistaken sense that we are acting on our own: 'All actions take place in time by the inter-weaving of the forces of Nature; but the person lost in selfish delusion thinks he himself is the actor.'[58]

It is not only Eastern sources like the *Tao Te Ching* and the *Gita* that offer insightful comments about the nature of universe-friendly work. Another source of wisdom is the Native American tradition, which says of work: 'One does it in harmony, in union with all Creation'.[59] The *Gita* too refers to the harmony of authentic work: '"I am not doing any work", thinks the person who is in harmony.'[60] When our work is so marvellously in tune with reality it doesn't feel like work at all.

In similar vein, Jaworski says: 'We are most deeply satisfied when we are participating in that creative process, whether through being a parent, forming an organization, or working on a project.'[61]

A further consequence of being part of the Great Work is a certain feeling of detachment. Recommends the *Tao Te Ching*:

Do your work, then step back,
the only path to serenity [. . .]
He who clings to his work
will create nothing that endures.[62]

Detachment does not mean being disinterested. Indeed, work consciously done in alignment with the creative powers of the universe is the most interesting kind there is, and we will rightly bring to it all our passion and enthusiasm. But again, because it is not just *our* work, we never need get uptight about it, or be addicted to it, or be worried by failure and set-backs. We can afford to take regular breaks from our work to enjoy 'the serenity of leisureliness' in that lovely phrase of Josef Pieper.[63] Making our work part of the Great Work of the universe is both the antidote to worka-holism and the key to establishing a healthy work–life balance.

The wide appeal of Fox lies in the fact that one doesn't need to be a believer in God to identify with what he is saying. Nevertheless Fox sometimes does use religious-sounding language as, for example, in the following quotes: 'If the Earth is a living organism, then all our work should reverence the Earth.'[64] 'Nature and grace became so separate in the machine era that all sense of grace was believed to come from outside nature.'[65]

Fox himself would claim to be a believer, but he calls himself a panen-theist rather than a theist. The word 'pan-en-theism' means 'God in everything, everything in God'; thus a panentheist is one who focuses on the divine operating in and through the cosmic order, rather than from outside it. In the present chapter we have omitted Fox's more overtly religious type of quotation, but this is to leave out a dimension that he himself regards as important. We shall look at Fox's more ostensibly religious reflections on the universe story at the beginning of Chapter 7.

We round off this chapter with a striking quote from D. H. Lawrence, who speaks of our connectedness with 'all our relations':

> If we think about it, we find that our life consists in [the] achieving of a pure relationship between me and another person, me and other people, me and a nation, me and the race of men, me and the animals, me and the trees and flowers, me and the earth, me and the skies and sun and stars, me and the moon: an infinity of pure relationships, big and little [. . .] This if we knew it, is our life and our eternity: the subtle, perfected relation between me and the circumambient universe.[66]

7

Connecting with Higher Power

If we once admit that we are spiritual beings, then the whole game takes another turn. Instead of patching wrecks, or even realizing potentials, we are dismantling the barriers which are keeping us away from the divine.

John Rowan[1]

People of all faiths and none participate in the SaW movement. Conceptions of higher power are therefore many and varied. For some, higher power is the higher self, or the collective unconscious, or the super-conscious, or Gaia, or the universe, or the divine within, or divine intelligence, or the sacred within, or the source, or the spiritual source, or the spiritual force, or the unified field, or the implicate order, or the generative order, or the quantum vacuum, or virtual reality, or the ground state of the universe, or a transcendent God . . . and perhaps several more we haven't come across! Or there can be various combinations of these. It is interesting to see how people claiming to have no religious faith are generally happy with *some* notion of the transcendent or higher power.

Traditional believers – and many such are found within the ranks of SaW – might wish to adhere to a more orthodox-sounding view of divine transcendence, whereby God is considered to be 'outside' or 'beyond' the cosmos. They would hold that God exists 'before' the universe and creates it out of nothing. (Actually, unbeknown to many Western Christians, Christianity does include the idea of 'God within' in its overall teaching about God – see Appendix 2.)

The universe story: the religious interpretation

We noted that there were things Matthew Fox wished to say about the universe story and the Great Work which had a more traditional religious flavour, and we will mention this aspect of his thinking now.

'Our work', says Fox, 'is interconnected with God's work'.[2] He quotes the medieval mystic Meister Eckhart's views on this subject: 'God and the soul are very fruitful as they eternally do one work together'; and also those of Thomas Aquinas who said, 'God works at the heart of all activity'.[3] When connected with the work of the universe, says Fox, our work 'flows from the "sheer joy" of the Creator, as Aquinas puts it'.[4]

Sometimes Fox aligns our work with that of the Holy Spirit: '(The) Holy Spirit who works through our work and moves our heart to work is the same Holy Spirit [. . .] who ignited the first flickering light of the original fireball',[5] and who is also 'committed to the work of co-creation with us'.[6]

Alternatively, Fox speaks of our work with reference to Christ. 'We give birth to the Christ when we give birth to the depths of ourselves, when we participate in the Great Work of creation in the universe'.[7] 'What we give birth to is bigger than us [. . .] it is the image of God operating through us; it is Sophia – Wisdom – the Cosmic Christ born from within us'.[8]

Another Christian writer who speaks of the work of God and of humans in the context of the unfolding creative universe is Jesuit priest and scientist Teilhard de Chardin (1881–1955). He uses new insights from evolutionary science to develop further the sweeping cosmic vision – one embracing the whole of nature – of St Irenaeus (second century CE).[9] Teilhard sees the universe as a total system that progresses through each successive evolutionary advance to ever greater complexity and ever higher consciousness. The process will culminate at what he calls 'the Omega Point'. He speaks also of a growing 'centration' or centredness, as the universe, under the influence of the Cosmic Christ or the divinity within its heart, evolves towards a unitary Mind. Once this mind has fully emerged the physical universe will fall away and all that has gone before will be gathered up and made immortal.

A fuller yet still concise account of Teilhard's philosophy is provided by Ruether,[10] who finds many elements of it extremely valuable, such as his affirmation of the world as a living organism (cf. the Gaia hypothesis). She is critical, however, of the notion that Western Christian civilization, including its modernist phase, is somehow a privileged axis of world evolution. Nor does she like the idea of the material world being tossed aside at the culminating stage – a notion which she believes 'contradicts the foundational insight of consciousness as the interiority of complexified matter'.[11] Among Teilhard's own writings, we strongly recommend *Le Milieu Divin*.[12] For a modern study of Teilhard, see Ursula King.[13]

Ruether also provides a summary of the process theology of Alfred North Whitehead and followers, and this too has its supporters within SaW.[14] This has many points of similarity with Teilhard.

Higher power in transpersonal psychology

Those of a religious bent are no longer alone in speaking of higher power in terms of connecting with the divine. John Rowan describes entering the transpersonal realm as 'facing and exploring the holy, the numinous, the divine'.[15] The term 'transpersonal' appears to have been the invention of Jung. Transpersonal psychology as such began about 25 years ago – with earlier foreshadowings, for example, in the work of William James,[16] in the writings of Jung himself and in several Asian systems such as Buddhist, yogic, Vedantic and Taoist psychologies.[17]

Our chief guide in this territory is Rowan.[18] Most of the authors cited in this section are referred to by him, often at length. Stanislav Grof describes transpersonal experiences as involving 'an expansion or extension of consciousness beyond the usual ego boundaries'.[19] Cohen and Phipps speak of these levels of consciousness as higher states. Yet, they claim, they are 'not higher in the sense of being unattainable or requiring great dedication to obtain. They are potentially present in all of us, and have to do with things like intuition, creativity, imagination and the like. They are part of being human, and even children may have access to them.'[20] Nor are they just the property of the religious person.[21]

The idea of the transpersonal has been made more acceptable by the notion of 'peak experiences', largely because such a large proportion of the population has had such experiences.[22] Again, these may happen at any stage of our spiritual development. They don't necessarily indicate that one is a budding spiritual genius. In the words of Anthony and colleagues, they are 'only temporary glimpses beyond the mundane ego-conscious-ness and do not involve true transformation to a more transcendent, encompassing state'. However, 'glimpse experiences [. . .] can be pro-transformative and can foster spiritual development in many ways'.[23]

Rowan gives many examples of such an experience. Here is just one, taken from Hay:

> I was walking across a field turning my head to admire the Western sky and looking at a line of pine trees appearing as black velvet against a pink backdrop, turning to duck egg blue/green overhead, as the sun set. Then it happened. It was as if a switch marked 'ego' was suddenly switched off. Consciousness expanded to include, *be*, the previously observed. 'I' was the sunset and there was no 'I' ex-periencing 'it'. No more observer and observed. At the same time – eternity was 'born'. There was no past, no future, just an eternal now; . . . then I returned completely to normal consciousness finding myself still walking across the field, in time, with a memory.[24]

Maslow had a great deal to say about peak experiences. They were of special importance, he concluded, for the most creative type of scientist, who 'lives for the moment of glory when a problem solves itself, when suddenly through a microscope he sees things in a very different way [...] The moments of revelation, of illumination, insight, understanding, ecstasy. These are vital for him.'[25]

Such experiences are often referred to in terms of an 'altered state of consciousness'. John Wren-Lewis, though, regards this as 'a complete misnomer', for his own experience was felt to be

> no more and less than 'just the way things are' [...] one of complete normality. It seems, rather, as if my earlier state, so-called 'ordinary' human consciousness, represents the real alteration – a deviation from the plain norm, a kind of blinkered or clouded condition wherein the bodymind has the absurd illusion that it is somehow a separate individual entity over against everything else.[26]

Maslow also speaks of 'plateau experiences'. These represent 'a new and more profound way of viewing and experiencing the world. This involves a fundamental change in attitude, a change that affects one's entire point of view and creates a new appreciation and intensified awareness of the world [...] It is a state we can call upon at any moment, in case of need.'[27] Unlike peak experiences which are fleeting and don't fundamentally change a person's spiritual centre of gravity (the glimpsed level is not 'held on to'), plateau experiences represent a more permanent abiding at a very high spiritual level.

Transpersonal experiences begin at Wilber's level 7[28] where 'nature mysticism' occurs.[29] Also emergent at this stage is the sense of having a higher or deeper Self. The latter is sometimes called the Witness, because it is able to observe the ego- or bodymind-self from 'above'.

The transpersonal comes more fully into its own at Wilber's next level. This is where nature mysticism gives way to 'deity mysticism', marking the beginning of a union with deity. Here people experience the divine according to the archetypal forms of their own culture. 'A Christian might see it as Christ or an angel or a saint, a Buddhist [...] the bliss body of the Buddha,'[30] or however the divine is conceived in any given belief system. Fresh, brand-new insights appear, and are 'seen as coming from a source other than the self',[31] and people at this stage say of their creative acts, 'I was just the channel, it was not me doing it.'

The subtle stage is also marked by feelings of intense bliss 'and expansive affective states of love and compassion'.[32] At this level, says Wilber, 'you are looking at the basic forms and foundations of the entire manifest world. You are looking directly at the Face of the Divine [...]

here is God within.'[33] We cited earlier Heron's remark about there being a point at which self-assertion gives way to surrender. This is another 'level 8' feature.

At Wilber's level 9, 'there are no symbols or images to speak of'.[34] This is the stage at which a person has transcended even deity mysticism and has entered the phase of formless mysticism, and at level 10 the self thoroughly merges with the divine. Needless to say transpersonal psychology at its present stage of development is able to say little about such exalted states.

Bohm and his disciples' conception of higher power

We have already referred to the thinking of physicist David Bohm.[35] We look again at his views, this time in order to examine their implications about the nature of higher power and how we connect with it. In *Wholeness and the Implicate Order* – let us remind ourselves – Bohm points to a deeper order of reality which is constantly seeking to break though the surface reality we currently perceive. He distinguishes between reality as so far manifested, which he calls the explicate order, and the implicate order, the higher order reality which, when conditions are appropriate, bursts through and then itself becomes part of the explicate order. But there always remains an inexhaustible reservoir of implicate reality underpinning or 'enfolding' the whole – enfolding being another meaning of the word 'implicate'. Bohm alternatively calls the implicate order 'the generative order', and as such is the source of novelty and creativity at all levels and stages of cosmic evolution, from the Big Bang to those precious moments in the lives of individual human beings when new harmony, connectedness, awareness – or some other aspect of wholeness – is perceived.

Bohm believes that we can connect directly and personally with the generative order. We can, depending on our state of consciousness, 'participate in how reality unfolds'.[36] Or as Zohar puts it, 'the ground state of the universe, the quantum vacuum, is in constant dialogue with the excitations of energy which are existence'.[37] Many in the SaW movement are imaging God, or the divine, in terms of the quantum vacuum or the implicate order. (Traditional Christians will probably baulk at this, but the naming of the divine in terms of the science of the day is a long-established Christian habit. A good example is the identification of Christ with 'the *logos*'[38] early on in the Christian era.)

Reality as Bohm conceives it is expounded in a more simplified form by Deepak Chopra.[39] He describes what he calls 'the reality sandwich of physics' (see Table 3).

Table 3: The reality sandwich of physics

Material reality, the world of objects and events

Quantum reality, the transition zone where energy turns into matter

Virtual reality, the place beyond time and space, the origin of the universe

---

'Virtual reality' is Chopra's term for the quantum vacuum or implicate order, 'material reality' corresponds with explicate order and 'quantum reality' refers to the transitional stage at which implicate is turned into explicate.

Special mention must again be made of Joseph Jaworski's book *Synchronicity*. Jaworski, whose debt to Bohm as his mentor is acknowledged throughout the book, sees synchronicity happening in 'those perfect moments, when things come together in an almost unbelievable way, when events that could never be predicted, let alone controlled, remarkably seem to guide us along our path'.[40] The conditions for this were Jaworski's own unswerving dedication to his call and an openness to whatever gifts the generative order willed to bestow.

Gillian's story

I can testify to a more modest, but nonetheless personally significant, experience of this. In the spring of 2002 I had the privilege of attending the Spirit in Business Conference in New York where major thinkers and prominent business leaders came together to further debate this emerging topic. On the second evening at dinner I walked into a room of over 500 strangers and felt immediately overwhelmed by the huge crowd! Almost simultaneously, however, I also had a deep sense of inexplicable peace and purpose. I actually felt that there was a *particular* table I needed to sit at and I began to wander around this huge room. As I passed one table which was almost full, I felt a clear signal to sit down.

As I sat down on the remaining empty seat we began to go round the whole table introducing ourselves. After the last person said that he worked downtown, at St Paul's chapel, he received a hushed, almost reverent silence. I didn't understand the reference at first, but my neighbour whispered to me that it was the church right by Ground Zero, scene of the devastating attack of 9/11 only five months previously. It was this chapel which was still offering physical, emotional and spiritual care around the clock for the emergency workers burdened by their huge task. After sharing his own remarkable story with the table, he invited anyone who wished, to go down to Ground Zero and visit the chapel. I went that afternoon and it turned out to be one of the most profound emotional and spiritual experiences of my entire life.

Peter Senge, in his guest Introduction to *Synchronicity*, shows how deep commitment on Jaworski's part was required to ensure the 'miracles' continued. He contrasts Jaworski's level of commitment in his best moments with what normally passes for commitment: 'In our traditional image of commitment, things get done by hard work. We have to sacrifice. If everything starts to fall apart, we try harder.' The deeper level of commitment is 'a commitment of being [...] of surrender [...] *When this new type of commitment starts to operate, there is a flow around us. Things just seem to happen.*' Senge refers to the 'attraction' exerted by people in a state of surrender.[41]

Looking back at the times when things really flowed, Jaworski reports: 'I had no fear of failure, and had cared deeply about the dream for its own sake [...] I was serving the dream itself because I felt deep down that this was what was intended to happen. I was so intent on the vision that I operated with complete spontaneity and freedom.'[42]

Like all others who walk the spiritual path Jaworski sometimes found himself regressing to pre-spiritual modes of consciousness. This was where his own ego got in the way, or where he came to feel everything depended on him, or where fear of failure caused him to work excessive hours. This was where the forces of evil threatened to wreck the whole project.

Evil

We have left our main treatment of evil until this point because we wish to follow the suggestion of Zohar and Marshall that, in essence, evil is a symptom of disconnection from the centre – from higher power, God, the ground of our being.

Evil is something that may afflict us at any stage of our spiritual journey. Every transition from one level to the next is fraught with danger and it is quite common for things to go wrong. Each level has its associated pathology. If the transition is not made cleanly, bits of our personality get split off and the split-off bits can sap our energy and reduce our chances of progress, 'sabotaging the main self with neurotic or even psychotic symptoms'.[43] Or these aspects of us can be projected on to others. This is the evil associated with the shadow self, which we touched on briefly in Chapter 4.

Just as there are different levels in the upward spiral towards goodness or spiritual enlightenment, so there are varying degrees in the downward spiral of evil. One type of evil is *addiction*. To be addicted is to allow something that may well be harmless or even good in itself to take over our lives and throw the whole self out of balance. A more serious type of evil is *possession*. To be possessed is to be 'in thrall to an archetype that itself has come loose from its moorings in the centre'; it is to be 'in the grip of psychic forces that have become anarchic'.[44] Zohar and Marshall believe that all archetypes have their shadow equivalents. They exert a pull on the rejected, split-off parts of ourselves. We fall under their spell when we see in them the call to wholeness, 'but it is a misguided call because possession is archetypal energy that is not rooted, energy that is split off from the centre'.[45] 'Evil is archetypal energy which is out of control.' The ultimate archetype of evil is the Devil, 'the most loved of God's angels, who out of pride rejects heaven (the centre)'.[46]

Zohar asks, 'Can anyone really *be* evil, or are some people just in the grip of evil?'[47] She speaks of her own experience of dialogue with the vilest sorts of prisoner, including serial rapists and child killers. She regards the intense anger she found in them as 'a cry to be recognized as human'. She observed how 'in being given voice some basic human quality did shine through, something irresistibly likeable'.[48] So her conclusion is that 'there are no evil people as such, but anyone of us might be capable of evil. It is a human potential – an extreme potential of the fragmented, decentred, spirituality stunted self'.[49] Margaret Wheatley too believes that people, though capable of getting seriously out of control, are 'still basically good and caring [. . .] We still desire learning, freedom, meaning, and love.'[50]

Pat Sullivan, in private conversation, has spoken of her time with a group called Pathwork when she and her colleagues 'explored the deepest parts of the self, not just the shadow but the negative intent', a phrase suggestive of the traditional Christian doctrine of 'original sin'. This is a teaching that Jung took seriously. He wrote, 'Blindly he [the human being of modern times] strives against the salutary doctrine of original sin, which is so prodigiously true.'[51] But we should not deduce from that remark that he saw original sin as the *primary* truth about us.

Matthew Fox believes that 'original blessing'[52] is the intrinsic nature of things. He recognizes that evil is present in history, but as distortion and alienation from original blessing, not as primary reality. Here Fox is following an honourable strand of Christian teaching. The over-emphasis (in his view) on original sin stems from Augustine, whom he believes to have been allowed far too much influence over Western Christianity. The view of Zohar, Wheatley and Fox (and we guess Sullivan and Jung too) is the more widely accepted one within SaW.

Evil may also manifest itself as negativity or even despair. This is a path which we all have to go down repeatedly in the course of our lives.

Matthew Fox calls it the *via negativa*. Mystics refer to 'the dark night of the soul', a phrase which derives from St John of the Cross (1542–91). Wilber and others are clearly alluding to the same experience when they describe the agony we feel every time we leave behind the old ways of being self in order to progress to a higher level. This invariably involves stepping right out of our comfort zone and entering entirely new territory – often a terrifying experience. Evil is manifested when a resultant pathology seriously impedes the soul's progress.

Michal Levin[53] is extremely illuminating on the subject of 'the dark night of the soul'. Speaking on the basis of personal experience, she writes:

> It is the moment we all dread. You feel you can't go on. You feel all power has deserted you. You feel you don't know anything. You feel you can't depend on anything. You don't understand [...] This is the dark night of the soul [...] You feel the fire has gone out, and you are facing the dark [...] When you know and recognise this point in yourself, and you know how to deal with it, this is a most exciting place – you are on the brink of a breakthrough. It is part of a pattern[54] [...] The dark enfolds [...] Now is the time to die back [...] For you, the experience of descending to what might seem like a dark, cold wilderness allows the mystery of life to re-form, deep in your subconscious[55] [...] But rather than resist [...] or see the change as damaging, I simply submit. I die [...] [Then] the new growth that led to my death [...] takes on a vigorous life.[56]

Zohar is speaking of the self-same process when she refers to the need to embrace chaos as the necessary prelude to creative breakthrough. Christians will see a parallel in Jesus' demand that we be prepared to lose our selves in order to find our true selves. There is much teaching in the New Testament about Jesus' followers being required to 'die with Christ' (cf. chaos) in order 'to live with him' (breakthrough to new life, resurrection, new creation). Interestingly, Zohar – who is not herself a Christian – believes the recognition of this pattern is Christianity's most profound insight into how both the universe and our own personalities creatively unfold.[57] She also uses this insight to encourage business leaders operating 'at the edge of chaos' (see Chapter 9).

Such uncomfortable experiences are therefore to be welcomed. Says Catherine McGeachy, 'Crises are the fast route to our spiritual core, because in an instant all the other ego-props and cultural layers are taken away and we are forced to examine the deepest levels within us.'[58] As Bill DeFoore beautifully expresses it:

There is a beauty in our endings, a lesson in our losses, a gift within our problems, a healing within our illnesses, and joy in the depths of sorrow [. . .] Is rebirth possible without death? Can electric exist without magnetic? Would we know masculine without feminine? Anyone who has gone through personal transformation (brought on by heart attack, cancer, near-death experience, spiritual crisis, psychological trauma, loss of loved ones, loss of job, financial failure, war) or corporate transformation (restructuring, re-engineering, downsizing, merging) knows that endings are always followed by new beginnings of some sort [. . .] For many of us, however, the rebirth explains the death.[59]

Thomas Moore says, 'We become persons through dangerous experiences of darkness [. . .] Any real initiation is always a movement from death to new life.'[60] 'Nor is it minor forms of melancholy that offer unique gifts to the soul; long, deep bouts of acute depression can also clear out and restructure the tenets by which life has been lived.'[61]

As in all areas of life, evil is manifested in work situations. André Delbecq has adduced evidence from a large number of business leaders of the existence of disruptive individuals in organizations, whose influence can only be described as evil.[62]

Roger Harrison also writes about evil in organizations, noting that 'even high-performing organizations have their inhumanities. They burn people out; they take over private lives; they ostracize or expel those who do not share their purposes; and they are frequently ruthless in their dealings with those outside the magic circle – competitors, suppliers, the public.'[63]

Harrison speaks of 'the daimonic' which is

that aspect of man which seeks to express itself and have impact on the world no matter what the cost or consequences [. . .] If unchecked [it] tends to take over the whole person. We find the daimonic in all sorts of obsessions [. . .] in the expansive dream of the entrepreneur, in the limitless personal ambition of the dedicated careerist, and in the dedicated money-making of the financial genius where it is checked and balanced by other parts of the personality, its energy fuels great achievements and contributions. Where it gets control of the person, it turns against nature.[64]

No doubt we should see the recent corporate financial scandals in this light. They are the result of an unbalanced desire to serve the bottom line, whatever the cost. They are an example of addiction. For what else can we call it when we see otherwise sane and good people (as we may suppose) being so obsessed with making their organizations appear profitable?

There is also the sort of evil reflected in the events of 9/11 and in the way some have responded to them. Ruether offers some valuable reflections on this aspect of evil:

> [The] capacity to imagine better alternatives is essential to the human capacity to invent artifacts and ways of behaving that incrementally improve daily life. But the danger of translating this capacity into absolutes is that we imagine that these absolutes actually exist, that there is an absolute good that can be set against an absolute evil, and that humans can strive to realize one side of this duality by repudiating the other.
>
> This problem is compounded when the evil side of this polarity is identified with other people and things: with other groups of people over against our group.[65]

Such demonization of the 'other' (the shadow aspect of Wilber's level 4 self) can so easily happen – indeed might be judged inevitable – in a world where there exist such huge inequalities of wealth, opportunity and quality of life. This is another manifestation of gross evil, which we shall be taking up when we speak of 'structural evil' in Chapter 11. We have already noted, in Chapter 1, the positive aspects of 9/11 – a remarkable instance of immense good emerging from the darkest evil.

Spiritual praxis

We conclude this chapter by looking at some of the practical aids, tools and practices that can help us make the spiritual journey and win the battle against evil. Some of these can be followed up using Chapter 15.

Meditation
That the practice of meditation can benefit organizational life in all sorts of ways is well documented in the SaW literature.[66] The beauty of meditation is that it is a technique anyone can use, irrespective of their spiritual or religious beliefs or lack of them. Meditation may be used simply to relax, calm the nerves, quieten the mind or reduce stress. At the other end of the scale, it is used to access the deepest layers of the self, as a way of connecting with the very ground of our being, with the holy, with God.

Typically, the meditator sits upright in a quiet place (ideally in the lotus position, but we Westerners are usually advised to sit on a firm chair!). We start by focusing our attention on breathing, or on some sound (called a mantra) or object in front of us. While one meditative technique is to notice every sight and sound with a view to heightening awareness of our surroundings, more often the aim is to still the mind and empty it of all thoughts. If thoughts still arise, as they almost invariably do, they should be allowed to float away like passing clouds. By detaching ourselves from our conscious mind or ego-self, we allow our higher self to emerge. This deeper level of meditation, at which profound insights may emerge, is often hard to reach at first. But those skilled in these matters promise us that if we are patient we shall be rewarded.

Here is a story of how meditation can help in a work situation.

Joan's story

I think I'm more productive now, even though working less hours. I find that daily meditation especially helps me to bring more clarity and creativity to my work, which enables me to solve problems more quickly and more simply. Like yesterday. I had started writing a software program which I thought would take about four days of work. After meditation last evening, a simpler way of writing the program came to me, and I was able to get the whole thing finished today, with about ten percent of the lines of code I had originally planned to use.[67]

Kabat-Zinn,[68] one of the leading medical researchers in the field of stress reduction, has adapted techniques of meditation and mindfulness from the Buddhist tradition which have the effect of creating stillness and greater peace at one's work.[69]

Those wishing to explore meditation further will find the following helpful: *Sadhana: A Way to God – Christian Exercises in Eastern Form* by Anthony de Mello;[70] *The Tibetan Book of Living and Dying* by Sogyal Rinpoche[71] and *Enlightened Management* by Dona Witten.[72] See also Rowan.[73]

Prayer

This is a way of approaching and communicating with the divine. On the face of it, prayer would seem to be most appropriate for those who have a 'personal' conception of the divine, i.e. God as 'Someone to talk to'. But it is also a form of surrender, and a means of letting go, which allows us to engage with spirit at the deepest levels of our being. Bohm and Zohar both speak of the interactive nature of our relationship with reality. Zohar says, 'When we "talk" or pray to God, we are doing the best we can to reach that innate wisdom within the heart of our deepest being, which puts us in touch with the whole of reality.'[74]

Zohar particularly favours that key aspect of monastic prayer, recollection. Drawing on the teaching of the mystical writer Thomas Merton, she summarizes recollection as 'the bringing together of our world inside and our world outside, the meeting of the deep, inner self and its innate wisdom or spiritual intelligence, with the outer ego and its worldly concerns, strategies and activities'.[75]

Pat Sullivan gives much attention to prayer. She refers to Fox who:

> defined prayer not as a request to God for answers or favors, but as an engagement with God in an ever-changing journey filled with questions. Sometimes we will be called to savor fully the wonder of Creation; other times, to experience emptiness and pain [. . .] Many of the joys and challenges of prayer come from the fact that prayer will always take us past our comfort zone.[76]

Sullivan finds prayer especially helpful in our daily work. She says, 'The most important formula for meaningful work I know is to pray for guidance and pay attention.'[77] She goes on to emphasize practising the presence of God in even mundane tasks,[78] citing Brother Lawrence.

Sullivan reports that many groups at work are deriving great benefit from the *Spiritual Exercises* of St Ignatius Loyola, founder of the Jesuits.[79] Of these she says, 'St Ignatius developed exercises filled with questions that can be readily adapted to the workday such as "What about my work this week (or today) has been most life-giving? What about my work has been most life-draining? [. . .] To what might God be calling me in these situations?"'[80]

Retreats

Spiritual retreats involve ordering one's day around practices that reveal the beauty and wonder of God's creation and being anchored in the rhythm of prayer, some of it alone and silent, some of it chanted in community. They also involve doing menial tasks on the one hand, and on the other provide opportunity to examine one's innermost thoughts and motivations.[81]

Direct experience of nature

This was covered in Chapter 6, but we would just like to draw readers' attention to an essay by Grace Ann Rosile. Commenting that 'the direct experience of nature is acknowledged to be a common path to greater spiritual awareness,'[82] she goes on to speak movingly of her own experience of working with horses.

Practising synchronicity

By this we mean trying to maintain that open state of mind that will result in 'predictable miracles'. See Jaworski; Deepak Chopra[83] is also illuminating on this subject.

Practising generosity, giving and compassion to others
As mentioned in Chapter 5, Cicero wrote, 'In nothing do men more nearly approach the gods than in doing good for their fellow men.' To give of our time, energy and money is to express love through service. When we truly give we experience our own divine nature, and pass on to others something of this divine essence.

Dialogue groups
This is a practice advocated by Jaworski. 'Taking the time to come together on a regular basis in true dialogue gives everyone a chance to maintain a reflective space at the heart of the activity – a space where all people can continue to be re-nurtured *together* by what is wanting to happen, to unfold. It must be a regular discipline.'[84]

Psychotherapeutic practices
Among these we would list active imagination and/or working with images, guided fantasy, dreamwork, journal writing (or keeping a spiritual diary), various sorts of counselling (different sorts being appropriate to dealing with the psychological problems arising at a particular 'level' – uncovering therapies for levels 1 to 3, self-building techniques for the middle levels, transpersonal methods for higher levels). Peppers and Briskin,[85] Rowan, and Wilber should be consulted.

Spiritual direction (coaching, having a 'soul friend')
Many find it highly beneficial having an experienced person to accompany them on their spiritual journey. Writes Elizabeth Guss:

> There is a longstanding tradition of this type of companionship [...] to help integrate our spiritual journey with our work. Variously called spiritual guidance or direction, it is a relationship of another's loving listening to us as we search for deeper understanding [. . .] Historically seen in a context of personal growth and often only within religious denominations, Spiritual Direction is now being recognized as relevant to workplace decisions and behavior.[86]

Ritual
Human beings are ritual animals, and it is natural for us to find spiritual support in worship, ceremony, song, dance and other ways. Such activities may be engaged in by groups in a faith-community setting, in the home or in workplaces. Matthew Fox speaks often of 'art as meditation'.[87] He advocates telling the universe story through ritual and worship. 'Our ritual ought to include all other species, all the other galaxies and stars and supernovas, all the elements and molecules and atoms, and the original

fireball that first blessed us all by preparing things for the coming of life.'[88] He has interesting suggestions about how this might be done.[89]

Other practices used in workplaces
In addition to the aforementioned practices, chanting, yoga, hypnosis, guided visualization, thought management, colour therapy, music therapy, sound therapy, aromatherapy, mountain climbing, sweat lodges, massage and other spiritual techniques are being increasingly used within organizations. 'Prompted often with a desire to solve a specific problem (frequently stress related) [people at work] [. . .] find those practices create a quiet space and centering that opens up for them an awareness of deeper issues that need exploration. Those places of quiet and stillness are often where we meet the Sacred within.'[90] Of the items just listed we would particularly highlight the use of music. The language of music is universal and joins together people of different cultures.

Spirituality at Work Conversation Groups
This technique was pioneered in San Francisco by Whitney Roberson, an Episcopalian priest. Designed specifically for use by workpeople 'of all faiths and none' and typically run during people's lunch break, these conversations focus on a reflective passage from any of the main faith traditions or from modern inspirational (often business) literature, which participants then apply to their own work situations.

Generally looking after ourselves
Levin[91] has some good material on care for our bodies, highlighting the need to release and balance our various types of energy. Nicholas Janni talks about re-engaging with our bodies.[92] Capra writes on 'wholeness and health' in *The Turning Point*.[93]

Short times of reflection
It is appreciated that many people at work are extremely busy and therefore find it difficult to find the time to meditate, pray or whatever in any depth, at least during the working week. But it shouldn't be impossible to devise a regular, preferably daily, pattern of, say, fifteen minutes' quiet time before beginning work, plus a similar short period of reflection, or recollection – perhaps journal writing – at the end of the day. It is good also to take a short breather, have a moment of quiet centring, go for a short walk etc. during the course of the day.

Pat Sullivan believes even a single sentence to prepare oneself for the working day can be of benefit, such as 'I welcome divine inspiration for my day'. Another example she gives comes from Biogenex CEO Khrishan Kalra: 'Lord, I am at your service. What is it you want me to do? Lead my day.'[94] Her suggestions for spiritual praxis in the midst of the working day include blessing our work, blessing others as we walk past them, prayer that each task might be done for the highest good and 'exercising attunement and reflection prior to decision making'.[95]

Those who imagine they haven't time for any workday spiritual practice might care to reflect on these words attributed to Gandhi: 'Normally I meditate for two hours each day. When I'm busy I meditate for four hours. When I'm exceptionally busy I meditate for six hours.' And Gandhi was someone who got an awful lot done!

8

Religion and Spirituality: Our Journey in Faith

Without context, such as scripture and rituals that shape many religions, spirituality can be vapid. Without community and its demands for discipline, spirituality can be lost in individualism or illusion.

Pat Sullivan[1]

There are several different paths by which people in SaW are making their spiritual journeys. Many travel the way of one or other of the world's religions, and it is to the role of religion in SaW that we now turn our attention. We deal principally with the mainline religions, but in the light of the allegation made by many in the religious mainstream – that SaW is simply the infiltration into the world of business of New Age spirituality – we shall add an appendix on the New Age. This appears at the end of the book as Appendix 3.

An intense debate is taking place in SaW circles about the respective merits of spirituality and religion. Some claim to be deeply 'into' spirituality while firmly rejecting religion, which they see as alien, or divisive, or out-of-touch, or simply redundant.

Here are some sample quotes from the SaW literature:

- Lois Hogan: 'Spirituality is a more universal experience, unbounded by any particular belief or dogma.'[2]
- Paul Gibbons: 'Spirituality, once an aspect of religion, has turned the linguistic tables and religion is now seen as one of many possible spiritual paths.'[3]
- Catherine McGeachy: 'Spirituality is seen as a "leveller" of people because it is non-denominational, inclusive, universal and allows for diversity of expression [. . .] Religion is seen as divisive in that it requires compliance with a certain set of traditions/ceremonies/dogmas.'[4]

- McGeachy again: 'Spirituality in the workplace has a much broader feel to it than religion: it addresses more of the factors that are common denominators across humanity and, therefore, it has a unifying effect.'[5]

British theologian Nicola Slee has this to say about the relationship between spirituality and religion: 'The spiritual can be distinguished from the religious and understood as something wider than religiosity; on the other hand, it can be understood as the deepest and most central element of religion.'[6] Some in SaW would agree mainly with the first part of that statement, some with the second part, and others with both.

There are those in SaW for whom their spirituality and their religion are one and the same thing, though we guess this is truer of people in workplaces than of academics who write about SaW. There are also those who continue to adhere to their religious tradition but long for it to recover its spiritual roots and become more relevant to their lives at work.

In this chapter we shall be giving examples of these various positions, but first we need to say what we mean by 'religion'. The literal meaning of the word is 'linking back', and we could say that a religious person is one who links back to one of the historic world faiths: to Christianity, Judaism, Islam, Hinduism, Taoism, Buddhism or some other recognized faith tradition. (There is a debate as to whether Buddhism, with its lack of belief in any deity or transcendent divine power, qualifies as a religion – many describe it as 'a spiritual science'. But it is certainly to be numbered among the great world faith traditions.)

Because SaW is a movement in which many faith traditions are involved it is necessary, in order to understand SaW, for us all to have at least a rudimentary grasp of the main world religions. It is not our intention here to summarize the distinctive beliefs of each, but rather simply to point readers to a book which many regard as the best introduction: Huston Smith's *The World's Religions*.[7]

In view of the influence of Buddhism on SaW, and also because its 'monistic'[8] conception of ultimate reality is so different from the mainline Western religion with which most of us are familiar, we suggest that readers go further than study just the chapter on Buddhism in Huston Smith. Two books we would recommend, both by Buddhist authors (and it's always good to get the insider view), are: *The Heart of the Buddha's Teaching* by Thich Nhat Hanh,[9] and Sogyal Rinpoche's *The Tibetan Book of Living and Dying*.[10] Both are written with Western readers in mind.

Those too busy to study these books might care just to have a look at Chapter 5 of Pat Sullivan's *Work with Meaning, Work with Joy*,[11] which gives a two- or three-page summary of the key beliefs of most of the major world religions and with an emphasis on the insights they provide for working life.

Religion as experienced

We have pointed out that many in the SaW movement identify with one or other of the world's religions. As SaW has so far developed mainly in the West, the main allegiance is still perhaps to Christianity. But in the course of his sabbatical study in the San Francisco Bay area, David found many Christian SaW practitioners very critical of their tradition in its current form. This was true both of those directly operating in the world of business and of Christian ministers, academics and consultants offering spiritual resources to business people.[12]

André Delbecq is a practising Roman Catholic and a professor at the Jesuit University of Santa Clara. He has commented in private conversation on what he regards as the lamentable failure of the churches to support people in their business roles, being particularly critical of his own church. He reckons that the Roman Catholic Church has always been alienated from business through its over-emphasis of the dangers of Mammon and its preoccupation with injustice in the business world. The average RC parish church 'does not connect with people's business lives'. Delbecq has also made a point of telling theologians about God's presence in the world and of urging them to find out what God is up to there, but to no avail. 'They persist in seeing the divine presence only in the church.'

Episcopalian priests John Huntington and Kevin Phillips speak of their church's alienation from the world of work with a result that their adherents 'haven't known how to be spiritual there'. They speak of the need to recruit corporate chaplains for Silicon Valley but do not expect to enlist suitable candidates via the seminaries. They reckon that in terms of equipping students to relate to the world of work, 'seminary training is a disaster', adding that 'the church at large hates business'. Such sentiments are widely echoed among Christians involved in the business world, both in the USA and the UK.

Religion as it could be

But things could be so different, and sometimes they are. Pat Sullivan, President of Visionary Resources, Oakland, California, has offered this comment in a private communication: 'When religion is out of touch with people's lives it doesn't enrich or connect. When it is grounded in everyday life, it's magnificent!' André Delbecq hopes that his religion will focus less on dogma and more on contemplation. And use silence more.

Many of the people David met are pointing the way forward to a style of religion likely to appeal to people in the SaW movement. They are placing greater emphasis on the mystical aspects of the religious traditions, and adopting a more interfaith approach.

André Delbecq manifests both these features. A Catholic himself, he has been much influenced by a book by the Jewish mystic Zalman Schachter-Shalomi. In preparing for putting together a course on spirituality for leaders (see the next chapter) he studied both Christian and Buddhist materials. Pat Sullivan draws her insights from all faith traditions. Episcopalian priest Whitney Roberson has prepared Spirituality at Work Conversation notes (described in Chapter 7), drawing inspirational material from many world faiths. Kevin Phillips tries to connect people to ancient wisdom traditions both Christian and non-Christian. John Huntington runs a course which focuses on saints and mystics, and again not just Christian ones.

It is felt that whereas theology and dogma divide, a mystical emphasis brings those of different faith traditions closer together. If faith practitioners were to adopt such an emphasis, one of the major objections to religion, that it is a source of division, would be overcome. What people at work find most disturbing is the prospect of Chief Executive Officers of a particular religious persuasion trying, when bringing spiritual principles to bear in their companies, to force their particular brand of religion on their workforce. Not only would this be resented – for workplaces generally contain people of all faiths or none – it would also, in the United States, constitute an infringement of the Second Amendment to the American Constitution, which stipulates that people should be free to pursue the religion of their choice.

What then would be the features of a religion that would help and support, rather than hinder and frustrate, the practice of spirituality in today's world of work? Perhaps we could apply the concept of a new paradigm to religion, as in Table 4.

The left-hand column represents how religion tends to be perceived by those who regard it as a hindrance to the SaW cause, whereas the right-hand column represents a style that people would respond to more positively.

A common complaint made by both those who have abandoned a formal religion and those who are still adherents, but uneasily so, is that the traditional religions have all but abandoned spirituality. Spirituality is largely intuitive and right-brain, it is relational, it is about connectedness at all levels. It is about a mystical sense of oneness with reality. It is deeply meaningful and life-changing. A religion which emphasizes dogma and intellect is often none of these things.

Alongside an emphasis on dogma often goes a theology which sees God as 'male' and wholly transcendent. The view we are setting forth in our new paradigm is a both-and God: both 'male' because characterized by creativity, power and purpose, and 'female' because loving, forgiving and relational; both transcendent to account for the incidence of radical newness in the

Table 4

Old Paradigm	New Paradigm
Emphasis on dogma and intellect	Emphasis on mysticism and intuition
Belief in a 'male' transcendent God/ultimate reality	Belief in a divinity/ultimate reality which has both male/transcendent and female/immanent aspects
Belief that one's own tradition alone possesses 'the truth'	Willingness to draw insights from other faith traditions
Accepts no insight or wisdom from 'outside'	Accepts and learns from science and all other sources of human wisdom and knowledge
Refuses to come to terms with the modern world	Accepts, while remaining creatively critical of, the modern world
Ignores business life	Is engaged with business life
Has no cosmology	Cosmology is a main focus
Is not much concerned for Planet Earth and its future	Is deeply concerned for, and engaged with, Planet Earth, and keen to work alongside all others dedicated to co-creating its future

universe, and immanent because we both desire and experience a God who is with and alongside us in our daily walk in this world.

Intellectual knowledge breaks up reality in order to analyse it; it learns about things by noting their differences from other things, and sees things in the world as mere objects. It has an 'exclusivist' conception of truth, holding that if *this* is true (and the 'this' often turns out to be my or my nation's or culture's or religion's way of seeing reality) then that which is different cannot be true. Hence the belief that one's own tradition alone possesses the truth. An intuitional, more mystical approach, places less reliance on precisely formulated ideas and sees reality more poetically, artistically and metaphorically. It is able to live with mystery and not-knowing.

Those taking this approach are more open to other angles on the divine mystery, and indeed often feel themselves closer to those in other traditions who are similarly able to live with mystery and not-knowing than to those in their own tradition who claim to know. The Christian mystical writer Thomas Merton had this to say about fellow mystic and Viet-namese Buddhist monk Thich Nhat Hanh: 'Thich Nhat Hanh is more my brother than many who are nearer to me in race and nationality, because he and I see things in exactly the same way.'[13]

One of the monks at Douai Abbey, near Reading in the UK, tells the story of a group of Catholic monks and priests visiting some Buddhist monks. The Catholic monks got on famously with their Buddhist coun-terparts whereas the priests found they had little in common with their hosts.

John Renesch believes that 'we are finally at a point when we may find radically new ways of being religious'. He outlines his vision for renewed religion: 'Imagine a world in which each individual could cultivate an intelligent and comforting theological vision that would not only be tolerant of all other points of view, but would positively appreciate and gain from alternative convictions. That is what, in my book *Soul Mates*, I label "conviviality".'[14] Perhaps the most remarkable example of convivial-ity was the thirteenth-century Sufi mystic poet Rumi, who declared: 'I am not a Christian, I am not a Jew, I am not even a Muslim.'[15]

As well as being willing to learn from the insights of those of other faith traditions, the new-paradigm religious person will be open to truths of science and other sources of human wisdom and knowledge. Sara Maitland, for example, is grateful to new science for enlarging our idea of God. 'Scientists, far from pushing us into an apologetic God-of-the-gaps sheepishness, are in fact opening up for us a vision of God infinitely bigger, cleverer, wilder than our somewhat stunted imaginations have allowed us; a God who is not tamed and constructed by our definitions.'[16] As we learned when looking at the universe story (in Chapters 6 and 7), modern science can be a source of mystical inspiration, providing as it does the 'creation story for our times'. After hundreds of years of separa-tion, religion and culture can now begin to draw together again.

There is a sense, though, in which religion must always remain counter-cultural. In relation to business, while religion needs to be interested in business as such, and to affirm the basic business enterprise, it must at the same time play the role of critical friend. Certainly business as usually conducted, and the economic system as it currently functions, must be challenged in the name of both its own best interests and those of humanity and the planet (see Chapter 11).

When we say that old-paradigm religion has no cosmology we mean that it pays no attention to, does not operate in relation to, the world as such. It has no conception of the divine indwelling of the cosmos and hence of the world itself participating in sacred reality. By focusing on the eternal destiny of individuals whom it has plucked out of a (in its view) literally godless world, old-paradigm religion shows itself to have little concern for our planetary future and little sense of its own responsibility to help co-create that future. (It may believe we should respect the earth as the creation of God, but that's about as far as it goes.) New-paradigm religion, however, sees co-creation as central to its very *raison d'être*, and will naturally make common cause with all others wanting to co-write the next chapter of the universe story.

Diarmuid Ó Murchú tells the story of a young man, Ian, who was passionately keen to make a difference in the world. He had joined CND because he wanted to save the planet. Curious about religion, he investigated Buddhism and Sikhism, and eventually came to the Church of England to see whether *it* would support his 'cosmic' intent. He made an appointment with his local vicar, whom he told about his quest at length and with great passion. It soon became clear, however, that the vicar was bored by Ian's story, for suddenly he interrupted him in mid-flow to ask, But do you believe in Jesus Christ? The implication was that Ian's interest and intent were misdirected.[17] One wonders what kind of Christ this vicar believed in!

A 'new-paradigm' religious writer

We illustrate new-paradigm religion with reference to a writer whose views we have extensively discussed and who is much admired in the SaW movement – Matthew Fox. An ex-Roman Catholic – he was expelled in 1993 from the Dominican Order for his radical views – Fox is a leading figure in the Creation Spirituality movement. He has written more than two dozen books. We have already referred to a number of them and we shall now say a little more about three in particular.

Fox's basic exposition of Creation Spirituality comes in *Original Blessing*.[18] A major complaint of his is that for most of its history Western Christianity has failed to honour creation and human creative activity, having become preoccupied with the themes of fall and redemption. His mission is to correct that imbalance, so he emphasizes 'original blessing' as opposed to 'original sin'. His Creation Spirituality is about following four paths: the *via positiva* (which enjoys and celebrates creation), the *via negativa* (which is about the pain, loss and suffering which are also part of life within the created order), the *via creativa* (which is about creative action in the world) and the *via transformativa* (which is concerned with re-establishing justice based on the spirit of compassion for the world). We shall say more about these four paths in Chapter 12.

It is in *The Coming of the Cosmic Christ*[19] that Fox gives us perhaps the most profound picture of his brand of new-paradigm theology. The concern uppermost in his mind in writing this book was what the human race is currently doing to Mother Earth, which he describes as matricide.

The only antidote to this, he believes, is for the human race, and particularly those of us in the West, to rediscover the cosmic, feminist, right-brain, mystical aspects of spirituality.

Fox includes a summary of what mysticism is about, which he presents in the form of 'twenty-one running, working, experiential definitions', under the following headings: Experience – Nondualism – Compassion – Connection making – Radical amazement – Affirmation of the whole as a whole – Right brain – Self-critical – Heart knowledge – A return to the source – Feminist – Panentheistic (see p. 82) – Birthing images – Silence – Nothingness and darkness – Childlike playfulness – Psychic justice – Prophetic – Being-with-being – True Self – Globally ecumenical.[20]

In the Creation Spirituality tradition, everyone is regarded as a mystic, or a potential one; and Fox's later chapters illustrate ways of bringing out our innate mysticism – one of his favourites being 'art as meditation'. He talks about mystics in all the faith traditions rejoicing in their mutual discovery of common ground. He believes this global ecumenism, or deep ecumenism as he also calls it, offers hope both for world peace and the saving of Mother Earth. What binds together people of the different mystical traditions is recognition of 'the cosmic Christ', which for the sake of non-Christians Fox alternatively names Cosmic Wisdom. The central part of Fox's book traces the cosmic Christ/wisdom theme in the theology of Judaism and Christianity, with special reference to the Western mystical tradition (see Appendix 2).

Fox believes that this neglected tradition should be studied by every Christian theologian and should feature centrally in the training of every minister. He also draws out the general implications for a renewed Christianity, providing (for example) imaginative ideas on how to revitalize worship.

Some parts of *The Coming of the Cosmic Christ* might be rather taxing for the general reader, but the gems scattered throughout the book, plus several sections which are highly accessible, are guaranteed to bring illumination to a wide variety of readers.

Matthew Fox's most referred-to book in the SaW movement is *The Reinvention of Work*.[21] We have already quoted from it extensively in expounding the universe story. But we would also like to indicate some of the other 'goodies' from this remarkable volume. Fox begins the book by explaining why so much in modern working life crushes our spirits. He shows how the isolation, insecurity and alienation inherent in many jobs can be overcome by authentic 'soul work'. He envisions a work-world where intellect and heart come together in work which celebrates the whole person. Fox shatters old-paradigm industrial-age models of work by applying the principles of new cosmology, as we have seen. He quotes from those of many backgrounds who are asking critical questions about the way we work, and gives special attention to mystical writers of all ages and traditions.

The contribution of world religions to SaW

There is much common ground between all, or most, world religions as to which are the principles that should be applied to working life and workplace spirituality. Kriger and Hanson reckon the following are among the values honoured by all the major traditions: honesty and truthfulness, trust, humility, forgiveness, compassion, thankfulness, being of service, and stillness and peace.[22] Compassion, for example, is a quality honoured in both Buddhism and Judaism, but each has an interestingly distinctive way of emphasizing it.[23] The Golden Rule – treating others as you'd like them to treat you – is also embraced by all the religions.

Another commonly held idea is that all types of work are sacred. Thomas Moore tells us that 'in many religious traditions, work is not set off from the precincts of the sacred. It is not "pro-fane" – in front of the temple – it is *in* the temple. In Christian and Zen monasteries, for instance, work is as much a part of the monk's carefully designed life as are prayer, meditation, and liturgy.'[24] This message is neglected in much religious teaching today, with the result that 'workers assume that their tasks [. . .] are purely secular and functional, but even such ordinary jobs as carpentry, secretarial services, and gardening relate to the soul as much as to function.'[25] Moreover – and this too is a point on which most religions agree – 'all work is a vocation, a calling from a place that is the source of meaning and identity.'[26]

The Eastern religions

Among the main Eastern contributions to SaW is the 'spiritual science' aspect of its wisdom, from which so much of modern psychology, particularly of the neo-Jungian variety, derives. Jung himself made an extensive study of Eastern philosophy, and we saw how the work of Grof and other transpersonal psychologists represents the discovery of a whole body of knowledge known for centuries in the East but hitherto largely hidden from the West.

Margaret Wheatley traces an 'Eastern religion' parallel to the 'all strands in the great web' view of new science: 'In Hinduism's Rig Veda, there is an image of Indra's net. We are all individual jewels [. . .] gleaming on the same web, each sparkling outward from our place on the net, each reflected in the other.'[27]

SaW is deeply indebted to Hindu author Deepak Chopra. An admirer of Ken Wilber, Chopra in *How to Know God*[28] uses a Wilber-like model of spiritual development to provide an illuminating history of religions, and he draws sympathetically from many faith traditions. He also fruitfully employs the insights of modern quantum physics in speaking of 'higher order' religious experience and spiritual development, and has much to say about prayer, miracles and synchronicity. He manifests in a remarkable way the new-paradigm qualities of global ecumenism, openness to modern science and critical solidarity with the modern world. Chopra has also distilled spiritual laws from the Vedic tradition into 'seven spiritual laws of success', in his book of that title.[29]

Karma Yoga (Hinduism) speaks of the importance of bringing the right attitudes to one's work, for these will determine one's experience of it. 'With love and enthusiasm toward our work, what was once a chore and hardship now becomes a magical tool to develop, nourish and enrich our lives.'[30]

Hinduism also recommends an attitude of 'non-attachment', which is 'a willingness to relinquish the results of any action to God'.[31] (See again the quotes from the *Bhagavad Gita* in Chapter 6 on this and other work-related points.)

We demonstrated the wisdom of Taoism in our quotes from the *Tao Te Ching* – also in Chapter 6. That document also has some wonderfully up-to-date teaching on leadership.

The Jain principle of *ahimsa* (non-violence) is another contribution of Eastern religion, and has many practical implications for working life.[32]

Buddhist writers are much in evidence in the SaW literature. We've already mentioned several of them (see our section on spiritual praxis in Chapter 7). Another is Lewis Richmond who, in *Work as a Spiritual Practice*,[33] makes the interesting point that 'the Buddha himself found enlightenment out of a serious case of job dissatisfaction as an Indian prince some 2,500 years ago'! The Buddha's contribution is highly relevant to our working lives, for it included 'practicing mindfulness, compassion, and meditation at work and a career journey that emphasizes "right livelihood"'.[34]

Philosophies like Zen Buddhism, Confucianism and Shintoism emphasize loyalty to one's group and looking to find a spiritual centre in any kind of work or activity.[35]

Levin points out that the ancient book of Chinese religion, the *I Ching*, 'has many wonderful teachings on friendship. For example, it points out that real friendship is based on sharing common values and a common end that is greater than yourself.' This puts a question mark against the current business view of 'friendship as networking', which often amounts to no more than making friends merely to gain a mutual business advantage.[36]

The Western religions

For Judaism and Christianity, we human beings are created in the image of the Creator God. Thus creativity is a key mark of our being human, and exercising our creativity in the world and forwarding the purpose of the Creator is a primary responsibility. As Sullivan puts it, 'Whatever our work, we are called to co-create with God a world that is just and loving'. She quotes from *The Eighth Day of Creation*[37] where Elizabeth O'Connor says that 'in every person is the creation story', and goes on to speak of our investing our gifts in 'the continuing creation of the world'. Catherine McGeachy draws out the business lesson that organizations should always bear in mind people's desire to create. They should 'look for the many ways in which creativity is stifled in their organisations – not just to re-motivate their employees, but to tap that creative pulse that is critical to the survival of the company'.[38] Matthew Fox sees creativity as the place 'where the divine and the human meet'.[39]

In his book about the teachings of the Jewish-mystic Kabbalah tradition, *The Power of Kabbalah*, Yehuda Berg speaks of our 'creator genes'.[40] This book also shows the affinity of Kabbalah with new science.[41]

There are many references in the SaW literature to the teachings of the Jewish rabbi Abraham Heschel. Here, by way of a sample, is Tracey Marks' summary of Heschel's definition of meaning, stated – says Sullivan – in a way that 'beautifully applies to meaningful work: "Man experiences his life as meaningful when he lives in God's presence – not simply by encountering God in the world, but primarily by serving God in everyday life, infusing every moment with the spirit of God, and by dedicating himself to ends outside himself."'[42] This reminds us of the spirituality of Brother Lawrence and his 'practice of the presence of God' as he went about his daily chores in the monastery kitchen.

We would also emphasize the importance to SaW of the Judaeo-Christian *prophetic tradition*. In his book *The Prophetic Imagination*, Walter Brueggemann shows that the prophetic tradition, from Moses to Jesus, insists that the new does not emerge smoothly from the old but rather through the death of the old and always as a divine gift. The process, in other words, is not a reformative one (for reform means simply ameliorating the old) but a transformative one, in which the old is comprehensively superseded.[43] We are already familiar with this line of thinking in the teaching of Wilber, Bohm, Zohar and others.

An important piece of teaching deriving significantly, though not exclusively, from the Judaeo-Christian prophetic tradition is the need to feel compassion for, and champion the cause of, *the poor and disadvantaged*. In business life this translates into according respect to, and valuing the contribution of, the lowliest employee.[44] It also means operating in ways that benefit rather than harm the poor of the earth (see Chapter 11).

Closely related to this last point is the emergence in the mid-to-late twentieth century of *liberation and feminist theology*, which represents a modern revival of the Old Testament and Christian prophetic tradition. Jacqueline Haessly writes eloquently on this subject in her contribution, Chapter 8, to the Renesch and DeFoore volume. Her whole chapter should be read, but we have space for just two quotes. Following Mary Jo Weaver, Haessly sees as the foundation of liberation theology 'a belief that . . . God's primary passion is to free humans from oppressive situations, and God's self-disclosure occurs when we recognize and accept God's summons to us to participate in the historic struggle for liberation'.[45] Liberation and feminist theologians are highly critical of the current economic and political structures, and urge their replacement by 'structures and systems that are life-enhancing'.[46]

McGeachy tells us about Limerick businessman Dan O'Connell who used to say, 'You never take maximum profit – you always leave some for the other man.'[47] This reminds us of the Old Testament stipulation that when a farmer harvests his crops he should always leave a proportion of them around the edge of his field for those less well off.

A vital Jewish contribution to working life today, given the ridiculously long hours some people work and the failure of many to achieve a work-life balance, is teaching about the Sabbath with its stipulation of one day of rest each week. 'Although it is difficult to find sabbath time in a wired-up world, August Turak, CEO of the Raleigh Group International software company [. . .] refuses to carry a cellphone after hours, and he doesn't work on a laptop during plane trips,' reports Pat Sullivan.[48] She also cites CEO Carisa Bianchi of the advertising agency TBWA/Chiat/Day, who declares: 'I draw a clear line between my work life and my personal life, and I expect my co-workers to do the same . . . When people don't take time out, they stop being productive.'[49] Sullivan also mentions an arch-violator of the sabbath principle, a senior manager who boasted: 'I am so loyal to this firm that I missed the births of all four of my children.'[50]

The idea of *covenant* relationships also comes from the Jewish tradition. As opposed to a mere contract, which is a legal agreement, a covenant is a personal agreement between parties who are deeply committed to one another – as in the relationship between God and Israel. In his forthcoming *Book of Agreements* (to be published by Berrett-Koehler), Stewart Levine sees the potential for business agreements to be covenant-based.[51]

Robert Greenleaf's 'servant leadership' philosophy (see Chapter 9) is taken directly from the teaching of Jesus on servant leadership.[52]

An important insight from the Christian tradition is the need for repentance and forgiveness and the transforming effect of this process. Kiefer and Senge have introduced the notion of the 'metanoic organizations',[53] i.e. those seeing themselves as shapers rather than victims of reality. In Christianity *metanoia* is about a revolutionary turn-around in your life's purpose, a complete change of heart and will, a turning away from an orientation that separates one from God and a reorientation towards God's purpose and ways. And the result of this reorientation, which is at the same time an experience of reconciliation (or, in terms of this book, reconnection) with God, is freedom from past guilt, a sense of present forgiveness and a confidence in final personal and cosmic transformation. (We shall be applying this understanding of metanoia to business organizations in Chapter 14.)

Before leaving Christianity we must mention the importance it attaches to the symbol of 'the resurrection of the body'. This implies a belief in the ongoing spiritual importance of 'the material', whose destiny is to be taken up into the spiritual rather than be superseded by it. This reminds us of Wilber's transcend-and-include principle, and of Teilhard's belief about spirit as 'the interiority of matter'.[54] We contend that this understanding of matter is important to a spirituality of work, for so much of human endeavour involves working with and upon matter.[55] The idea that through our work we are co-creators of Planet Earth (Chapter 6) itself implies a high regard for things material.

The Muslim religion well integrates faith and life. 'If you are a Muslim, you are a Muslim in the workplace, in the street, and carry your teachings with you everywhere,' explains Abdul Patel.[56] Islam places great emphasis on prayer, and the way Muslims at work quietly and unobtrusively demonstrate their commitment to their 'five times a day' prayer – one of the pillars of Islam – is impressive.

Bayrak speaks of the insights we can learn from the Sufi tradition – the mystical branch of Islam. He says that of the 99 names for God in that tradition, compassion and mercy come top of the list. Also closely aligned with these virtues is that of 'inner surrender, so that we can identify and ultimately merge with "the beloved"'.[57] Kriger and Hanson tell us that Sufism's teaching on compassion is based on the conviction that 'we exist in relationship – with the physical environment, the plant and animal kingdoms, and within human communities – and cannot survive outside of relationship with these. In compassion, we extend the realm of what is central and important beyond ourselves. We come to recognize that it is our connection with the "apparently other" that makes us human in the deepest sense.'[58]

In his book *Thinking Like the Universe: the Sufi Path of Awakening*[59] Pir Vilayat outlines the belief of Sufism that it is in the midst of the problems and concerns of everyday life that we must attain and sustain illumination. Rather than regard these as 'permanent roadblocks on the spiritual path', we should see them as 'creative catalysts for spiritual evolution'.[60]

Sufism is principally concerned about 'giving birth to the Universe's unborn qualities'.[61] A Sufi initiate 'is considered a vice-regent of God who takes responsibility for the human condition'.[62] According to Pir Vilayat, Sufism sees the spiritual journey as 'about much more than detaching from the illusory conditions of life; it is creative and transformative'.[63] Judging from the number of times David Bohm is referred to, this book shows how modern Sufism readily identifies with new science.

A much-quoted figure in SaW literature is the Sufi mystic Rumi. Here is a sample of his wisdom: 'Let the beauty of what you love be what you do.'[64] We mentioned Rumi's remarkable inter-faith stance earlier in this chapter.

Indigenous native religions

The Sufi insight about our need for, and intrinsic connection with, all others, including 'all our relations' in the natural world, is powerfully reflected in the teachings of native peoples throughout the world. Matthew Fox often refers to the contributions of those in the North American Indian tradition – such as Hobday (see Chapter 6) and Starhawk. Margaret Wheatley also acknowledges the importance of the indigenous religions: 'Too many of us have forgotten that we live in a web of life. However, the knowledge of our proper role has been taught by many indigenous peoples.'[65]

Pat Sullivan is another SaW writer who greatly appreciates the insights and practices of indigenous religions. She notes how 'common to tribal people throughout the world is an ethic in which all work is enfolded into community and spiritual life [. . .] Work tools were blessed and work was infused with ritual and prayer.'[66] She acknowledges native environmental wisdom: 'The earth and its inhabitants are expected to be protected, as in the Iraquois commandment to consider the impact of one's actions to the seventh generation.'[67] She refers to drumming as a way to pray with the body, and commends the practice of sweat lodges, which involves pouring water over heated rocks. Anita Roddick tells us what she has learned from her experience of sweat lodges: 'I was not on *top* of nature. I was *part* of nature.[68] It taught me not respect. It taught me reverence.'[69]

Sullivan feels we have much to learn from the custom of tribal people sitting in a group at the time of twilight and sharing their stories and their wisdom. By contrast, 'today [. . .] most of us lose twilight to commute time or TV news or game shows', believing that 'we're too busy to sit together under the night sky and ponder the mysteries of life'.[70]

An expert SaW writer on indigenous religions is Angeles Arrien, who contributes chapter 6 in the Renesch and DeFoore volume. Her book *The Four-Fold Way* should also be consulted.[71]

Can the religions renew themselves?

There is much in the religious traditions that is still highly relevant to the modern world and to the concerns of SaW. The religions do therefore have a contribution to make to SaW – a contribution which adds a depth and breadth of spiritual experience without which SaW would be much the poorer. Why should people be left to do the spiritual equivalent of reinventing the wheel? Why not draw on the centuries and (in many cases) millennia of accumulated spiritual wisdom?

The trouble is that religion as taught and practised today often serves to conceal rather than reveal religion's true treasures. However, were the religions to renew themselves along the new-paradigm lines we outlined earlier in this chapter, and give more regular expression to the wisdom that we have just been examining, they would be more in tune with modern people's spiritual quest, more sympathetic to their needs and more equipped to make their distinctive contributions. In Chapter 15 we list many religious groups currently emphasizing the relationship of faith and working life.

PART THREE

MAPPING THE TERRAIN: THE CORPORATE JOURNEY

9

Becoming an Authentic Leader

Life is a mystery to be lived, rather than a problem to be solved.

Aspire to be more rather than to have more.[1]

The aim of this section is to make connections to the corporate outworking of spirituality and explore how the 'four connections' may be applied organizationally. Chapter 10 explores the corporate parallel to 'connecting with others'. The themes of 'connecting with nature' and 'connecting with higher power' are both assessed in relationship to organizations in Chapters 11 and 12. But first we turn our attention to the 'connection with self' and its natural relation to leadership.

In one sense this whole book is devoted to leadership issues since leadership, like spirituality itself, is multi-dimensional. It's about an individual's capacity and personality, as well as about different ways of leading and working with others, and ultimately it's about our impact on the world. The literature on leadership is vast and yet, as Warren Bennis has said, 'Without question, leadership is the most studied and least understood topic of any I can think of.'[2] It is not our purpose here to expound on the vast array of leadership theory. Rather we want to explore what role spirituality has to play in developing our capability as leaders.

Our capacity for leadership

One of its first contributions is the suggestion that *we can all be leaders* in our own way. There is wide agreement that leaders are made not born, which implies that any one of us can choose to become a leader. We each lead our own lives through the choices we make and we can choose to be the change we want to see in the world since 'I am my contribution'. We should not allow hierarchy, power and role-position to obscure our view of what leadership is. As Gillian has already indicated in Chapter 5, leadership can be informal, it can emerge amongst a group of people and differ depending on the context and what the group needs in order to survive and grow.

Organizations are full of people who may be using their leadership skills voluntarily outside of paid work – in communities, sports, clubs, churches, charities, in education, at home and in their social lives, even if they wouldn't always think of these activities as involving leadership. But there is something which leadership activities have in common, wherever they take place. Peter Drucker says that truly effective leaders don't ask 'what do I want' but 'what needs to be done'.[3] Their purpose is to make a difference.

Kippenberger examines the research of Buckingham and Coffman, published in their 1999 book *First Break All the Rules*,[4] which suggests that 'effective leaders appear to be people who do not need to pretend to be someone else; they are generally at peace with themselves, recognise their own strengths and weaknesses, and fit themselves into the right roles. They look for ways in which their natural talents can make a big difference.'[5]

This sense of wanting to make a difference is connected to our authenticity as individuals, which is ultimately spiritually motivated. Our earlier chapter on self (Chapter 4) shows some of the depth of this journey towards authenticity. William Guillory emphasizes the centrality of personal development being at the heart of the leadership path: 'Leadership begins with self [...] [and requires] a sufficiently in-depth knowledge of ourselves that our external activities naturally carry commitment and passion.'[6] Leadership entails self-development in the total and truest sense – intellectually, bodily, emotionally and spiritually. Bennis argues that leadership is based on learning – learning from one's own life and experience, understanding one's self and the world. Leadership, he argues, can and must be learned.[7]

Tom Heuerman supports this view: 'We can only change ourselves by becoming more aware, authentic, courageous and then we can contribute our unique gifts and influence the systems around us in life-enhancing ways.'[8]

Developing leadership qualities

According to Bennis two of the criteria that can make or break a leader are judgement and character. These qualities are acquired and tested as part of our whole life experience; they are part of who we are, not an 'add on' that we can adopt for a season when it suits us. Perhaps the second contributing factor of spirituality to leadership, then, is a deepening appreciation of the holistic nature of our development as part of our life's overall journey.

This is particularly pertinent for leaders in business to take notice of since it signals that there are no quick fixes. As Mintzberg points out, 'Key managerial processes are enormously complex and mysterious.' Managers are constantly 'drawing on the vaguest of information and using the least articulated of mental processes. These processes seem to be more relational and holistic than ordered and sequential and more intuitive than intellectual.'[9]

How do leaders develop their intuitive judgement skills? How can we enhance our capacity for dealing with complexity? Only by taking up the subjective path of individual learning and development, desiring to become more self-aware, authentic and courageous about our convictions. Here is where spirituality makes its presence felt since genuine learning and spirituality get to the heart of what it means to be human.

'The spiritual leadership approach finds the solution in contemplation,' argue Korac-Kakabadse and colleagues. This involves approaching situations 'with an attitude of discernment rather than one of intervention; acceptance rather than control; letting go rather than holding on; lightening rather than doing; and in humility rather than competence'.[10]

Leadership retreats run at Waverley Learning (see Chapter 15) stress that a self-reflective process is necessary if people are to extract wisdom from experience. When they become 'centred', leaders can be more effective at developing relationship awareness and communication skills that enable them to create a genuine community of purpose with those around them.

André Delbecq focuses on this self-reflective process in his illuminating course 'Spirituality for Business Leadership' which he runs at Santa Clara University in California. We have extracted details of this course from the *Journal of Management Inquiry*[11] at some length because it provides huge insights to us about the whole terrain of leadership and what it's all about in the business context.

Delbecq's course, as described, defined spirituality as 'lived experience'. The course design paired CEOs with MBA students and the MBAs were 'profoundly touched by the depth of spiritual sensitivity and leadership complexity' disclosed by the CEOs. A number of key insights arose about spirituality and leadership from their experiences on the course together. One of the revealing truths that emerged was summed up by an MBA student: 'If business is essential to society, and most people must participate in it in order for society to function (as opposed to being full-time charitable volunteers or monks), and if all people are called to a life of full spirituality and holiness, then it must be possible to live a full spiritual life in business.' Such a statement has recently been verified at a conference run by the Christian organization, CIEBN, who featured Rich Marshall, author of *God@Work*,[12] as their main speaker. It is safe to assume that the development of leadership is a part of our life's work, and our work is a part of the way in which our spiritual life is developed.

The importance of 'being', and personal integration, are prioritized over 'doing' if a leader is to avoid cynicism, despair and burnout in the intensity of the leadership role. Such qualities of 'being' were, in Delbecq's course, found through a process of discernment, which revolved around prayer and listening. The prayer experience alternated between a contemporary, informal and spontaneous kind as well as a deeper, more meditative type of reflection. The course also explored the shadow or 'dark side' of leadership which, as we have previously highlighted, is a key to understanding the struggle within ourselves. Symptoms of the shadow include pulls to power and greed, the lure of wealth, the temptations to narcissism, self-delusion, over-control and vanity. It was agreed that, to counter these pulls, humility and God's grace were needed.

Another particular insight from this course was the paradox between poverty and wealth as part of a spiritual path. Successful CEOs naturally become wealthy. The issue of what to do with the riches gained necessarily raised questions about the nature of the consumptive West and what to do about injustice and inequality amongst the less advantaged. Interestingly, Delbecq's leaders found it difficult to resolve this complex area but all took the issue seriously and assessed their own part in changing the system. The timing of this part of the course was interesting, as these issues came up just before a module on contemplative practice coupled with a retreat. By this stage the participants were ready for such an experience and many facets of group life had come to bind them together. Delbecq says, 'The sharing of gifts and challenges just before dinner highlighted the diversity of talents within the group and the mysterious way in which we need and bless each other.'

The intensive retreat, which included a variety of religious forms of mindfulness, led to the next part of the course, which was to step outside their comfort zone in order to engage in a place of suffering that they most feared. 'If you feared death, to have an encounter with the dying; if you feared being severely disabled, to visit those who are disabled, and so on.' This assignment was possibly the hardest on the course, but the learning was vast.

'I learned the value of basic things in life: food, shelter and friendship. I learned how small the personal cost of a smile and friendliness is. I knew that these things had value [. . .] but I just never realized how priceless they could be' (MBA student). Class participants ended their experience with 'a new sense of the dignity and grace with which many carry their burdens, an overcoming of the fears that keep us from contact with those less fortunate, and the realization that once we engage in the encounter, simply to be with the sufferer, we often gain more than we give'.

This part of the course might appear to have little to do with business leadership, but the premise of Delbecq's course is that an adequate spirituality for business leadership must acknowledge the reality of suffering as part of the leadership journey. Examples of suffering might include

- the selflessness required by the leadership role with its demand on time, emotional energy and the absence of privacy;
- the criticism and backbiting often directed towards leaders; the loneliness of office and the demands of confidentiality; the anxieties when addressing new strategic challenges;
- the special burdens of bearing bad news in firings and lay-offs; the humbling uncertainties when stepping down from high prestige roles; anxiety and doubt, and so on.

The relevance of lessons from the earlier module began to become clear – the need to be fully present, to *be* with one's colleagues even when you cannot *do* what you would wish. The need to avoid hiding behind activity as a shield from pain. By mindful attention to heartfelt suffering, the group had learned how to deal with the difficulties often faced in a leader's journey. They had also gained a deeper insight into their own part in making a difference to the world order.

The conclusions from the course were rich and deep. 'We had touched deeply an aspect of life and leadership that is not often discussed in the instrumental managerial literature. We had uncovered that moment when one can only proceed by faith, by surrendering to the unknown mystery, however each person defines the mystery.' Delbecq comments that the 'need for such a course is greater than I could have anticipated'.

Desire for others to live more authentically

Developing our internal capacity for leadership opens the door for us to lead externally. When we appreciate the changes that are required in us, then we are better able to lead change in others.

Turner says:

> Organizational transformation begins with the willingness of an organization's leaders to examine their own values and behaviors. Leaders who endorse workplace spirituality will envision an environment in which all employees are given the opportunity to reach their highest potential both in terms of their work and as human beings. Unfortunately [. . .] most leaders in organizations today have not reached that higher level of consciousness.[13]

In fact, for many of us, the leadership in our organizations is killing our spirit. Jobs can be dispiriting and we absent our true selves from them.

Russ Moxley suggests that we end up colluding with those who exercise command and control when we give away our power and act co-dependently. We complain about 'them' and what they are doing to 'us'[14] but we don't choose to be authentic and honest when we have a chance to talk. We choose the safety and security of the status quo over work that would allow us to use our gifts and talents in life-giving, energy-producing ways.

And yet Moxley also claims that there is an understanding and practice of leadership that elevates spirit, honours the whole self, and encourages us to use all of our energies in the practice of leadership. This understanding makes use of our spiritual energy. Indeed, spirituality is the essential factor in creating inspired performance.

Many writers have put forward their ideas on how to tap into the spiritual as part of leadership, for example Robert Greenleaf (servant leadership), Peter Block (stewardship), Stephen Covey (principle-centred leadership). Greenleaf espoused the idea of a leader being a 'nurturer of the human spirit'.[15] His philosophy of 'servant leadership' contains the idea that individuals should want, above all, to serve. The identifying signs of such a leader are found in the answers to the following questions: 'Will all of the people touched by that leader's influence grow as persons? Will they while being served become healthier, wiser, freer, more likely themselves to become servants? And what will be the effect on the least privileged in society; will that person benefit, or at least not be further deprived?'[16] The stewardship concept fundamentally aligns with the importance of service: 'Stewardship begins with the willingness to be accountable for some larger body than ourselves – an organization, a community. Stewardship springs from a set of beliefs about reforming organizations that affirms our choice for service over the pursuit of self-interest [. . .] We serve best through partnership.'[17] Covey suggests that the set of beliefs behind such an approach are based on principles, or natural laws, that govern human effectiveness. He attests to the need for character and integrity, emphasizing that you reap what you sow in life.[18]

All of these concepts are also biblical. The SaW idealists recognize them as essential truths and champion them. We recommend those interested to pursue these ideas through further reading of the books just mentioned.

Such approaches show how theories of leadership are moving away from control and towards influence, collaboration and partnership. Peter Senge writes, 'Leaders are visionaries who see possibilities and orient themselves toward creating rather than maintaining [. . .] Leaders are teachers, facilitators, "growers" of human beings.'[19] So a third aspect of spirituality's contribution to leadership is that it is not enough for leaders to bear their own responsibility; they must seek to liberate others' responsibility for choices and actions and so encourage their personal growth.

As Greenleaf puts it, 'Work exists for the person as much as the person for the work; the growth of those who do the work is the primary aim.'[20] We have to look 'at our glasses as well as through them' and ask whether we really believe that business exists to provide meaningful work for a person as much as it exists to provide a product or service to the customer. This is the challenge offered to us by spiritual leadership.

Spirit in Business

Many leaders are already tuned into new-paradigm leadership thinking, and forming networks to support the expansion of this ideology. The growing network Spirit in Business (SiB) is encouraging such a viewpoint. SiB's strategy focuses on adding value at the highest level by connecting 'leaders in a global community of inquiry, learning and action, to release the creative power of individuals and organizations for the benefit of the whole'. SiB works from the simple assumption that personal character and conscience is informed and inspired by spirit; this in turn informs business ethics which are essential for business success. Their mission is to enhance business performance by integrating personal inspiration from spirit with ethical leadership, and thereby encourage a values-based approach to everyday business practice. By addressing fundamental personal, organizational and systemic questions, the SiB community is striving to transform business into an agent of world benefit. We highly recommend that you take a look at their website – www.spiritinbusiness.org.

Founded in May 2001, they have held a number of conferences and retreats and have established a leading-edge, web-based knowledge platform, using the flower model in Figure 2, which provides excellent resources on how spirit can work to transform different areas of business. The model clearly shows that spirit is a source of many evolving knowledge domains with relevance to all aspects of our organizations.

The spiritual/scientific domain is the source of the whole flower which, as we have described, offers new perspectives on reality.

The domain of creativity and emotional intelligence is the source of personal expression, represented by the first petal of the 'personal' section of the flower. This domain is the source from which business performance springs and where know-how regarding all subsequent knowledge domains can be developed.

The domain of health and well-being is based on the fact that without a healthy body one cannot function or develop. It also refers to holistic complementary health care.

The domain of effective leadership is where new insights, based on a scientific integration of principles of spirit, take place and from where

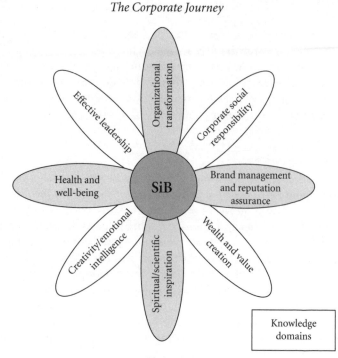

Figure 2

change in organizations will begin. It is the culmination of the personal side of the SiB wheel.

The domain of organizational transformation (OT) begins the public development of the flower, taking the personal insights of effective leadership and incorporating them into OT and learning.

The domains covered so far refer to the 'soft' aspects of management. With the domain of corporate social responsibility (CSR) we enter upon the 'harder' aspects because CSR is not the exclusive property of human resources and organizational development management but more often that of line management with profit and loss responsibility. In this domain SiB complements the conventional, but obviously limited, legal approach to enforcing business ethics.

The domain of brand management and reputation assurance involves marketing, sales and public relations. While the previous domains are primarily internally driven, this one makes a clear connection to external markets.

The final domain, wealth and value creation (both material/financial and non-material/social/ecological/spiritual) is in fact the outcome of the integrated SiB approach and links it to the bottom line. As true wealth creates personal fulfilment and inspiration, this petal closes the circle. To put it differently, SiB's belief is that any organization whose outcome is other than staff fulfilment and inspiration will gradually deplete its most valuable resource and become unsustainable.

SiB's web-based knowledge platform offers the latest thinking in each of the domains via research from leading writers, speakers, universities and institutes, and translates it into appealing and inspiring content and programming for the business community. To unleash the power of the knowledge domains, the SiB global network interacts with people and companies to build new business wisdom in each of the eight areas.

SiB shows that whatever our unique gifts, or however we fit into the system, all our contributions are affected by spirit. The holistic and integrated approach to being human which spirituality offers is critically needed after centuries of fragmenting and compartmentalizing our lives and work.

The significance of our worldview

Spiritual leadership encompasses the ideals of being self-aware and other-aware, but also 'world-aware'. Jaworski, whom we have highlighted previously, reminds us of this in his easy-to-read and inspiring book, *Synchronicity*. He personalizes inner leadership work by telling us the story of his own journey, featuring all the events and experiences he encountered along the way. He began to reframe the way he saw the world, shifting from an attitude of resignation to seeing the world as full of possibilities. 'If we are to participate in the unfolding process of the universe, we must let life *flow* through us, rather than attempt to *control* life.'[21] Instead of trying to make things happen, he began to trust and be open to simply 'being'. This is why his book is entitled 'Synchronicity'. When he adopted such an attitude, all manner of people and events came along in his life which strengthened and guided him on his new journey towards personal growth and understanding.

Jaworski went on to found The American Leadership Forum based on a mission of helping to free others from their limits, adopting the philosophy of servant leadership, enabling people to align to broader visionary purpose in their lives, one founded on love not fear. His book makes for a compelling read and we highly recommend it.

One of the key moments in Jaworski's journey was his meeting with David Bohm who, as we have seen, has been very influential. Whilst Jaworski is not explicit about spirituality, the journey he describes and the ideas Bohm articulates portray the underpinning change that SaW ideas promote. Jaworski realized that Bohm's ideas had far-reaching implications.

Since Bohm, other writers such as Zohar and Wheatley have confirmed and supported the changes in how we can think about the world brought about by the new science perspective. Everywhere in the new sciences – in living systems theory, quantum physics, chaos and complexity theory – there are changing perceptions of the organizing principles of life. We are observing life's dependence on participation and the freedom to self-determine. This knowledge is affecting leadership theory, which now recognizes we can no longer survive under the command and control leadership that was inspired by a mechanistic worldview. Wheatley suggests: 'No-one can hope to lead any organization by standing outside or ignoring the web of relationships through which all work is accomplished. Leaders are being called to step forward as helpmates.'[22]

Zohar says,

> Servant leadership is the essence of quantum thinking and quantum leadership [. . .] To qualify as servant leaders in the deepest sense, I think that leaders must have four essential qualities. They must have a deep sense of the interconnectedness of life and all its enterprises. They must have a sense of engagement and responsibility, a sense of 'I *have* to'. They must be aware that all human endeavor, including business, is a part of the larger and richer fabric of the whole universe. And perhaps most important of all, servant leaders must know what they ultimately serve. They must, with a sense of humility and gratitude, have a sense of the Source from which all values emerge [. . .] The servant leader serves from a base of love.[23]

In organizations this attitude of service is revealed in our respect for relationships. Returning to Wheatley:

> To live in a quantum world, to weave here and there with ease and grace, we need to change what we do. We need fewer descriptions of tasks and instead learn to facilitate process. We need to become savvy about how to foster relationships, how to nurture growth and development. All of us need to become better at listening, conversing, respecting one another's uniqueness, because these are essential for strong relationships. The era of the rugged individual has been replaced by the era of the team player. But this is only the beginning. The quantum world has demolished the concept that we are unconnected individuals. More and more relationships are in store for us, out there in the vast web of life.[24]

If we act on the belief that we are part of a great whole, then not only are we becoming more fully alive as we reach out to wholeness, but we become engaged with reality in a way that enlivens others to their own potential. These two strands can combine to change our actions in the world, and the world itself. This is transformational leadership.

The difficulty is that most people have a block to going this far. We feel we could never make a difference, and so we don't face the possibility – it's too disturbing, too frightening, it seems to require too much of us. Dealing with the block in our consciousness and the outworking of this in our lives is what spirituality can contribute to leadership.

Learning spiritual leadership values

The SaW network is full of people who are promoting a variety of ways to support a deepening appreciation of the learning that we need to become authentic, transformational leaders. Some of these are incorporated into our next chapter. But perhaps, to conclude this chapter on leadership, it is helpful simply to state some of the values and terms that are associated with and attached to the notion of spiritual and transformational leadership (Table 5).

Table 5

Reflection	Wisdom	Love
Discernment	Caring	Meaning
Humility	Intuition	Integrity
Commitment	Service	Healing
Compassion	Vision	Dignity
Honesty	Nurturing	Fairness
Listening	Patience	Character
Trust	Mission	Truthfulness
Encouragement	Freedom	Forgiveness
Openness	Learning	Abundance
Stillness	Thankfulness	Peace

Gillian's story

It is so easy just to scan a list of values such as the one just given and move on. But we must think about what they really mean, how hard they are to live out consistently and how long they take to develop. And yet these concepts are not simply theoretical or empty buzz-words, but they are actually what employees look for and expect from their leaders, as a recent initiative in our organization proved.

We have been looking at how best to develop excellence in the area of leading others. We gathered together a significant number of managers who were interested in up-skilling themselves, and asked them to think about their best experience of excellent line management and then go out and spend one hour asking other colleagues the same question, before coming back together to draw out common themes.

The answers given were instinctive, heart-felt and consistent, matching the above list almost entirely. When we grouped together all the responses and stepped back to consider what they meant, we were humbled by what employees at all levels and across various functions and countries were asking of their leaders. The message was clear and compelling – most of those interviewed made the link between line managers who exhibited these qualities and an increase in what they were prepared to give to their job in return. Therefore a causal link was established between the practice of these qualities, enhanced employee fulfilment, increased productivity and a healthier bottom line.

Spiritual leaders challenge taken-for-granted opinions and ideas but they want to work in a way that develops both themselves and those around them positively. They seek to build a shared understanding of vision, meaning and values. They are enabling, using their influence and power to support others' growth. In the next chapter, let's explore some of the approaches that can help to develop these qualities.

10

Spirituality and Learning: Being in Community

The best that can be done is to make organizations places where individuals can know themselves and speak their truth.

Nancy Dixon[1]

In this chapter we want to look at the organizational parallel to 'connecting with others'. Our connection with others in organizations goes beyond our day-to-day work, and involves our deeper hopes and fears for our work and our lives. As Gibbons suggests, 'It seems clear that organizational behaviour could benefit from understanding how deep beliefs (e.g. about transcendence, human nature, personal change, guilt and shame, etc.) affect thinking, emotions and behaviour at work.'[2]

Vaill argues more strongly:

I want to show that human organizations are inherently spiritual places where, far from a spiritual life being a matter of survival and self-protection entered into reluctantly and in desperation, a spiritual life is *invited* by human organizations. Indeed, the more I reflect on it, the more it seems to me that without a willingness to try to lead a more spiritual life, we cannot understand what is going on in a human organization, we will not be able to see very clearly how to be personally effective there, and we won't get much personal pleasure out of being there.[3]

We have already seen (in Chapter 2) that the field of Organizational Development (OD), which Vaill defines as 'basically a process of continual learning',[4] is giving way to the notion of Organizational Transformation (OT). OT 'wants society to change, it wants people to more fully discover themselves in their lives, their thoughts, their actions'.[5] OT aims at helping leaders and managers towards this fuller discovery, and simultaneously to deepen their understanding of what it means to 'be in the world with responsibility'.[6]

OT, and SaW, point out that, as humans, we have wide-ranging and deep needs that organizations must recognize if they are to maximize the potential of their human resources and release our creative spirit. We focus in this chapter upon a range of ideas about how these deeper needs can be met within an organizational setting.

The learning organization

We begin by reviewing some ideas about the concept of a learning organization. This has grown in popularity through books such as Peter Senge's *The Fifth Discipline*.[7] Senge's five disciplines, which presented a model for a learning organization, include:

- systems thinking (the interrelatedness of everything);
- personal mastery (balancing vision with current reality to create a future we care about; being proactive by taking greater personal responsibility);
- mental models (examining and overturning limiting personal beliefs and assumptions);
- shared vision (a purpose that arises from a collective process of reflection and conversation);
- team learning (building alignment by enhancing a team's capacity to think and act in new synergistic ways, through knowing each other's hearts and minds more fully).

Since this ground-breaking book, research on organizational learning has grown rapidly.[8]

There is general agreement that organizational success is increasingly dependent upon learning as the 'dynamics of rapid change, heightened global competition and advancing technology' call for the ability to 'continuously build new capabilities' in order to retain competitive advantage.[9] The capacity to create and to innovate is prized. Such capacity is sustained by organizational learning and requires a fundamentally different managerial approach – one which unleashes the human spirit.[10] The learning organization is espoused as being the type of environment that can encourage creativity to flourish by tapping into the human potential in deeper and more enriching ways. Only by developing a thorough understanding of the nature of our humanity can this be fully achieved.

Gratton argues the case for putting people at the heart of corporate purpose because it is only people who can sustain the competitive advantage of a company through their ability to create rarity, value and inimitability. She suggests that if we do emphasize the importance of people, we have to take full account of the fundamental characteristics of being human. These characteristics are:

- that we operate in time (requiring a long-term rather than short-term approach to success);
- we search for meaning (we seek to understand our role amidst the contradictions that abound in organizations);
- we have a soul (we have hopes, fears, dreams and want to be trusted, inspired and treated fairly).[11]

It is becoming clearer that models of learning in an organizational setting are based on a set of humanistic assumptions that more and more are in alignment with spiritual teachings. The fields of philosophy and theology are a rich and time-tested source of wisdom from which organizations are beginning to draw. As Cunningham argues, this is partly because our understanding of the OT notion of 'being in the world with responsibility' requires a moral basis. 'We need to start managerial learning on a base of examining issues of morality, ethics, values and social responsibility. The decision of what is right and good for a manager to learn must start from rightness and goodness being treated as moral questions.'[12]

Whatever we do, we can't get away from organizational events that challenge our feelings, our sense of wholeness, and our self-respect. Our spiritual lives are bound up in organizations. Vaill presents a picture of two approaches to business: the material-instrumental which ultimately focuses on taking and making money, and organizations as valuing-systems. The latter approach involves recognizing that the energy that keeps things going comes from the joint actions of people (individuals and groups) as they work out their sense of what is important, meaningful and fulfilling. There are five categories or dimensions, which are:

- the economic (valuing resources);
- the technical (valuing know-how);
- the communal (valuing each other);
- the adaptive (valuing environmental relationships); and
- the transcendent (valuing meaning).[13]

Vaill cuts through some of the myths that we use to disguise reality in organizational life. We are prone to collude with an illusion of unity and solidarity, but there is a different truth under the surface. His ideas have encouraged many other SaW writers and thinkers. Different authors stress different processes and characteristics to enable positive outcomes to be achieved, but Porth, McCall and Bausch have simplified the field to three main themes:

• Employee development and continuous learning within the organiza-
  tion.
• Information sharing and meaningful collaboration.
• Team-building and shared purpose.[14]

We take up these themes as they offer a useful foundation for further exploration.

Employee development and continuous learning

We cannot in one chapter hope to do justice to the huge territory that is captured under the title of employee development and continuous learning. This is a professional field with masses of literature, differing theories and a variety of practices. Neither employee development nor continuous learning is as simple as it sounds. Two excellent books which convey some of the complexity of these areas are *Management Develop-ment, Strategy and Practice* by Jean Woodhall and Diana Winstanley,[15] and *Management Learning: Integrating Perspectives in Theory and Practice* edited by John Burgoyne and Michael Reynolds.[16]

The term 'management' has both a general and a more specific meaning. In general terms, 'managing' is used to describe how human beings accomplish things in everyday life. The specific meaning of 'managing' and 'management' is everyday organizing and is associated with the governance of work and, more specifically still, with operational practices and positions. The use of the term 'management development' is inclusive of a variety of developmental approaches which can be used with all employees. Woodhall and Winstanley regard management develop-ment as taking place at three levels: the individual, the group and the organization. Its purpose essentially is to enhance effectiveness in practical ways. It encompasses a range of processes, and needs to take into account the individual's motivations to learn as well as the organizational climate in which learning is to take place.

Burgoyne and Reynolds suggest that the field of management learning also ranges from the personal to interpersonal and to organizational. But management learning theorists have become a critically reflective voice examining the underlying theories of management development practices. From this position they seek to question the values and assump-tions upon which much that goes on in organizations is based, and suggest we need to challenge our mental frameworks and perspectives.

The focus first on development and subsequently on learning in organizations has provided a platform upon which to engage in critical questions about ourselves, our workplaces and our world.

Diverse conflicts and inconsistencies are encountered in every kind of human organization, and managers routinely struggle with conflicting loyalties and moralities. 'Managerial work involves having to cope with a lot more than the list of tasks we see in typical management textbooks. These individuals are struggling to manage their lives, their identities, their value-based conceptions of "the sort of people they are" as well as their formal managerial responsibilities,' says Wilmott.[17] The emphasis has moved towards a focus on 'human becomings' rather than on 'human doings' or 'human beings' *per se*.

Such understanding has shifted the emphasis in approaches to learning. Academics involved in management learning are interested in the realities we deal with and the contradictions we encounter in trying to carry out our jobs. Focus is now upon the internal frames of reference of individual learners, their values and beliefs, as well as upon the social communities of practice in which the learner is situated. Coaching, in its various forms – life coaching, performance coaching, executive coaching etc. – has emerged as being particularly useful in helping individuals to uncover their true values, and achieve balance within their lives. For those who would like to know more about this area, we recommend two books: John Whitmore's *Coaching for Performance*, and *The Therapist as Life Coach* by Patrick Williams and Deborah Davis.[18]

Critical thinking about learning goes further still and explores the political agendas, emotional dynamics and power plays that abound in organizational life. Wilmott describes learning in this way:

> Learning refers to the acquisition of ways of relating to the world. It includes the development of our relations with others, through which a (precarious) sense of identity and autonomy is constructed. In learning to become separate, purposive beings, it is easy to overlook the interdependence of human action and, not least, the interdependencies within contemporary work organizations.[19]

Perhaps the point here is that living, learning and working with others is most likely to be a complex task, hard to predict and fraught with uncertainty.

One way to deal with the ambiguities and complexity is to understand that we need to learn with one another, exploring tacit and intuitive knowledge which contribute to the dynamic of workplace communities and networks. Holistic approaches to learning, which emphasize the whole person, have come to be seen as providing more connectedness within daily personal and professional life. The focus of Arie de Geus, whose books include *The Living Company,* is that the most enduring businesses treat their organizations as work communities where a company must learn and become a living community in order to survive.

Management learning has become an applied philosophy which seeks to address what can be regarded as a good or desirable state of affairs, as well as the nature of action. 'There (still) seems to be a need to establish values, principles and morality which looks further than the expedience of day-to-day performativity.'[20] 'The values associated with this position are that with appropriate organization (created by good management and learning) human beings can be emancipated (made free through a full knowledge of their situation) so that they can formulate and achieve their highest needs and potential.'[21]

Gillian's story

So what does it mean in practice for a company to learn and become a living community whilst actually getting the job done?

We are encouraging our line managers to create community by bringing their teams together to explore the 'what' and the 'how'. 'What' the business is specifically asking them to deliver and 'how' they, as a team, agree they can best achieve it. This approach begins to turn on its head the notion of 'command and control' leadership where both the targets and the means of achieving them are decided by the manager and then communicated to members of the team whose job it is merely to execute.

More often than not the destination is already defined by the business strategies. However, we are finding that those teams who explore together individual ways of working preferences and then agree as a community how best to use these as levers to deliver their targets, tend to be happier and more productive work groups. The conversations which are the basis for the final agreements often cover subjects such as 'how can we live out the core values of this business in what we do?', 'what is important to me in my workplace relationships?', 'what do I believe we are ultimately trying to achieve?'

Unsurprisingly, it is the 'usual suspects', the high performing managers, who pioneer this approach with their teams, but it is the responsibility of the business to encourage all managers to embrace these methods so that developing such living communities is the default. The organization can only do this by learning itself through carefully choosing what it appraises, rewards, promotes and role-models to ensure that it sets the standard and encourages the desired outcome.

Wisdom from spirituality

When writers in the field of development and learning speak of 'values, principles and morality' and 'highest needs and potential' they are clearly moving into spiritual territory. For SaW literature holds that spirituality is intrinsic in everyone and that if we awaken our awareness of spirit then we will have new motivation, and new capability, to pursue development in other aspects of our lives such as personal emotional maturity and improved relationships with others.

One area where we feel SaW can make a particular impact is on its exploration of our motivations and comprehension of change, transition, and transformation. Mezirow believes that perspective transformation is the 'central process of adult development',[22] and that 'making meaning is central to what learning is all about'.[23] He suggests that learning is the process of achieving personal knowledge and creating meaning for ourselves. As individuals we have acquired our social frames of reference (meaning perspectives), our ways of knowing, believing, feeling and valuing, from our complex personal history of making sense and meaning in our own particular set of contexts. It is these 'meaning schemes' which are held up for assessment during processes of reflective learning, individually and collectively, about our assumptions of the way the world is or our expectations of how it is supposed to be. Mezirow suggests that 'examining critically the justification for our interpretations and the meaning schemes and perspectives that they express is the major imperative of modern adulthood'.[24] Transformative learning results when our 'meaning schemes' are transformed, and a transition occurs that takes us 'from the present state to an altered future state'.[25]

It is when we are at the point of a crisis of meaning that we are first truly able to engage with the realities of life in a new way. On an individual basis, we have already referred to the 'dark night of the soul'. In an organizational context the point of crisis might be precipitated by an external event (e.g. loss of a major customer, deregulation, changes in technology, unexpected litigation) or an internal situation (merger/acquisition). These circumstantial crises become transition points, signalling that it's time to change.

Transition points, which occur throughout our lives, can be used to help us become mature. During stages of transition and at times of decision, meaning is becoming clarified through an ongoing process of reflective judgement. Freire used the term 'conscientization', which is defined as the process by which adults achieve a 'deepening awareness of both the socio-cultural reality which shapes their lives and [. . .] their capacity to transform that reality through action upon it'.[26] Such a deepening awareness of reality can lead us to see the relevance of spirituality's contribution to a new mindset, or paradigm shift. Transitions provoke us to think about who we are, where we are, and what life is all about. We can shift our mindsets and see reality differently.

This is a deeper appreciation of what learning offers us. Gregory Bateson proposes that there are 'logical categories of learning and communication'[27] built on a classification of the types of error which are to be corrected in the various learning processes. At the lower levels of learning there is 'no place for death'. The image is of constant adaptation and growth; of more and more effectiveness. Level II learning, he suggests, can lead to survivor mentality, always adapting to the vagaries of market opportunities, customer demand and social change. But Bateson's level III learning represents a 'corrective change in the system or set of alternatives from which choice is made'. This suggests that our whole way of perceiving the world has been based on questionable premises and that learning involves a change in our assumptive frames of reference. Level III learning implies a shift to the spiritual and transpersonal realm. Such learning addresses the fundamental question of *purpose*: what are we striving to be efficient and effective for? At level III learning, where our focus is shifted from organizational survival to planetary survival, 'we have to replace helicopter thinking with satellite thinking, where we can see our own organization in the context of planetary consciousness'.[28]

Transformation, then, 'is the organizational search for a better way to be [...] The essence of transformation lies in the odyssey or passage of the human spirit as it moves from one manifestation to another.'[29] It is through awareness, reflection and review of our encounters with external or internal events, from within a conscious system of personal beliefs, values, needs and purposes, that we begin to learn and to restore meaning to our personal and professional lives. However, whilst different thinkers (Wilber, Bateson and others) use the term 'levels' to categorize difference in some way, adult development is not seen as always taking place in a linear way, but rather includes being more dialectical and contextual. We can find a better way to be, but we need each other to help us see things afresh.

People at work are discovering meaning by developing their capacities of awareness and reflection collaboratively. 'Process wisdom' focuses on participatory methods of communication since it values relationships. We therefore turn our attention to these forms of communication.

Information sharing and meaningful collaboration

We live in a world which is saturated with information and we are daily bombarded with messages and images of all kinds that we must try to make sense of. In the workplace information has an immediate effect on markets and share prices. The speed of business life has encouraged the recognition that knowledge and the ability to share knowledge internally is directly relevant to competitive advantage. Managers are continually faced with new data and new challenges, and decisions have to be made.

In addition, there is an increasing acknowledgement that the diversity of beliefs and perspectives inherent in employees, customers and other stakeholders, are important to consider and can contribute to business success. We need to work with rather than exclude difference.

An inclusive approach brings 'new voices, new perspectives, and new energy to the process'[30] of business planning and allows organizations to tap into the knowledge and diversity of their people. Bateson argues that the most important task facing us is to learn to think in new ways.[31] The emergent view from a new-paradigm perspective is that the current way we think separates us from our experience, from each other and from the rhythms and patterns in the natural world. New forms of thinking together are emerging and these are important – perhaps we can think of these as 'new voices'. But simultaneously, the knowledge we have developed during the course of life – which is more than simply information, and which now has become associated with competitive advantage – provides us with 'new perspectives'. Businesses have begun to recognize that when people have the chance to participate in creating the solution to problems they are more committed and innovative. Such thinking together, and the sharing of our insights, contributes to a sense of rejuvenation of meaning – which gives us 'new energy'.

This premise is supported by shifts in educational techniques. Management education has moved from a mainly pedagogical (i.e. tutor-led, tutor-as-'expert' approach) to a more andragogical approach. Andragogy is the art and science of helping adults to learn. 'In particular, andragogy assumes an equal relationship between teacher and learner and accepts that both participate in the learning process.'[32] The rationale for this is that our forms of 'knowing' are not simply about the acquisition of rational facts about things (propositional, conceptual knowledge) but include awareness 'from the inside'[33] (experiential knowledge that encompasses feeling, intuition and judgement). That is, when people deal with one another they need to give attention to the whole person they are engaging with.

Alan Harpham's story
When I took my MBA at Cranfield I thought I would learn all about being objective, and the use of rational and logical thinking. I did, but I often tell people the most important thing I learnt through working in groups on case studies was how to listen to my own 'gut feel' or intuition. This was not knowingly taught by the faculty.

We have to draw upon many guiding factors to determine a wise course of action. Sometimes 'gut feel', or intuitive insight, is a more reliable guide than intellectual knowledge alone. Business decisions are very often made in this way. Sometimes intuition is attributed to our emotional intelligence, but recognizing it takes us a step further and 'reverses the direction of operation by which we habitually think'.[34] Intuition is emergent: it unfolds within each situation we encounter. Chia suggests that unfolding events give rise to a necessary 'toing and froing characteristic' – a dynamic and ongoing process of reciprocal influence between the perceiver and the perceived.[35] That is, our understanding of a situation orients us towards particular types of response, which in turn affects the shifting pattern of relationships. 'In this way our construction of what we understand shifts us nearer to embracing a particular version of reality, to which we then oftentimes unreflexively respond.'[36] This fits in with the notion that 'reality is always in a process of becoming and this becoming consists of an emergent dynamic web of inter-related events'.[37] Here, located in the flux of change, we are working with the very real energy at the centre of things.

The recognition of 'organization as energy' is very relevant to any focus on how information is shared, and how we communicate with one another at work. It was Heraclitus, an early Greek philosopher, who first asserted that reality is a process whereby all things flow and are in a process of becoming. Chia transfers this line of thought to a modern context suggesting that each managerial situation we encounter 'carries with it a range of possibilities in terms of future outcomes'.[38]

Ackerman Anderson says, 'Energy flows through the communication networks in the organization.' Energy can either flow or it can be blocked. 'People's attitudes and beliefs can act as obstacles to the energy flow, as can negative emotional states, fear and distrust.'[39] If we want there to be a positive flow of energy then, Ackerman Anderson suggests, we have to learn to manage 'the flow state', or 'go with the flow'. 'The concept of flow can be traced back to the Eastern Philosophy of the Tao, which urges harmony with the natural order of things [. . .] Being in the flow state means working in harmony with others and looking after the good of the whole, not just the favored parts of the system.'[40]

Those who write about managing the flow state suggest that it involves trusting the connection between one's intuitive inner knowing and the reasoning power gained from seeing the big picture of what's happening all around. It's a combination of using both left- and right-brain thinking and ultimately it seeks to facilitate higher levels of performance, and to empower others to act on their best intuition and skills. 'One accepts that every individual is unique, and that the greatest gift one can give is to free up people's internal energy [. . .] Through delegation, giving away responsibility and authority, and demonstrating trust, a manager can unlock a tremendous amount of motivation and excitement.'[41] One particularly popular book about the concept of flow is *Finding Flow: The Psychology of Engagement with Everyday Life,* by Mihaly Csikszentmihalyi.[42]

Flow state managers encourage the best efforts from everyone and value a work environment that supports learning, exploration, and creativity. In their efforts to ensure harmony among the parts of the organization they also promote opportunities for group synergy and group recognition. Lievegoed says that such exchanges 'are concerned with spiritual potential, which [are] dependent on the interrelationships resulting from [our] confrontation with other human beings'.[43] Inter-relationships are central, and collaborative learning is key. 'Process wisdom' has been highlighted as key to understanding the way we approach each other and the problem in hand. Process wisdom is based on the premise that we are 'neither passive recipients, nor dominant agents [but rather] reciprocal influencers'.[44]

Participatory forms of communication, conducted in communities or networks, provide methodologies which can help us to engage with one another in deeper, truer, more collaborative ways that support a positive flow of energy. Chapter 5 introduced this concept and the importance of dialogue. At the heart of any significant progress in organizations lies some form of conversational sharing. This is the way in which individual persons are restored to the human community.

Gillian's story
One of the ways in which we sought to merge two separate arms of the Organizational Development team was through a process of conversation sharing. We did a simple exercise that took no more than one hour, which involved each person identifying their top five personal values, and then in pairs, through the medium of pictures or stories, sharing what these values meant and why they were so important to them.

We spent 15 minutes at the end reviewing together what we had learned through the exercise. Everyone had found it very powerful. There was a deep understanding of each other and a sense of the importance and benefit of spending time talking about what really matters. The result was that people began to relate and work together powerfully, which benefitted the individuals, the team and the quality of the work produced.

Richard Barrett experienced a growing desire amongst individuals to meet together to discuss matters related to their spirituality at work; their meetings became known as the Spiritual Unfoldment Society. These groups had a significant impact on the way in which work was experienced, personally and professionally, in the World Bank. The success of this group led to media coverage, an international conference and ultimately a consulting career. Richard's story shows the influence a small group of people can have.[45]

Georgeanne Lamont's work with organizations involves the process of reflection using eight tools of reflection: Stillness, Listening, Story, Encounter, Celebration, Grieving, Visioning and Journalling. These simple tools allow people to move quickly towards working at a deeper level with one another.[46]

A variety of approaches are put forward within SaW literature suggesting alternative ways to commence conversational sharing (see Chapter 15 to pursue these in more depth). For example:

- Storytelling – storytelling is one of the best ways for individuals, groups, organizations and societies to learn. It helps people to unmask and explore the myths, symbols, metaphors and rituals that live in minds and hearts and portray a sense of how people see the organization.
- Spirit at Work Conversations – a series of short focused writings about SaW which can be used to engage small groups in an exchange of ideas (see Chapter 7, p. 97).
- Large Scale Interventions such as Real-Time Strategic Change, Future Search and Open-Space Technology – processes to engage large groups in sharing ideas about the business, or to address particular business projects.
- Appreciative Inquiry – an approach which stresses the positive aspects rather than the negative. 'What enables contact with the core spirit of an enterprise or community is a process of honoring not of altering.'[47]
- Cooperative Inquiry – a form of research where everyone contributes to the research agenda.

Team building and shared purpose

We have already seen that SaW shows we need to understand things in more relational ways. A strong sense of community is vital to the creation of strong work teams. As Senge states,

At the heart of building shared vision is the task of designing and evolving ongoing processes in which people at every level of the organization, in every role, can speak from the heart about what really matters to them and be heard – by senior management and each other. The quality of this process, especially the amount of openness and genuine caring, determines the quality and power of the results. The content of a true shared vision cannot be dictated; it can only emerge from a coherent process of reflection and conversation.[48]

Senge's books focus on team learning rather than team building. Teams are defined as 'any group of people who need each other to accomplish a result',[49] and this means sometimes including people in team learning processes who have traditionally been excluded, e.g. suppliers, customers, and associates. The organizational system is 'open' and not 'closed'; there is an openness and a willingness to learn. Positive energy is released in such a learning community, which offers both support and challenge, and the chance to raise one another to higher levels of motivation and morality.

Gillian's story

An example of such an open learning process occurred during one of our recent Human Resource (HR) development workshops. We were in the process of understanding how we, as a function, could optimize our service to other parts of the business. As part of this review, we invited some of our 'clients', senior leaders from functions outside HR such as Manufacturing and Commercial, to attend.

The first part of the session involved the clients sitting in a circle talking about their expectations of what HR should be offering and their experience of interacting with us. As they talked, the HR community sat observing and listening, reflecting on what was being shared and identifying themes and patterns. The second part of the session took place in smaller groups with each HR group containing one of the non-HR senior managers. In these groups, HR reflected back what they had heard and entered into a dialogue, which built on what was said in the first session, asking questions that deepened understanding in order to develop an optimized strategy.

There was a great sense of two-way learning through moving towards one another in such an open manner. In addition, there was an evolving understanding of what was required from HR and what it could deliver.

The discipline of team learning goes beyond conventional team building skills and is described as being the 'most challenging discipline, intellectually, emotionally, socially and spiritually'.[50] Dialogue is once again highlighted as being a central process to improve the quality of thinking together; it enables shared purpose, and learning from and with each other, to rise to the fore.

When such learning is encouraged an air of excitement, energy and optimism is released. The findings of MODEM's 'Hope of the Manager' research project, which was conducted to investigate whether spiritual energy is at work among managers, offers some interesting insights[51] into how people feel when a strong team spirit, aligned around a shared vision, is in place. The researchers deduced that exceptional energy is released when three conditions are present:

- An inspiring purpose – something achievable, worthwhile and stretching, requiring special effort.
- A liberating and empowering context – one in which the participants were free to take decisions, to develop their potential and to work creatively with others.
- An attitude of hope, confidence and commitment – ready to seize the opportunities on offer.[52]

This seems to confirm that 'essentially people want to give, especially if it's to something they think is needed and worthwhile. That's why it's important to develop ways for people to see clearly how their daily work makes a real contribution to the organization's success.'[53]

The sense of a shared purpose goes perhaps even deeper than building a shared vision. It comes about by building shared meaning with one another in community. Seeing organizations as communities offers a new image of working life, one which provides a more involved sense of ourselves in relationship to a larger whole – a place where we can serve the common good. Healthy communities provide opportunities for the full diversity of members' talents, and each person's unique gifts, enabling the community to develop. Community perspectives allow organizations to have a wider concern, where people can commit themselves to a truly engaging purpose and therefore have good reason to talk and learn together.

Concluding thoughts

Our corporations are populated with individuals who are striving for meaning, trying to understand what the company is about and what they have to do to succeed.[54] We do not work in isolation but adopt shared patterns of belief that allow us, when we work together, to create and engage in collective viewpoints. Our individual frames of reference exist within a collective frame. Our conversations and discussions with colleagues create a dominant reality of the group of which we are a member, providing a sense of what needs to be achieved and how it can be achieved.

Adult learning and development are characterized by the need to acquire new perspectives in order to gain a more complete understanding of changing events and individual purpose. This requires a fundamental shift from thinking in 'bits' to thinking systemically. Spiritual teachings are fundamentally consistent with the model of a learning organization when it comes to the importance of collaborative participation and providing opportunities for full development of human talents.

Whilst there are some unresolved issues and differences between spiritual and business perspectives, there is the possibility of expanding our theories to accommodate spirituality as an intrinsic part of our dealings with others in organizational and community life. If we begin to work in a process way with spirit then it is more likely that people will begin to see the value of becoming more explicit about spirituality for themselves.

11

Doing Well by the Planet?

Spirituality at Work might help businesses to become humane, socially active and environmentally responsible.

Paul Gibbons[1]

We are in the midst of a change of consciousness of what organizations are all about.

Dorothy Marcic[2]

Robert Haas, CEO of Levi Strauss, has coined the phrase 'doing well by doing good'. In so doing he represents the aspirations of the increasing number of companies intent on being socially responsible. Corporate Social Responsibility (CSR) is the mantra of our time. But is it believed in seriously enough and widely enough to change general corporate behaviour? Those in SaW insist it must be believed in and acted upon.

Why CSR is essential

The case for environmental responsibility was made in Chapter 6. It will be made again here, only more strongly and urgently. There are, for instance, scientists who say that life on earth is heading for its 'sixth major extinction'.[3] Then there are the warnings of the Japanese Science Council who, in a report of July 2000, stated that by 2050 there would be no human race or living planet left if we continued to be driven by our consumerist, energy-hungry, resource-depleting lifestyle.[4]

As these words imply, the challenge must be taken up by all of us – by businesses, by governments, by ourselves as consumers – but most importantly by businesses, since they are the dominant institutions on the planet. As John Adams puts it, 'Whatever future we realize [. . .]will be strongly influenced by business practices.'[5] In Peter Senge's words, 'Today, the global corporation transcends national boundaries and has an impact in the world that goes beyond even that of governments.'[6] The point is reiterated by Ryuzaburo Kaku, chairman of Canon, Inc.: 'The role of business is becoming increasingly important [. . .] If they do not assume a leadership role, who will save the world?' Kaku points out that in the increasingly borderless world created by the global economy, politicians and bureaucrats, who tend to serve just their own countries, would not be the ones to turn to.[7]

The good, the bad and the ugly

Those in SaW are in no doubt about the key contribution of business. Often they speak of the corporate role in almost 'messianic' terms, as some sample quotes from Adams and colleagues in *Transforming Work* will demonstrate.

First Adams himself, who urges businesses to 'focus on our becoming custodians of a sustainable future, and collectively to develop a trans-organizational, global mind-set'.[8]

Say Allen and Kraft: 'Clearly the seeds of transformation are already planted in the organizational world [. . .] Organizations are not only products but producers of our social environments [. . .] [They] are appropriate places to instigate change, because their hierarchical structure makes it possible to institute change programs quickly.'[9]

Kiefer and Senge talk about 'the role of metanoic organizations' [those who believe we are reality's shapers not its victims] in 'creating a sustainable society'. They see emerging in the business world the 'belief "we can collectively envision and create the society we want"'.[10]

Richard McKnight sees as a vital business aim '(clarifying) the organization's relationship to the larger purposes of human evolution and environmental health – the spiritual uplifting of the larger culture'. McKnight cites with approval Gail Sheehy's notion of 'being in love with the world', which she believes stems from having 'a transcendent purpose'.[11]

Lawrence de Bivort is another writer to bang the evolutionary drum. He refers to 'evolutionary managers', i.e. managers who are focused on the next stage of human evolution; or as Matthew Fox would put it, those who see themselves as writing the next chapter of the universe story, or forwarding the Great Work. These are people (de Bivort again) with 'a sense that a world that works must be built as a matter of highest priority'. A company too can become 'an "evolutionary manager", that is, a catalyst and guide of the evolutionary development effort'.[12]

The cynic in us finds it hard to believe that global capitalism, widely seen as the arch-enemy of Earth and most of her inhabitants, might suddenly do a *volte face* and become the saviour of the planet. How might globalization, currently a vicious process of shifting jobs from one country to another depending on who bids for the lowest wages and has the fewest environmental protections, become a virtuous process of protection and enhanced quality of life? How might today's heartless exploitation become tomorrow's beneficent stewardship?

Sharp criticisms of the current form of global capitalism, together with suggestions about what should replace it, are offered by David Korten[13] and George Soros,[14] among many others. Korten tells the chilling story of how the current system, dominated by the financial institutions, draws as if into a vortex the world's corporate capital. This situation, he points out, is beyond governmental institutions to control. It is moreover hugely wasteful of good companies and good people, and indeed whole economies, whose futures can be wiped out in an instant as a result of fickle movements of a financial market operating on whim or rumour. Korten seems to suggest that the only real hope lies in the virtual super-seding of large-scale multinational businesses by smaller-scale, more community based, locally financed intermediate technology companies. E. F. Schumacher introduced many of these ideas in his ground-breaking book *Small is Beautiful*.[15] Soros appears to place hope still in the big companies, but calls for tighter regulations.

Hope is placed in the latter also by Sir John Egan and Des Wilson in *Private Business – Public Battleground*,[16] but with the proviso that there is wide acceptance of CSR combined with stakeholder capitalism. This new British book on CSR, with the subtitle *The Case for 21st Century Stake-holder Companies*, gives a very balanced consideration of 'the good, the bad and the ugly', as might be expected when authorship is shared by a leading business person and one of our most hard-hitting social cam-paigners, recently fellow directors on the BAA board. Through an extended case study of BAA's deliberations with stakeholders over the con-troversial fifth terminal at London Heathrow, they give a lively account of the possibilities and the difficulties involved in dealing with the diverse wishes of various stakeholder groups. This is a significant and hope-inspiring book.

The anti-nature type of capitalism is contrasted with what is termed 'natural capitalism' in a book of that title by Paul Hawken, and Amory and Hunter Lovins.[17] Hawken has been developing the theory of natural capitalism since 1994. A key element is that companies should move their emphasis away from *human* productivity to *resource* productivity. This, claim the authors, would both improve world-wide living standards and reduce humanity's impact on the environment. Natural capitalism's key tenet is the pre-eminent value (or 'capital') of nature. These writers show how this might work out in relation to transportation, power generation, building design, food and many more. They criticize conventional wisdom's assumption that there has to be a trade-off between economic, environment and social policies, believing rather that it is possible to integrate all three. Many, including such well known figures as Jonathon Porritt and Anita Roddick, believe this to be a very important book.[18]

Two recent articles have pressed the cynical case but ended on a more positive note. The first, contributed by Mark Goyder as a guest paper in the Egan and Wilson volume, is called 'Connected Economy – Disjointed Society: What can we hope for from global capitalism?' Goyder, who is a major player in the UK stakeholder debate as Director of the Centre for Tomorrow's Company,[19] tells the dispiriting story of a seed company luring local Indian farmers to abandon the type of seed they had been using for centuries in favour of a new hybrid variety which cannot be saved but has to be purchased again year after year – from the company of course! This new seed, as it happened, was not resistant to local diseases and the farmers were reduced to abject poverty. Goyder also tells of companies taking out patents – which are meant to be for new inventions – on traditional rice varieties, but getting away with it because they haven't been officially 'registered' before – again with devastating consequences for the local people. As we indicated, the article does end on a more hopeful note, but we are here focusing on the more pessimistic part in order to illustrate the 'bad and the ugly'.

The other cynical-yet-ultimately-hopeful article we wish to draw attention to is 'Who Cares Wins' by Stephen Cook, which appeared in *Management Today*.[20] Its aim is to assess the real state of play regarding CSR. Cook rehearses all the usual charges – that only lip-service is paid to CSR, that companies behave responsibly just for reputational reasons, or under pressure from lobbyists and consumers, or in response to diminishing sales, or after suffering media exposure. Reference is made to, amongst others, fraudulent energy giant Enron who made proud boast of their tree conservation achievements in Bolivia. Cook next tells us about the pressure groups and non-government organizations making their 'greenwash' awards – spoofs of the Oscars – at the Johannesburg Earth Summit of 2002. He speaks about the chairman of a large oil company arguing that his organization is trying hard to behave responsibly. Comments Cook, 'It's a disconcerting, looking-glass world when a lifelong oilman starts talking renewables and sounding like Greenpeace.' However, the tone of the article gradually changes and by the end we are assured that many expressions of good intent deserve to be taken seriously. Perhaps after all a sufficient number of leading businesspeople are persuaded by the CSR case.

We refer to just one more book about globalization and CSR, *Globalization and the Good*, edited by Peter Heslam. This volume rightly argues that globalization can be a force for good in the world, and indeed stresses how essential the role of global business is to the development of Third World countries. The book clarifies what globalization is, showing its positive as well as its negative features, and suggests practical alternatives to current forms of globalization where these have negative effects. Drawing on Christian insights about 'creation', its authors find encouragement in the 'number of non-governmental organizations (NGOs), economic think-tanks and businesses addressing environmental and social concerns in ways that resonate deeply with the insights of the Judaeo-Christian faith'. Heslam concludes that 'such groups are among those which represent the greatest hope for the future of global capitalism', and finds grounds for believing that businesses are making the right 'difficult choices' to guarantee sustainability and success.[21]

What is the purpose of business?

No doubt the eventual outcome of CSR will largely depend on what people believe businesses are ultimately for. The traditional view of course is, 'we exist to maximize profit/return on investment/shareholder value'. This understanding is derived from Adam Smith, who believed that society also stood to benefit from businesspeople pursuing their own self-interest. Smith famously wrote in *The Wealth of Nations* (1776): 'It is not from the benevolence of the butcher, the brewer or the baker that we expect our dinner, but from their regard to their own self-interest [. . .] By pursuing his own self-interest, he frequently promotes that of society more effectually than when he intends to promote it.' It was as if there were some 'invisible hand' behind this process, ensuring that this arrangement worked for the good of the whole. What modern-day subscribers to this philosophy tend to forget is that Adam Smith also wrote another book called *Moral Sentiments*, in which he made clear his own adherence to the values of the Christian society in which he lived. This was a time before the dissociations of modernity set in (see Chapter 2) and when 'doing the right thing by others' was still the norm. Such 'sentiments' would suffice to prevent people thinking it didn't matter if their actions – intended or not – harmed others.[22]

There are clear signs that the invisible hand has faltered. No one can look objectively and dispassionately at global capitalism – surely the ultimate outworking of Adam Smith's philosophy – and deny that it has served to create massive inequalities in our world, both within and between nations. To cite just one fact, it is reported that in 1996 some 447 billionaires had a net worth equal to the combined income of the poorest half of the world.[23] This trend continues.

The beneficent invisible hand is just one of seven myths which have obscured the dangers of our traditional way of operating. The second myth is that competition is an unmitigatedly 'good thing'. This has led people to define as a business purpose the need to out-compete everyone else, which suggests they have a Darwinian 'survival of the fittest' understanding of business life. Sandra Waddock, writing in Biberman and Whitty's *Work and Spirit* symposium, says we should learn from today's natural scientists, who are keen to qualify this Darwinian view of nature. They 'tell us quite directly that life derives from processes of symbiosis – collaboration and community – at least as much as from competition'.[24] Margaret Wheatley makes the same point: 'Competition among individuals and species is not the dominant way life works. It is always cooperation that increases over time in a living system'.[25]

As in nature so in human and business affairs, 'it is cooperation that forms the interstices of both meanings and relationships'. Therefore we need to move away from 'the dominant management, business, market paradigm [. . .] of cutthroat competition, even hypercompetition [. . .] which is now being touted as a desirable way to force communities to become "world class"'. The logic of this perspective 'is a sort of amoral winner-takes-all competition'.[26]

Lois Hogan, another contributor to the *Work and Spirit* symposium, detects in the business world a move from 'business as a competitive war for profit' to business 'as a cooperative force for good'.[27] She speaks of the evolution under way from a 'self-absorption' to a 'relationship' focus. The former approach stresses the organization and its needs and corporate self-interest, while the latter emphasizes stakeholder relationships, corporate citizenship, ethics and socially responsible business practices.[28]

A third myth affects businesses' self-understanding at the national economy level – i.e. the level of 'US or UK plc'. It is that the Gross National Product (or its variant, the Gross Domestic Product) is a suitable measure of economic health. Schumacher criticized 'GNP mania', and the related notion – myth number four – that an economy must always be growing to be healthy. Matthew Fox aptly comments: 'How can we have infinite growth on a finite planet without someone or something having to pay a dear price? And isn't that exactly what industrial societies have subjected the planet to – an infinite plundering of limited resources of fossil fuels, forests, water, air, plants, animals, people?'[29] A similar myth – number five – equates wealth with money in the bank. Fox again: 'The environmental revolution requires a new definition of wealth, even a new kind of currency – one not backed by gold in the bank but by health on the planet.'[30]

Swimme and Berry expose myth number six – the myth of automatic human progress. Behind this stands the destructive notion 'that human well-being could be achieved by diminishing the well-being of the Earth, that a rising Gross Domestic Product could ignore the declining Gross Earth Product; this was the basic flaw in this Wonderland myth'.[31]

Myth number seven is the illusion that our primary task in relation to nature is to *control* it. Berry invites corporations to ask what kind of world it is that they have given us after a century of control.[32] He also calls for the overthrow of the traditional economic view in which 'the natural world is considered a resource for human utility, not a functioning community of mutually supportive life systems within which the human must discern its proper role'.[33]

Shareholders versus stakeholders

We have introduced the word 'stakeholder'. A debate has being going on for at least two decades as to whether a business is obliged simply to have regard to the interests of its shareholders, or whether it should also have regard to, and seek to balance, the needs of all its stakeholders.[34] Both sides of the argument have been presented in two successive issues of *Faith in Business Quarterly*.[35]

The vote of the SaW movement has unreservedly been cast in favour of the second of these positions. Dennis Heaton of the Maharishi University of Management advocates 'a more holistic framework of business planning which considers how the business creates value for multiple stakeholders – including employees, managers, investors, local/global communities, government and civil society, suppliers and business partners, future generations and the natural environment'.[36] Sandra Waddock again: 'Stakeholder theory helps somewhat because it is relational, especially when it is framed in terms of mutual collaboration and interaction [. . .] In this view, stakeholder relationships involve entities embedded together in a web or interwoven context where the actions of any one person affect all the others.'[37] She here draws on the insights of physicist Fritjof Capra.[38]

In SaW and other literature the multiple stakeholder idea is often coupled, naturally enough, with the concept of the 'multiple goals' of business, as contrasted with the 'single goal' of profit. The joint editors of *Work and Spirit*, Jerry Biberman and Michael Whitty, joined by Lee Robbins, write: 'Without spirituality the normative goal of business is profit, an objective which has shown demonstrable effectiveness in increasing industrial output.' However, they point out, this is 'a one-pointed goal'. They prefer to see profit either as the means to a greater end or as one goal alongside others. In this case 'profit becomes a constraint, a necessary condition to achieve multiple objectives, rather than a single varied objective to be maximized'.[39]

So what *is* the purpose of business? Its main and proper purpose, argue those in SaW, is service – working for the common good, understood in its widest sense as embracing all people and the whole natural order. This is 'the new bottom-line' that is so heart-warmingly expounded by John Renesch, Bill DeFoore and colleagues in their book of that name.[40] One of the contributors to that volume, Joel Levey, puts it like this: 'As the world becomes more of a global village, the sustainable values of consciousness and caring increase in immediacy and urgency. The changeless human spirit in an ever changing environment is a reality that challenges us to expand our view of "profit" beyond the limited confines of a financial index to encompass the totality and intricate inter-weaving of our universal interdependence. Understanding the impact of this larger balance sheet, and expressing it through our commerce in the global marketplace, is the Tao of business.'[41]

The more enlightened amongst British companies are championing what has come to be known as the 'triple bottom line'. This involves equal consideration of (1) the financial – balancing the books, (2) the social – considering the well-being of the employees and other stakeholders, and (3) the environmental – ensuring the planet doesn't suffer from the firm's activities.

Some people- and planet-friendly companies

In Chapter 13 we shall be giving examples of companies which have embarked upon the spiritual journey and seek to live out their spiritual principles. Here we mention some that embody the particular principles we are focusing on in this chapter.

First, two brought to our attention by Matthew Fox. Fox tells us about Dutch architect Ton Alberts, whose design for the ING Bank in Amsterdam is

> based on environmental consciousness and spiritual principles. As he [Alberts] puts it, 'Nature is the source of inspiration for my work. The beauty of nature is linked with organic architecture.' The greatest possible use of the sun is guaranteed by using solar collec-tors, sloped walls, and a ceramic energy retrieval wheel that draws heat from the air. No air conditioning is needed. Plants and water fountains within the building provide the needed humidity. The results are that the building saves two million dollars annually in electrical cost and the atmosphere is so friendly to the 2200 employees that a 25 percent reduction in absenteeism is reported. This demonstrates that creation-centered architecture is a sound financial investment.[42]

Another example Fox cites is Ben & Jerry. 'They deliberately support family farmers [. . .] They consciously contribute to defending the rain forest by purchasing Brazil nuts from people in the rain forest and calling their product "rain forest crunch" in order to raise consciousness about the rain forest.[43]

A similar example is Anita Roddick's Body Shop. The first Body Shop was opened way back in 1976 in Brighton, UK. 'The company pledges itself to the pursuit of social and environmental change; workers are vetted to ensure they live up to this philosophy, and staff at HQ spend a day a month working with disadvantaged children.'[44] Anita Roddick reports the effect of such experiences on her staff: 'When a member of our staff, after three exhaustive weeks refurbishing a Romanian orphanage holding babies with AIDS, or campaigning for human rights looks you dead in the eye and says "This is the real me" – take heed, for she is dreaming of noble purposes, not a moisture cream.'[45]

Some enlightened organizations give their employees paid time off during company hours to do voluntary work in their local communities. This has been a regular practice of the American Leadership Forum members.[46]

> Disney has promised one million hours of voluntary service from its employees to a mentoring programme for children at risk in city areas. K-Mart will allow its 2,150 stores to be used as safe havens for children at risk. Nike has created 'Zone Parks' in primary school playgrounds to tackle bullying [. . .] Coca-Cola has pledged money to train volunteers to act as mentors to disadvantaged children and it has distributed thousands of leaflets in Africa on Aids.[47]

Hewlett-Packard have been running a project in Third World countries designed to enable business people in those countries to jump straight into the information era without having to work through an industrial stage, with the inevitable pollution of the environment and damage to health that would cause.

Hass' principle of 'doing well by doing good' is well illustrated by James Collins and Jerry Porras in their much referred-to book *Built to Last*.[48] One of their model firms is the US pharmaceutical company Merck. They decided to give away a drug that cured river blindness because their customers in the Third World couldn't afford it. George Merck II explained that this was 'to express the principles which we in our company have endeavoured to live up to . . . We try to remember that medicine is for the patient [. . .] for people. It is not for profits. The profits follow.'[49]

Bill George, CEO of Medtronic, speaks of his firm's priorities: 'Medtronic is not in the business of "maximizing shareholder value" but, rather, our purpose is to "maximize patient value". We like to say "the real bottom line" for Medtronic is the 1,300,000 patients who were restored to full life and health last year by Medtronic products.'[50] Wagner-Marsh and Conley report a further statement of Bill George, that 'Medtronic decided to pull out of one country because the organization couldn't tolerate some of the practices there'.[51]

British science and technology research company QinetiQ have developed an advanced image processing system to help spot early signs of sight loss in diabetics. With Philips they will be providing technology for monitoring vital functions in foetuses. For the Mayo clinic they are developing de-blurring technology for body scanners. QinetiQ's fuel cell research has enabled them to develop more eco-friendly power systems than were possible using batteries, by converting hydrogen gas into electricity and where the only by-product is water. The company has also devised a waste management system which can process almost any material, including sewage and garbage, for safer discharge at sea.[52]

Danah Zohar gives us the example of Japanese businessman Katsuhiko Yazaki, owner of a global mail-order company. His business was successful and he became very wealthy, but felt something was missing. After reading a book about Zen he went into a monastery, where he found peace and liberation. He was able to see the beauty of the world for the first time. After receiving lots of new insights, Yazaki rededicated his business life and renamed the company 'Felissimo' ('most happy'), because he now saw as the proper role of business increasing the sum total of human happiness. He attended the Rio Earth Summit Conference in 1992, and dedicated himself and much of his money to saving the environment.[53]

Another example of people- and nature-friendliness is the attention some companies give to providing a pleasant internal environment. One such is Nortel Networks' Head Office in Brampton. This example is provided by Heather Skelton, an advocate of healthy environments to support the whole person. She suggests that

- employees be allowed to decorate their own workplaces with fabrics and colours that uplift the spirit;
- company restaurants provide healthy food;
- there are available quiet 'nature spaces' where people can reflect, meditate or just enjoy sunshine and fresh air.[54]

But lest we become too euphoric, we also need to take fully into account the darker aspects of corporate life and behaviour. Recalling what we said about paradox in Chapter 4, true spiritual wisdom holds in tension both the heights of human goodness and the depths of human evil.

Structural evil

We mentioned earlier Mark Goyder's dispiriting accounts of corporations causing mayhem in the Third World. It can be argued that these are results not so much of deliberate ill-will but of companies playing the game they are forced to play, and operating by the rules needed to ensure they meet the demands of their shareholders. The latter would take their investments elsewhere if these companies relaxed for a moment their relentless drive for profit. To the extent that this is true, those companies are victims of what theologians call *structural evil*. St Paul in the Bible refers to 'the rulers, authorities and cosmic powers'[55] – his name for the more-than-human structures which hold human beings in thrall. Partly we are victims to such, and partly we collude with them, even give ourselves over to them. The net result is to strengthen them further, and there can come a point when our moral sensitivities become deadened. We can then become ruthless, greedy, totally materialistic and unconcerned about riding roughshod over others, disregarding the suffering our action causes. We can even come to believe that bad is good, as was the case in the 1980s when, inspired by Milton Friedman, business teachers were lauding greed as a virtue – 'greed is OK, greed is good, greed is cool', business audiences were assured. When one of the seven deadly sins becomes a primary economic virtue, it is clearly time to take stock.

Structural evil that has got people, companies and even whole systems under its spell is one of the most serious types of evil, and one of the hardest to eradicate. This is all too apparent to those who campaign tirelessly for fairer trading arrangements, remission of Third World debt[56] and other seemingly intractable problems. Failure to make progress in such areas can make people cynical when businesses do try to adopt more socially responsible practices. This can lead to other kinds of evil: self-righteousness and the inability to believe that there can be any good in, or real improvement in the behaviour of, those they castigate. This is a pity because those who do try to achieve something in this area – for example, Sainsbury's and others who promote Fair Trade products – need support and further encouragement.

A spiritual mapping of the good, the bad and the ugly

A spiritual development model which we have mentioned so far only in passing is 'the chakras'. This model is expounded in Michal Levin's *Spiritual Intelligence*[57] in a way that is helpful to our current discussion. Those wishing to explore the chakras further should consult Levin's book. It is sufficient here simply to say that the chakras – base through to crown – may be compared with the Wilber levels we have been working with. We mention just two of the chakras: the second chakra and the heart chakra. The second chakra corresponds broadly with Wilber level 4 and the heart chakra with Wilber levels 6 and 7. That is to say, chakra 2 is about me and my group, our self-interest and our drive to promote it, including exploiting others and the world for our own benefit – Adam Smith without the moral sentiments. The heart chakra is about global awareness and assuming responsibility for the well-being of all.

Thus Levin speaks of 'the heart chakra, whose domain is the world' and sees operating from the heart chakra as 'contributing to the life of our planet'.[58] For those at this spiritual level, she claims, 'it becomes impossible to gain [. . .] at another's expense. The implications of this for our relations to one another, all the inhabitants of our planet, and the earth itself, are revolutionary.'[59]

Also revolutionary is the form of behaviour now demanded of businesses. So it won't be a case of '"I'll dump this chemical waste a hundred miles away because then it won't affect our town" [. . .] Second chakra behaviour, in fact. But in the light of interconnectedness, and the teachings of the heart chakra, those sentiments are exposed for what they are.'[60] You won't in fact dump them anywhere if you are 'aiming to act from the perspective of the heart chakra, understanding interconnectedness and knowing that your remit is the world, not your own interest group'.[61] 'The challenge of this millennium is to move into the heart chakra, that observes no boundaries. To learn and display the love that is universal.'[62]

But how do we get there? What of the actual transformation process that moves us from chakra 2 – and there are elements of chakra 2 in all of us – to the heart chakra? How do we ensure that 'the seeds of transformation already planted in the organizational world' (to recall the words of Allen and Kraft) grow into strong, healthy, mature plants that can resist the metaphorical soil- or air-borne infestations that are an ever-present threat? Where does the spiritual strength come from that enables organizations to brace themselves against the chill winds of global capitalism and withstand all the other dangers, internal and external, that will continue to beset them? These are huge questions and we are not sure there are fully satisfactory answers to hand. We believe organizational transformation, which depends heavily on organizational members' relationship to higher power, is a significant part of the answer, and this is the subject we take up in our next chapter.

12

Unlocking Corporate Transformation: The Work of Spirit in the World of Business

Nothing is harder, yet more necessary, than to speak of certain things whose existence is neither demonstrable nor probable. The very fact that serious and conscientious men treat them as existing things brings them a step closer to existence and the possibility of being born.

Hermann Hesse[1]

Our world is turbulent and constantly fluctuating. Change abounds as corporations deal with global flows of currency and investment plus the internet and new technology, at the same time as contending with the growing power and effectiveness of pressure groups, and the threat of environmental crisis and terrorism. These elements combine in unexpected ways creating a sense of uncertainty and ambiguity in the business environment. The effects are demonstrated through fickleness of markets, power shifting to more sophisticated customers and stakeholders, transparency of pricing and pressure on margins, and cost control imperatives.

All this drives demand for managers and leaders with different capabilities from those appropriate in a more stable world. Management literature about organizational transformation is moving into new territory, and implies that more and more companies are becoming influenced by advances in scientific understanding – such as the ideas explored in this book. These propose that organizations are living, adaptive systems in which nothing is independent, everything relates to everything else and no one system is ever necessarily continuously in charge. Ideally, to succeed in today's world, organizations need information from every source. Not only from external signals in the marketplace environment but also internal ones. There is an increasing realization that hierarchical, command and control structures are unhelpful. The attitude that it is only the knowledge at the centre/top which counts, and that only the centre/top is in the position to transform information into knowledge, is redundant. Instead more responsibility is in the hands of middle managers and, in fact, all employees who have access to electronic information and can exercise immediate and widespread influence on customers and other stakeholders. Morgan says, 'Since organization ultimately resides in the heads of the people involved, effective organizational change implies cultural change.'[2]

Organizations are recognizing that the competitive environment demands that businesses be knowledgeable, innovative, flexible and adaptable. Such competencies arise from the turning of information into applicable knowledge in 'real time'. The ability to do this rests critically on individuals and teams of employees; hence people are more clearly highlighted as the primary strategic resource in business. Such attention to individuals has sharply enhanced the importance of management learning and development as critical to long-term organizational success. As management development has evolved, there has been increased acceptance of the need to align human resource strategies with those of the business. With this in mind, much of the focus of consultants and organizational/management development specialists is upon how to transform organizations.

Spiritual transformation?

But the danger is that people pay lip service to the ideology surrounding change and transformation in organizations. As Zohar puts it:

> Transformation is the great obsession of our fearful and dissatisfied change-conscious culture [. . .] I think that transformation is the great lie of the corporate world. A large part of the lie is the misuse and abuse of language – the distortion of words like transformation, recontextualizing, restructuring, vision and value, openness, from the heart, and change itself. Many corporate transformation programs are initiated by leaders who want greater control over their markets and employees. They see them as a step up in the battle against their competitors [. . .] Most (of the leaders) are terrified of change. The programs themselves are often run by consultants (witch doctors) who charge high fees to create the illusion of real action [. . .] but their purpose is to ensure that nobody becomes too uncomfortable, that nothing fundamental really changes. Even the *illusion* of change must be delivered quickly, in quantifiable data, to impatient clients.[3]

And so we find that in the midst of attempts to create these fast-moving adaptive systems, and amidst the business and management hype, significant stress, strain and workplace problems remain. The mismatch between business/academic ideals and our daily experience of reality take their toll.

Our own experience in working with organizations confirms this. The trouble is that people don't appreciate that, to be genuine, transformation must be grounded spiritually. The truth of this is found when people regard work as dispiriting. People find it easy to identify what a dispirited organization looks like, often because they have had their own experience of 'bad times' at work. The following list summarizes some of the words that people in Britain today use to describe their feelings about (their own) dispirited workplaces:

> Low energy, low creativity, despondency, hopelessness, poor rela-
> tionships, hard to go to work, unhappiness, stress, lack of personal
> development, poor teamwork, control focus, unable to be whole self
> at work, unconcerned for wider impact on society and environment.

What good is this type of culture to any business, to our society? Those in SaW believe that what is missing is attention to our deeper spiritual core. Only by concentrating on that can we help to create spirited organizations. These portray a different set of characteristics altogether:

> High energy and drive, high creativity, encouragement, hopefulness,
> good relationships, enjoy going to work, happiness, learning and
> developing, good teamwork, empowering focus, taking whole self to
> work, concern for society and environment, cooperation and
> community spirit.

Moxley[4] highlights the contrasts between dispirited and spirited organizations as in Table 6 (see p. 157).

The central thrust of this book is that we do want to create organizations that have more in common with the second, spirited, list than with the first.

The role of spirit

We don't however wish in this book to leave the impression that SaW is a Pollyanna-style panacea for all organizational woes. What it offers is a perspective to help us discern wisely and deal with our work lives, particularly in the face of current business realities. If you have read our chapters up to this point you will have realized the complexities inherent in taking into

Table 6

Dispirited	Spirited
Use physical and mental energy	Use all four energies – mental, physical emotional and spiritual
Work is a job	Work is a vocation
Sense of separation and disconnectedness	Sense of connectedness to others
More competition than cooperation and community	Community or family used as a metaphor
Lack of congruence between personal and organizational mission and values	Congruence between personal and organizational mission and values
Lack of meaning and purpose; workers drained of energy	Work has meaning and purpose: energized, animated workers
Leadership exercised in a top-down way	Workers involved in the activity of leadership

account the various dimensions of SaW: not only personal and individual development, but our appreciation of others, nature and our connection with a higher power. The acceptance that spirit is significant is the beginning of a journey that does not prevent us from struggle, and in many cases actually throws us into a deeper struggle than does ignoring spirit altogether. But how can spirit contribute to solving the problems we encounter daily in organizational life?

SaW literature portrays a number of benefits from integrating work with spirit – ranging from individual fulfilment to more productive and humane workplaces leading to the betterment of society. Yet in exploring some of the most critical research ideas about SaW we acknowledge that there are also likely to be numerous difficulties to overcome. For example, ambivalence over definitions of spirituality possibly diminishes the appeal of SaW initiatives for a wide cross-section of people. Also there is the concern that such initiatives may cause upset, opposition or offence; and there is the question of whether, or to what extent, individuals might *choose* to engage in this dimension in a work context. Since spirituality is such a personal area, where we are potentially very vulnerable, there are naturally questions about the exercise of power and whether organiza-tions might attempt the application of spirituality as a leadership tool without the necessary personal commitment (as Zohar implies above). These are valid concerns. In fact Michael Joseph concludes that 'it is neither desirable nor wise to be prescriptive in suggesting or proposing how spirituality might be specifically raised, presented, engaged with, or "implemented" in organizational settings'.[5]

Even more broadly, as noted in the last chapter, there is the issue of structural evil that abounds in society; this is something that is particularly hard to deal with.

So where do we start then? Maybe the most important decision we each have to take is that, in fact, we want to start at all! The potential difficulties, the well-founded concerns and cautions could easily result in our paralysis, and the alternative to act is – to do nothing. While concerned about the dangers of misusing spirituality, Joseph is convinced that inaction is not an option. He suggests 'that authenticity requires each person, each leader, to take well considered steps to act on their convictions'.[6] If we want to restore a meaningful perspective to our working life, if we want to find a career that seeks to make a difference or to make things better for our planet, then the commitment to change rests at our own doorstep. (Such a thought may have become clichéd, e.g. Change starts with me; A journey of a thousand miles begins with the first step; Evil wins when good men do nothing – but these are truisms that have relevance for each of us.) And our commitment has to be authentic and genuine.

Our personal authenticity is perhaps the most vital ingredient since, as we have shown, the view of SaW is that evil in the world, in ourselves, in our organizations, is the result of disconnection from 'higher power' (see the discussion of evil in Chapter 7). Consequently, as we have also suggested, the goodness people are seeking will depend upon reconnection with this higher power. To a large extent this connection has to be made by individuals before it can take effect in organizations.

There are various different spiritual paths and practices an individual can follow, and some of these have been discussed already. But, while taking seriously Joseph's cautions (mentioned above), the main focus of this chapter is on some of the frameworks, models and processes that are being tried, tested and put forward to encourage organizations to work in new and spirit-friendly ways. We attempt to answer the question: how can we take our authentic commitment forward and transform our workplaces?

Approaches to corporate spiritual transformation

Gibbons suggests that there are two primary types of approaches to spirituality in the workplace – individual and organizational.[7]

At the individual level, work contributes to the individual's spiritual path, and the individual's spiritual path contributes to their work. This encompasses ideas around leadership, individual creativity, intuition and well-being at work, as discussed in previous chapters.

The organizational journey towards the spiritual can include organizational efforts to nurture individual Spirituality at Work, but also organizational re-orientation toward spiritual goals and means. Gibbons' research led him to categorize the individual and organizational aspects of Spirituality at Work in terms of their interior and exterior attributes (building on Wilber[8]), the features of which he lists as in Table 7.

Table 7: Gibbons' organizing framework for spirituality at work

	Interior	*Exterior*
Individual	• Private meditation and prayer • Practising spiritual attitudes towards work and colleagues • Deep beliefs about the nature of God, the universe, humanity, order/chaos, grace etc	• Observable behaviours • Spiritual symbols and talk • Spirituality and leadership development • Spirituality and career development • Empirical research (well-being, task effectiveness, motivation)
Organizational	• Organizing principles (Mitroff and Denton, 1999b) • Values programmes • Climate, attitudes • Organizational history and mission • Culture, stories, myths	• Structural features (e.g. hierarchies, reward systems, measures) • Spiritual goals (multiple stakeholders, non-material outcomes) • Spiritual means (participation, no layoffs?) • Boundaries/statements of policy on SaW • Nurturing individual spirituality (e.g. time and space)

It is the lower right area of the organizational (collective) exterior that Gibbons suggests is the least well researched. Those in the lower left area, the organizational interior, have been experimented with more fully.

Gibbons refers to the most oft-quoted research about organizational spirituality, that of Mitroff and Denton.[9] They proposed five sub-types or models of organizational spirituality. These are the:

- religious – either positive towards religion and spirituality, or positive towards only religion, being somewhat negative towards spirituality;
- recovering – adopts the principles of Alcoholics Anonymous[10] as a way to foster spirituality;
- evolutionary – begins with a strong association with a particular religion and, over time, evolves to a more ecumenical position;
- socially responsible – founders or heads of the organization are guided by strong spiritual principles or values that they apply directly to their business for the betterment of society – particularly they are often more concerned with external stakeholders than with their own employees;
- value-driven organizations – founders or heads are guided by general philosophical principles or values that are not aligned or associated with a particular religion or spirituality.

Certainly, these organizational approaches rest on different individual understandings of spirituality, based on different religious backgrounds. As Mitroff and Denton point out, in most instances the five models came about as a result of a precipitating event in the life of a founder or head of an organization. In other words the initial motivation to pursue any of the models generally came as a result of a desire by an individual to confront major crises and surmount them successfully. (This fits in well with the idea of the *via negativa* or 'dark night of the soul' discussed previously.) Such research highlights the significance of the leadership role in helping SaW come about. It might be then that the link between leadership and spirituality is the most pragmatic to pursue further in order to understand transformation in organizations.

The leader as spiritual catalyst

We have discussed leadership more fully in Chapter 10, showing some of the considerable demands that are made. Joseph's own case study demonstrates that change towards a spirit-friendly organizational culture *is* possible but implies that:

i) the process is difficult and demanding
ii) absolute determination and clarity of purpose is required on the part of those promoting the change
iii) the change leader will need, in addition to a high degree of competence and skill, huge amounts of energy and commitment to hold to the vision
iv) it still takes considerable time for new or different cultures (particularly ethics, values and practice) to permeate through the organization and to be widely accepted and practised.[11]

The indications from Joseph's study are that spiritual conviction, and in particular conviction which recognizes a higher power as a source of inspiration and strength, may be significant in sustaining the required 'energy and commitment' (point (iii) above) and indeed in justifying the large sacrifice of time, effort and energy that is inevitably demanded. Further, with the protracted timescales required, the same spiritual conviction may provide motivation to persist both in the face of opposition or inertia and over the long term.

To truly transform an organization, leaders have to be committed to a long-term spiritual vision and have the ability to stick with it over time. Mitroff and Denton point out that such an organization will operate on a time-scale very much longer than the 'normal' quarterly and even annual focus of traditional organizations and may extend 'over the entire course of a person's – and organization's – life'.[12] Without authentic commitment, there is a danger that leaders will misuse spiritual principles, that their actions will hinder true transformation and take individuals and organizations into dangerous territory.

Is spirit profitable?

Each model represented by Mitroff and Denton also has a fundamental underlying principle of hope. The hope principle expresses the organization's basic optimism, i.e. if they do the 'right' thing, stick to their ethical principles and values, then profits will follow. So far there is insufficient research evidence to support this optimistic view. This is another stumbling block that we, the authors, encountered in discussions with MBA students at Cranfield who asked, 'If you follow spiritual principles, which may in fact cost more, will you be able to improve profits? Is business the right place to look for meaning and fulfilment?' It is understandable that business students ask such questions. But are they right to assume this is an 'either-or' matter? Could it not be a matter of 'both-and'? This issue gives an indication of the contradictions and tensions of organizational life but also an insight into the paradox of leadership.

Moxley points out that 'one of the important challenges facing us [. . .] is to learn to be "both-and" people: to be hardheaded realists while paying attention to spirit. To keep a focus on the bottom line while making meaning in our work communities.'[13] His suggestion, which the growing literature on SaW offers anecdotal evidence to support, is that those who do weave spirit into their leadership approach are doing well. The reverse is not true: 'Contrary to business school doctrine, we did not find "maximizing shareholder wealth" or "profit maximization" as the dominant driving force or primary objective through the history of most visionary companies.'[14]

What spiritual leadership writers point out to us time and time again is that organizations have to be focused on *more* than improving the bottom line, if they are to improve the bottom line! But both are important and necessary.

Despite the encouraging recognition of the relationship between development of personal insight amongst employees and strategic success in business, it is important to understand that spiritual leadership is not, nor should be, motivated by a desire for bigger profits. The ideas from new science caution that 'the use of spirituality for profit will not produce the profit desired because it is coming from an inappropriate motivation. This would be in line with the concept of the unified field in quantum theory – that our deep-seated primordial thoughts create realities. So, if my inner motivation is wrong, then I will create the effects of that wrong motivation.'[15] As we have shown in this book, the system which drives the insatiable requirement for higher and higher profits actually hinders their achievement. The vision for the organization cannot be confined to the financial bottom line as this does not sustain organizations.

It all boils down to the question of what we believe an organization is *for* (to recall the discussion in Chapter 11). Gibbons points out that

> spirituality and business are two belief systems with different ultimate goals: profit and God (or the equivalent sacred transcendent conception). SaW concerns itself with the coalescing of these belief systems. In this coalescing, some mutual accommodation must take place if these two belief systems are to coexist. However, right now, spirituality is doing most of the accommodating and in the process is losing its distinctiveness.

Taking spirituality seriously involves self-examination, self-discipline, study and sustained effort.

> If we are interested in making a significant impact on how people experience their work lives, or organizations conduct their affairs, we need to be careful how much we allow the currency of spirituality to be debased.[16]

The truth seems to be that there is no middle ground. Chaos theory in new physics holds that 'at a deeper level, organisation is implicit in apparent chaos',[17] for within chaos lie the seeds of new creation. To move forward we need to undergo transformation. This requires us to let go of the control imperative, and trust the design and control of non-material elements. Such understanding helps us to become aware of invisible fields of thought and belief that govern our experience and be ready to 'loosen our grip' on reality in order to let new wisdom come in. Having studied the process of spiritual transformation in a large number of organizations, Neal, Bergman, Lichtenstein and Banner observe: 'In all cases the transformations [...] were sparked not through rational efforts at all: the actual "cause" of transformation, according to the data, was expressed by these practitioners/theorists in terms of "grace" (Ellen Wingard), "magic" (Peter Senge), and "a miracle" (Bill Torbert).'[18]

A certain level of trust, or some might say faith, is needed to release our belief that working for something beyond profit will create value and wealth. There is also the kind of wealth that money cannot buy. Wealth in its broadest sense includes positive outcomes that are non-material, e.g. social, ecological and, of course, spiritual. After all, inner peace is not something you can buy, and love is priceless.

How to support transformation

The processes used to support transformation are varied and we have highlighted some of them throughout this book. It may be that there is no one right way, but rather that people simply make a commitment to start and then work with the tools, opportunities and gifts that present themselves. Drawing inspiration and encouragement from those of like mind is a great way to maintain momentum and find resources, and we recommend becoming involved in a network (see Resources, Chapter 15 for a useful listing). Knowing that good results can be achieved from undertaking SaW is also a strong encourager, which is why we have dedicated our next chapter to offering some positive accounts.

The many books in this field, particularly ones like Georgeanne Lamont's *The Spirited Business*, which testify to the practical benefits, give us cause for hope and action. Georgeanne offers a values-based approach to creating organizational vision and transformation.[19]

Whilst using the exploration of our values as a starting point is not seen as explicitly spiritual by many, it has become a popular way to open the door to discussion of spirituality by those who do want to go a bit further. We are aware of two key frameworks that are used to open up discussion around values: those of Clare Graves[20] and Richard Barrett.

We only have room to focus on one of these and we explore Barrett's contribution, as it seems to be the most widely known. We highly recommend his book *Liberating the Corporate Soul* for a more detailed appreciation of his ideas.

Barrett suggests that corporate culture is built around a set of complex beliefs and assumptions that make up a mental model of how people in the company believe the world ought to be. Organizations are living entities that share motivations similar to those of individuals, therefore corporate transformation is fundamentally about personal transformation. He takes us on a tour through seven levels of employee and organizational consciousness (similar to Maslow, Wilber and Graves levels). These are briefly shown in Figure 3.

		Positive focus/Excessive focus
SERVICE	7	**Service to humanity** Long-term perspective. Future generations. Ethics.
MAKING A DIFFERENCE	6	**Collaboration with customers and the local community** Strategic alliances. Employee fulfilment. Environmental stewardship
INTERNAL COHESION	5	**Development of corporate community** Positive, creative corporate culture. Shared vision and values
TRANS-FORMATION	4	**Continuous renewal** Learning and innovation. Organizational growth through employee participation.
SELF-ESTEEM	3	**Being the best. Best practice** Productivity, efficiency, quality, systems and processes. Bureaucracy. Complacency.
RELATIONSHIP	2	**Relationships that support corporate needs** Good communication between employees, customers and suppliers. Manipulation. Blame.
SURVIVAL	1	**Pursuit of profit and shareholder value** Financial soundness. Employee health and safety. Exploitation. Over-control.

Richard Barrett and Associates LLC. Corp Tools (UK) Ltd. Copyright 2001

Figure 3: Barrett: The seven levels of consciousness

The first level or need for employees and the organization is financial security and survival. But if organizations develop a preoccupation with the bottom line they become entrenched in survival consciousness and allay their fears through excessive control, and exploitation. They do the minimum to conform to regulations. There is a general belief that the world is hostile. People are territorial and see life as a series of battles.

The second need for employees and the organization is harmonious interpersonal relationships. However at this level of consciousness emphasis is on relationships not for what they can give but for what they can take. Employees are co-dependent; they suppress feelings and sacrifice truth for the security of belonging. Companies at this level are strong on tradition and image, and weak on flexibility and entrepreneurship. They demand discipline and obedience from employees; there is little trust.

The third need is self-esteem. This shows up as a desire for greatness. Employees want respect, and feelings of self-worth are derived externally. Companies are competitive and see management as a science focusing on improving productivity, efficiency, time management and quality control.

Training of staff must be seen to have an impact on the bottom line. Control is maintained through hierarchical power structures, which cater for the managers' needs for status, privilege and recognition.

At the level of transformation consciousness, or self-actualization, belief systems are re-examined. This may be due to a number of challenges either internal or external, personal or corporate. Introspection occurs and transformation begins when an individual takes responsibility for the way things are. There is a shift from reaction to choice. The spiritual questions (e.g. Who am I?, Why am I here?) begin to emerge, along with an awareness of the importance of values to guide decisions. As deeper motivations are discovered, a search to express the self in new ways begins. At the organizational level everyone is asked to take responsibility for making the organization a success. The culture of the organization shifts from control to trust.

Organizations at the level of corporate community recognize that real self-interest is intimately entwined with the interest of the common good – that we each form part of the pattern of the inter-connectedness of life. Modern management calls this the systems perspective. Success is measured not only in financial terms, but against a broader set of indicators. Work begins to be about meaning, values, learning and creativity. There is a focus on honesty and sharing as well as on self-knowledge and renewal. A sense of fun and play are brought to work.

At the level of community consciousness the focus is on making a difference in the world. Organizational members have an enlarged sense of responsibility that embraces not only the workplace but the community as well. They seek to achieve partnerships with suppliers and customers, supporting the local community. They are concerned with environmental and societal issues. Work is a way of fulfilling mission and goals. Rewards are more about personal fulfilment than finance. Organizations care for the needs of the whole employee – physical, emotional, mental and spiritual.

At the level of society consciousness the emphasis becomes service to humanity and the planet. Ethics, justice, human rights, sustainable development, social activism and philanthropy become part of the employee's and corporate strategy. Every aspect of an individual's life is meaningful, everything that they do is with a purpose. They will do what is morally and ethically correct. They are visionary. The inner life of these individuals includes deep silence, unshakable commitment and a frequent sense of joy and contentment.

Barrett and his European Associates[21] are able to offer a variety of assessment tools, which can be used to ascertain the cultural climate of any given organization. These can then be used to facilitate internal discussions about values and about change.

Gillian, whose story highlights the significance of Barrett's and Lamont's values-based approaches, explains what happened within her business when values began to be discussed, how these were vital to the vision of the business, and the process she used to help the values emerge:

Gillian's story

The concept of values being a focus in the workplace is of real relevance to me. With a change of management within the last eighteen months, our organization set about sharing an articulated vision for the first time in the organization's 90-year history. Before, it had been held effectively in the heads of the owners. Now, this vision was being shared with all our employees around the globe who were being asked to engage with it in a way that impacted how they went about their daily business. The expectation was that this shift would enable us to deliver our challenging business goals.

In terms of awareness, the impactful multi-media campaign that disseminated the vision did an excellent job. 'Engagement', however, was much trickier. Engagement is personal. It is also about values, and it is about the heart. Research shows that when an individual's values are aligned with the organization's values, productivity can increase by between thirty and seventy per cent. A worthy goal for any business!

But how to communicate meaningfully about values with thousands of people, from factory floor to senior management, who represent many different cultures? How can you tap into what they are most passionate about? What most motivates them? In short, how can you really get below the surface and encourage them to bring their true selves into the workplace?

Storytelling helps people to communicate values in a non-threatening way. For thousands of years almost every culture has used the medium of stories to share the things that really matter. We decided to harness the power of storytelling to engender a culture change in the business and create an environment where people can bring who they truly are and want to be to what they do each day. This, for us, is the essence of spirituality in the workplace.

The shadow is on the wall

We conclude by returning to the central theme: that personal transformation is the gateway to leading organizational transformation. Barrett emphasizes that 'we are not able to become true leaders until we become authentic individuals, and we are not able to become authentic individuals until we release our unconscious fears'.[22] Sullivan suggests that it is our pride, fear and self-will, which get in the way of our positive, resilient and compassionate core.[23]

Facing such fears and truths about ourselves means dealing with our unconscious 'shadow' (as briefly discussed in Chapter 5). These aspects of our personality combine in a group setting to form an organizational shadow. 'Each organization contains two organizations, one visible, articulated, expressed in stated goals, policy statements, and procedural manuals; the other invisible, lying quietly under the surface, but actually determining what will happen in the long run. We call this unseen but powerful force the organizational unconscious.'[24] As there is a need to confront our individual shadow, so in organizational life we must recognize and address the combined shadow that underpins the organizational culture.

There is a wealth of literature on organizational culture which we cannot do justice to in this book. But we believe that in its broad approach and host of methods, SaW attempts to get to the heart of the problem and deals with the real issues that lie underneath the surface. As we have explored, this can be difficult territory, but adopting the spiritual approach is the only way true transformation is ever likely to be made.

We referred in Chapter 8 to Matthew Fox's view of original blessing and the four 'pathways of creation spirituality'. His understanding of transformation, which is shared by many in SaW, is that we need to move through all four of the pathways of creation spirituality:

- the *via positiva*, recognizes the blessing of abundance and beauty originally gifted to us;
- the *via negativa*, confronts the evil in ourselves and society;
- the *via creativa*, trusts that we have the ability to co-create: 'Beauty and our role in creating it lie at the heart of the spiritual journey', 'Creativity is not about painting a picture or producing an object; it is about wrestling with the demons and angels in the depth of our psyches [. . .] This process of listening to our images [. . .] allows us to embrace [. . .] the shadow side of ourselves – as well as to embrace our biggest visions and dreams.'[25]

These pathways lead us finally to:

- the *via transformativa*, the culmination of the creation spirituality journey where we are called to be compassionate. We are called to work together in community with others to relieve suffering and to combat injustice.

Our spiritual journey results in the need for each one of us to take up the challenge to work with integrity. As Pat Sullivan writes:

> If spirit and work had to be summed up in one word, that word is *integrity*. When we live and work with integrity, we are authentic and whole. There is a beautiful resonance among body, mind and spirit, which leads to further resonance between our values and our actions, and between ourselves and the rest of creation. Thus, when we live and work with integrity, we can express our unique viewpoint and gifts while surrendering to the call of spirit to go beyond all sense of self.[26]

Such an attitude requires letting go of the spiritual arrogance that says 'I have it all together'. Instead we have to face our fears and process them, out of which we will recognize that in spite of all our faults we are always worthy of love and compassion. 'In the depths of our shared vulnerability we can forge new depths of wisdom and trust. This is precisely the kind of foundation we need if we are to build a new economy that works for us all.'[27]

13

Spirit-led Companies

Alvin Toffler foretold the technological 'third wave'. We suggest that an organizational fourth wave is mounting, the spiritually-based firm.

Wagner-Marsh and Conley[1]

You will know them by their fruits.

Jesus[2]

What does it mean to live out in practical terms the corporate spiritual transformation we referred to in the last chapter? To our knowledge, no one has yet attempted to produce a full list of spiritual companies – or spirit-led companies as we wish to call them. To produce any comprehensive account would entail a huge amount of research. All we shall attempt here is to illustrate what it can mean to be a spirit-led company.

We began this process in Chapter 11 where we mentioned a number of 'people- and planet-friendly' companies, and we refer to some of them again here. All of the varied organizations mentioned are widely recognized as examples of good spiritual practice. Our chief sources of information are Biberman and Whitty[3] and British author Georgeanne Lamont, and we start with examples from the latter.[4]

The central chapters of *The Spirited Business* (a volume which we recommend for the spiritual wisdom of its comments as much as for its encouraging documentary evidence) are devoted to case studies of seven 'soul-friendly companies'. They are of varying sizes and types and they are all either British or British branches of multinational corporations. Here are a few facts about three of them.

Happy Computers

A small company of just 40 people, Happy Computers provides a range of IT training courses for some 25,000 delegates a year. The highest quality of service to customers is matched by the quality of care each one in the company has for colleagues at all levels. Their training manager has received a string of awards for her training and motivational skills. That the company operates a 'no blame' culture was vividly demonstrated when a young woman inadvertently wiped out the company's entire accounts file. Instead of reprimanding her, her boss encouraged her to regard the incident as a valuable learning experience. So that everyone may find their work interesting, a list is kept of all the administration tasks, and every six months each person in administration selects the tasks they are happy to do, and the remaining boring jobs that no one wants are rotated.

We understand that three years further on,[5] Happy Computers' extraordinary way of working continues to get results and win main-stream accolades. In 2002, Happy Computers won the business-to-business category in the Management Today/Unisys Service Excellence awards, with Nationwide winning the overall award. In October 2003 Happy Computers won both its category (small business) and the overall award, with Happy being rated the best for customer service of any company in the UK.

Microsoft UK

The computer giant Microsoft employs 50,000 worldwide and 1,000 at its UK location near Reading. Georgeanne Lamont approached Microsoft with diffidence and, given all the adverse comments about the company in the media, wondered what she would find. But they had responded readily enough to her request to come in and talk with them about their 'company soul'. She soon found a reality markedly different from the media impression, a company that naturally speaks the language of, and lives the reality of, spirit – in manifold ways.

Microsoft sees creativity as a key feature, and believes its own creativity can change the world. Its fundamental aim is global delivery of affordable PCs and software with a view to enhancing human life. Staff are encouraged to reflect on their personal vocation, on what they were put on this planet for. Throughout the organization priority is given to people and relation-ships. There is a huge emphasis on teamwork, on creating 'superteams'.

Microsoft is outward-looking and takes helping the community seriously, sometimes by substantial charitable giving and at other times by direct involvement. During the Balkan War, at the instigation of certain staff members, Microsoft contacted the Red Cross to see how they could help those who were suffering. The answer was to develop special software to speed up the registration of refugees and the issuing of passports and other papers. The department that carried out this work failed to meet budget as a result, but the rest of the organization applauded them for getting their priorities right!

IMG (Industrial Maintenance Group)

Employer of 100 staff, IMG has an annual turnover of £6 million. The MD has deliberately based his company values on the 'fruits of the Spirit' in the Epistle to the Galatians.[6] The majority of employees spontaneously mention these values and regard them as 'making the job worthwhile'. There is a strong commitment to 'growing people' and an ambitious training programme, which highlights living by the values, and every employee goes through it. People are delighted that the company values match their own life-values. Teams discuss a 'thought for the day' taken from a management guru, work out how it applies to them, and keep a book for writing down their own thoughts for the day. Even telesales work is experienced as enjoyable, and when the group finds its energy flagging its members take time out to do a line dance or utter a Maori war cry!

We haven't the space to cover the other four case studies – Peach Personnel, NatWest Bank, Scott Bader and Bayer UK – all of which are equally inspiring in their own ways.

Reflecting on the visits she made to the seven companies, Lamont says that at times she wondered whether what she was being told was too good to be true, admitting that the cynic in her occasionally rose to the surface. But, just as often, she was impressed by the obvious sincerity and exuberance of her interviewees, including junior staff such as warehouse lads and receptionists. She reports that several of the companies were particularly keen that she should meet these people, because their views would justify the organization's claim that the company values permeated the organization as a whole.

Lamont draws some general conclusions. She sees 'the chief characteristics of soul-friendly companies' as:

- *Leadership* – the leaders have considerable, but gentle, authority; they share leadership with others; they are servant leaders.
- *The least is the most important* – those in the lowliest jobs are valued and seen as pivotal to the success of the company.
- *Balance* – recognition is given to the rich variety of people and the different gifts they bring.
- *Financial targets* – these are regarded as important and are rigorously pursued.

- *A greater purpose* – increasing shareholder value is not enough; the company also has a wider, caring purpose.
- *The intangibles* – regard is given to less measurable features like culture and team spirit.
- *The small detail and the larger picture* – everything from minute particulars like the colour of the walls to the wider purpose of the company reflect the spirit of the organization.
- *Agape* – they don't use the word, but these companies embody love.

Broadway Tyres

Since conducting her research, Lamont has been busy as Managing Director of Lamont Associates, a UK consultancy she has founded to encourage corporate expression of spiritual values and practice. Their August 2003 newsletter features Broadway Tyres (BWT), another British company that is seeking to honour spiritual principles. We reproduce extracts from a piece entitled 'Tyres, Tales and Radio Talk'.

Last week Radio 4 listeners were surprised to find themselves listening to a report on spirituality in business from the warehouse of Broadway Tyres, in High Wycombe. Phones ringing, trucks unloading, the place was busy with the daily work of distributing tyres. This was BBC Radio 4's first foray, as far as I know, into the world of spirit at work and the reporters were struggling to understand what it was doing humming away here in this noisy, down to earth warehouse.

Steve the young warehouse man explained, 'It's about team effort, team spirit, about real feelings, everyone being honest with each other . . .'

Bianca, the van driver whose job it is to go to all the garages and deliver tyres, was aware that the term spirituality was not a good one because 'the lads don't particularly want to know or show that vulnerable side'. But she found that in practice 'it showed me that different people in the warehouse have different abilities. So I just kind of feel now that I'm a lot closer to my work colleagues and it's nice. It feels more like a family now.'

Steve and Bianca had in fact just had a couple of hours' training in this new approach but others in the company, the MD, Jonathan the salesman, Billy the warehouse manager, Jeff, and the General Manager Guy, have put in many hours of training, reflection and application in order to release the full human spirit into their company. The results have been much reduced absenteeism and vastly increased profits. The culture has strengthened its buzz and harmony; it's a nice place to work [. . .]

A tip from Broadway Tyres: Take time for stillness; when a customer rings up and bawls down the phone at you or asks an impossible question, tell them you will ring back in 5 minutes; put the phone down and take a minute of quiet reflection; become still again and allow the calm to rise and allow yourself to find an answer in that place of stillness.

One of the remarkable features of BWT is that, whilst it emphasizes the intangibles such as 'buzz' and harmony and the importance of the human spirit, it has at the same time achieved a 49 per cent increase in profits over a 12-month period. It is growing at every level.

The next story comes from Phil Clothier of CorpTools (see also Chapters 14 and 15).

Gazeley Properties

This is a small but very successful distribution development company based in Milton Keynes, UK. Its Chief Executive and Operations Director are working hard to sustain and grow this vision-led, values-driven organization. Without offering guaranteed employment to anyone, which they feel is unrealistic in today's business environment, what they do offer to every employee is a fantastic opportunity in both professional and personal development while they work at Gazeley. Significant investment is made in people and this shows up in the capabilities and attitudes of company members as well as in Gazeley's reputation and healthy balance sheet. Gazeley's leaders are clear that the work on values and culture is not a short-term fad but an ongoing process that builds success.

Other stories of UK organizations adopting spiritual principles have been supplied to us via our Spirituality in the Workplace network.

Guildford College

When Lynne Sedgmore arrived in the late 1990s to take up the post of Principal and Chief Executive of Guildford College of Further and Higher Education it was with the firm intention of applying her own spiritual principles to the whole ethos and running of this large college. Her attempt to do so, and an assessment of the results, was the subject of the research conducted by our colleague Michael Joseph.[7] In Chapter 12 we presented his findings concerning the challenges facing a spiritual leader as deduced from this case study.[8]

University Hospital Birmingham NHS (National Health Service) Trust

The chaplaincy team leader of this large NHS Trust gained the supportive approval of the CEO to run an 'away-day' focused on the spiritual side of healthcare. A broad cross-section of staff attended and wide-ranging issues were discussed with great energy, commitment and concern. Often different groups gravitated to the same topics. In the round-up to the day a Filipina nurse declared that Filipina nurses are regarded as good nurses on account of not only their skills but their holistic concern for patients, which included spiritual well-being as a priority. With tears in her eyes, she reported that in the many years at the hospital she had rarely encountered empathy with her views on the importance of the spiritual perspective, so this day had been a unique experience for her. The Trust has begun implementing action plans arising from the day, and intends to hold a similar event in the future with as many new faces as possible.

We turn now to the American scene, beginning with some firms that have been studied in detail.

Southwest Airlines

Numerous studies have been made of Southwest Airlines. We draw on the one by Milliman, Ferguson, Tricket and Condemi who contribute a case study in the Biberman and Whitty volume.[9] Building on much previous research, their story is of a firm which cares deeply for its people and their families. Mistakes made by employees are seen as valuable learning experiences. Legendary stories are told about the lengths to which SWA staff have gone to please customers.[10] SWA, 'the Love Airline' as it calls itself, has operated a no lay-offs policy, even though downsizing has been a major feature of the airline industry generally in recent years.

Employees are also made to feel they are part of a cause. The company's mission is to offer the lowest air fares, frequent flights and a personable service characterized by fun and humour. When demand increases, SWA seeks to expand flights rather than increase prices.

SWA highly values humour and enthusiasm. For instance, the CEO, Herb Kelleher, is famous for his humorous and eccentric behaviour, such as singing and entertaining at company functions and telling jokes.

While SWA values community and having fun it also has a strong work ethic. Employees are expected to work hard and be flexible so that they can reduce staffing requirements to below that of their competitors. Both employees and managers are expected to do different jobs, top managers as well as pilots sometimes helping with boarding passengers or loading planes.

Milliman *et al* comment on the company's remarkable achievements, often against considerable odds, and on the numerous awards they have won over the years.[11]

Tom's of Maine

The 'Tom' after whom Tom's of Maine is named is Tom Chappell, the company's president. Looking for new insights, Chappell enrolled at Harvard Divinity School and, while there, resolved to bring soul back to the firm. He also subsequently arranged for staff and students from the divinity school to come into the firm as consultants. One of Chappell's claims to fame is being the author of a well-known book, *The Soul of a Business*.[12] (He is but one of many CEOs who have gone so far as to write books and articles elaborating on their spiritually based philosophies on leadership. Examples include Max DePree, former CEO of Herman Miller and author of *Leadership Jazz*;[13] Kendrick Melrose, CEO of Toro Company and author of *Making the Grass Greener on Your Side: A CEO's Journey to Leading by Serving*;[14] and Earl Hess, former CEO of Lancaster Laboratories, who has written an article entitled 'Character in the Market-place'.[15] Anita Roddick of the Body Shop is the author of several books, one of which is *Body and Soul*;[16] Ben Cohen and Jerry Greenfield have produced *Ben & Jerry's Double Dip*,[17] and so on.)

According to Burack, Tom's of Maine (ToM) well exemplifies the 'middle way' of Buddhism, having achieved a balance between 'living its values and being successful financially'.[18] Wagner-Marsh and Conley attribute ToM's success to two related factors: the quality of its leadership, and its core beliefs and value structure.[19]

Mitroff and Denton[20] also feature ToM, characterizing the company as an 'Evolutionary Organization', a chief feature of which is 'emergence out of a crisis' (a familiar spiritual pattern). These authors give an interesting summary of Chappell's personal odyssey, seeing him as a Joseph Campbell-style 'hero'[21] in that he experienced a crisis, withdrew temporarily from the world, heard the call to bring 'soul' to his business, returned to the world and then faced the further struggle of convincing his doubtful colleagues, eventually winning them over.

Ford Motor Company

In the view of Elmer Burack, 'Ford Motor Company is an outstanding example of a firm that made a complete turnaround in favor of people-centered approaches.' The latter are viewed as 'the main contributing factor to their outstanding performance in the highly competitive auto-motive industry according to a recent *Wall Street Journal* article (July 16 1998)'.[22] Burack elaborates:

The reinvention of the company [. . .] witnessed a complete scrapping of a 'Theory X' management style. This 'X' style dated back to the early years of the (20th) century and reflected the philosophy of (the senior) Henry Ford. 'Theory X', the view of people as essentially non-thinking tools requiring much direction and close control, was gradually replaced with a newer vision of human resource potential [. . .] Long-term business success would be the consequence of consistent progress as measured by *two* bottom lines – one financial and the other people.[23]

Another writer to be impressed by Ford is Lois Hogan. She writes, 'The revolutionary team production process at Ford Motor Company's Saturn manufacturing plant was designed to provide workers with an opportunity to be engaged in the whole process thereby also enabling a greater sense of satisfaction and meaning in the work.'[24] This was the lesson learned years ago by another car manufacturer, Volvo of Sweden.

Jesuit writer and researcher Gerald Cavanagh speaks of Ford's successful training programme for upper and middle managers, which was started in 1998. 'On the last day of the program', he tells us, 'Ford managers are asked to do a half-day of service work in the city. This work involves helping at a soup kitchen, homeless shelter, or building homes with Habitat for Humanity.' After enquiring about the rationale for this work, Cavanagh was informed in writing by a Ford executive that 'it is the company's fundamental responsibility to the community in which it exists. This community is the source of our sales and we have a responsibility to give back to the world in which we live. This is not about selling cars; it is about being good corporate citizens.'[25]

Dollar General

Another large organization, Dollar General, has been studied by Dorothy Marcic. Dollar General is a retail chain located in small towns and poor urban areas. 'The average sale is $8, and they like it that way, not wanting poor folks to spend too much in their store,' explains Marcic.[26] Cal Turner Jr (son of the founder) states, 'Our strategy is to hire ordinary folks, those with moral integrity, give them a sense of mission and then get out of their way.' He adds, 'Good people in pursuit of mission need the least amount of policies and control [. . .] It's the values that control them not the rules.'[27]

The first sentence of Dollar General's mission statement contains the words 'A better life for our customers'. Cal Jr's compassion is not limited to customers; employees are special too. Prospective employees 'see a short video of Cal, jr, describing just how Dollar General considers its workers "an honored and valued asset".'[28] Only those 'who share (the company) values and aspirations' are recruited. Workers make personal development plans, which often include active involvement with church and community and 'trying to make the world a better place'. Executives take pride in knowing their employees and their family circumstances.

The company 'maintains its values base by constantly challenging itself with policies and behaviors to see if they fit in with the values'.[29] Marcic visited a number of Dollar General stores to 'ask the clerks if they like their jobs', and uniformly got 'positive responses'. 'The difference between Dollar General and other companies who hang their values on the wall is that Dollar General started living out the values from day one and only recently wrote them down on paper.'

Cal Jr, a religious activist, seriously thought of going into the ministry. He decided instead to take on the family business. 'Rather than have only a few hours of impact on several hundred in a congregation, he now has forty hours a week of influence over 40,000 employees and has made life richer for 40 million low-income customers, most of whom live in crime-ridden inner cities or poor rural areas.'[30]

Other spirit-led organizations

Considerations of space mean that we can only mention other spiritual companies very briefly. Much of the detail can be found in Biberman and Whitty. We refer to these particular organizations because between them they well demonstrate the variety of histories and motivations lying behind the corporate pursuit of spiritual principles.

'Some business owners and founders such as those at Hewlett-Packard and Fel-Pro were committed to (people-centered) practices from their beginnings or shortly thereafter,' states Burack. Hewlett-Packard's purpose is 'to make technical contributions for the advancement and welfare of humanity'. Merck's is 'to preserve and improve human life'.[31]

'AT&T and Boeing, among others, invited poet David Whyte to speak to managers and employees about "The Preservation of Soul in Corporate America" [. . .] *Business Week* reported that Lotus Development created a "soul" committee to reexamine the company's management practices and values in order to build a strong culture'.[32] Reports Cavanagh: 'Chase Manhattan Bank, AT&T, Apple Computers and others have tackled the subject of contribution [to wider society] by including a new question in the search for vision, "What is our higher purpose?"'[33]

Wagner-Marsh and Conley list among 'a great number of highly diverse firms [who] are moving ahead with attempts to instill a spiritual approach to their corporate cultures: [. . .] Herman Miller, TD Industries, Lancaster Laboratories, Wetherill Associates, Toro Company, Sisters of St. Joseph Health Systems, Medtronic, Townsend and Bottum, Schneider

Engineering Corporation, Bank of Montreal'.[34] They elaborate on one of them: 'As an example, the president of WAI (Wetherill Associates, Inc.), a highly successful auto parts distribution firm, specifies that its field representatives hand over and discuss with potential customers an attractive piece of literature called a "Quality Assurance Manual" [. . .] The slightest perusal of the document reveals that the intent is also to communicate the spiritual basis for the firm's existence.'[35] They report other noteworthy features of this company: '[A WAI] employee stated, "We are not in competition with anybody. We just do what we have to do to serve the customer [. . .] If we are out of something, for example, we'll tell them our competitor's part number."'[36]

These authors also refer to the

> several spiritually based firms [who] incorporate spiritual values in their employee development and training programs. For example, Boatmen's First National Bank in Kansas City, Missouri includes spiritually oriented materials into its [. . .] leadership conferences for the bank's executive group [. . .] TD Industries is among *Fortune's* 100 best companies to work for in America [. . .] Xerox managers attend weeklong retreats where vision quests and council meetings based on a Native American model help Xerox professionals see their work in a meaningful way.

Other examples include 'Exxon USA of Houston's two-day spiritually geared component to its management training program and Bank of Montreal's spiritually oriented materials used in employee training for its 36,000 employees from all levels of the company'.[37]

Wagner-Marsh and Conley also mention Wayne Schmidt of Schmidt Associates Architects, Inc., who

> believes that 'the bottom line is there if people are working effectively with an attitude of serving others. That's the reward. Don't distract people with what the bottom line needs to be', he advises.[38] Schmidt explains that 'potential staff go through several interviews. The first is to determine if they are technically competent. The second [. . .] if they have an attitude for serving others. Every new staff member is required to read Robert Greenleaf's *Servant Leadership* (1977) and Stephen Covey's *The 7 Habits of Highly Effective People* (1989). New people are given a mentor who helps nurture the servant leadership attitude.'[39]

Muslim writer Abbas Alkhafagi mentions three business executives who believe that spirituality and business should be brought together.

They are: John D. Beckett, the president of R.W. Beckett Corporation; David L. Steward, the CEO of World Wide Technology, Inc., and Jeffrey H. Coors, president of ACX Technologies Inc.[40]

'A number of businesses (e.g. Mary Kay, Service Master, Chick Fil-A) are attempting to integrate spiritual values as the foundation for their corporate mission,' reports Conger.[41]

The question of size

On the basis of their case study of Tom's of Maine and other spiritual companies, Mitroff and Denton conclude that there may be limits on the manageable size of a spiritually based company. Initially, they say, Tom Chappell wanted to grow the company, reasoning that the bigger they got, the more money they could give to worthy causes – which had always been one of their key policies. However, he came intuitively to realize that for members of an organization to relate on a personal basis – a requirement in a spiritual company – the maximum feasible workforce number lay somewhere between 150 and 300 members.[42]

Must a company's size be restricted in the interests of preserving its spiritual qualities? The fact that many of the organizations we have discussed are large is enough to refute that contention. But there remains a sense in which Mitroff and Denton are correct. Business *units* need to be small. But they can still be units within a large corporation. The originator of the 'small is beautiful' philosophy himself, E. F. Schumacher, recognized this way back in the 1970s. Admitting that the 'large-scale organisation is here to stay', he believed 'the fundamental task is to achieve smallness *within* large organisation'.[43]

Along with Adams, Kiefer and Senge, and other SaW writers we cited in Chapter 11, we contend that it is on the globally influential spirit-led large corporations that we shall significantly rely to reshape both the world economic order and our social and political institutions. The future progress of SaW itself largely depends on their widespread embodiment of spiritual principles and practices.

14

The Progress and Future of Spirit at Work

What will we choose?
Will we allow ourselves to descend
Into universal chaos and darkness? [. . .]
Or might we choose to make
This time a waking-up event,
A moment of world empowerment?

Ben Okri[1]

Simply by holding a vision and daring to want its fulfillment, we call forth what is needed to turn vision into reality.

Pat Sullivan[2]

Given that the companies mentioned in Chapter 11 and the last chapter represent but a fraction of the organizations that are putting spiritual principles to work, we might feel justified in claiming that SaW is a movement of some significance. That impression is strengthened by the examples provided here of the literature, the media attention, the conferences, courses, consultancies and the various upbeat assessments by commentators that surround and support what is going on in the spirit-led companies.

Marks of progress

It is difficult to pinpoint precisely when SaW got under way. You could say it all started with Lao Tzu in the sixth century BCE. But its current manifestation, we reckoned in Chapter 2, began in the early 1980s in the United States, and was marked by such publications as John Adams' *Transforming Work* (1984) and Harrison Owen's *Spirit* (1987). An earlier date could of course be argued – for example, Robert Greenleaf's *Servant Leadership* came out in 1977, Fritz Schumacher's *Small is Beautiful* was published in

1973, and Joseph Campbell's *The Hero with a Thousand Faces* saw the light of day as early as 1949. However, we stand by our claim for the 1980s, largely because those were the years when SaW really began to take off.

One key indicator is the explosion of literature on the subject. A bibliography distributed at a session on spirituality in the organization at the 1998 Academy of Management meeting listed no fewer than 72 books on SaW. Amazon listings contained a similar number, and (at the time of writing) that number currently stands at 1,753.[3] Articles on SaW or SaW-related subjects now number thousands.[4] Between 1992 and 1999, the *Journal of Organizational Change Management* alone published 68 articles that mentioned spirituality, of which 36 made it their main focus. Comments Pat Sullivan: 'Thanks to feature articles about spirit and work in business magazines such as *Forbes*, *Industry Week*, *Workforce*, *Training*, and the *Wall Street Journal*, it's practically impossible for business people not to notice that there's been a major shift in public perceptions of spirituality and its place at work.'[5]

The appearance of dedicated networks is another feature in the development of SaW. Judi Neal, Associate Professor of Management at the University of New Haven, Connecticut, began publishing a quarterly newsletter, *Spirit at Work*, in 1994. Her subscription base has grown dramatically ever since and includes many human resource and organizational development specialists. Hers is not the only journal devoted to the subject; another is *Business Spirit*. And one that has just been launched in the UK is *Spirit in Work*.[6] Judi has also founded the Association of Spirit at Work (ASAW), based at the University of New Haven, Connecticut, and encouraged the setting up of Chapters of ASAW. At the present count these number 60 in the United States and one in the UK. In spring 2003 the Center for Spirit at Work was inaugurated.[7]

There has also been a steady increase in the number of courses offered on our topic. Lois Hogan notes, 'The Academy of Change Management has seen an increase in sessions with a spiritual theme. Increase in scholarly interest is also evidenced by approximately 30–50 dissertations in progress on the topic.'[8]

Cavanagh refers to the new courses on religion, spirituality and contemplation that are being offered in business schools.[9] Richard Barrett reports a poll in which 79 per cent of graduating MBA students across 50 graduate business programmes said that a company should consider its impact on society in such areas as the environment, equal opportunity, family relationships and community involvement.[10]

'In 1995 alone there were at least five major conferences for leaders in business that had a specific focus on integrating more soul or spirit into business,' reports Joel Levey.[11] The growth of interest in the subject was further borne out by a 1994 survey sponsored by the New Leaders Press, and by the 'International Workplace Values Survey Report' which involved 1200 people in 18 countries. The latter indicated that interest in spiritual development ranked ahead of physical development in its importance to people in business.[12]

King *et al* confirm this trend: 'A review of the syllabi and the course titles [in academia] makes it immediately evident that the topic of spirituality and work is being integrated into courses through a number of different avenues. Among the more explicit course titles were: HRD: Spiritual Values; Self-Leadership; Ethical, Moral and Spiritual Issues of Management; and HRD: The Meaning of Work'.[13] They also refer to the tools and techniques for enhancing self-awareness and spiritual growth that Senge and others have given as part of their programme for encouraging companies to be 'learning organizations'.[14]

Cavanagh says,

> It is becoming common for business schools to offer courses that require undergraduate and graduate students to do service for those people who are less advantaged in the community [...] Students can be asked to keep a journal and to reflect on such questions as: (1) What was the experience that you had? (2) What about the experience was most troubling? (3) What about the experience was most inspiring or empowering? and (4) How were you affected or changed by the experience? What did you learn?[15]

André Delbecq and Robert House interviewed many executives in Silicon Valley in the 1980s on the topic of the rapidly changing business environment. Delbecq was impressed by the quality of their spirituality. He writes: 'Let me forthrightly state that my interest in spirituality in the context of business leadership did not flow from my own inner inspiration. Rather it came from experiencing the intense spirituality of senior executives in Silicon Valley, and their selflessness of service flowing from the richness of their individual inner journeys.'[16] His own work had been mainly from a Christian basis and with Christian executives, but he found 'Taoist, Buddhist, Jewish and Hindu executives with a similar centeredness transforming their leadership'.

Delbecq, as we noted earlier, is a professor at Santa Clara Jesuit University, but the interest in SaW is shared by the other 27 Jesuit universities in the US. Having begun by taking their own organizational spirituality seriously they now seek to influence other organizations.[17]

'The Transcendental Meditation movement of the 1960s and 1970s has developed the "Maharishi Corporate Development Program" for the 1990s,' note Neal *et al*, showing the multi-faith involvement in this field.[18]

Judi Neal and colleagues state that 'the number of conferences about spirituality in business has gone from none to almost a dozen per year in the United States alone in 1998, and several throughout the rest of the world'.[19] Cavanagh reports that in 1998 conferences were held in Washington DC, Santa Fe, Minneapolis, Indianapolis, Loveland, British Columbia, Canada, and Puerto Vallarta, Mexico. The Puerto Vallarta conference attracted more than 500 attendees.[20] Also in the autumn of that year 'several courses were offered in schools of business on spirituality at work and on contemplation [. . .]: at University of Scranton, University of Detroit Mercy, and Chapman'.[21] Singled out for special mention is André Delbecq's course at Santa Clara University, which we described in detail in Chapter 9.

We referred in Chapter 7 to the upsurge of interest in spiritual direction. Again in 1998, the *Wall Street Journal* ran a front-page article about business and professional people seeking out a spiritual director.[22]

Cavanagh makes an interesting remark about SaW and a parallel movement: 'Business ethics has become a major concern of most business people over the last few decades. Yet the spirituality in business movement has developed largely independently of this related movement'.[23] He regrets this separation since they are committed to broadly the same ends. This is an area that warrants further attention.

André Delbecq told David in a private conversation in 2000 that two separate surveys, one conducted by himself and another by Ian Mitroff, had both found that a staggering 88 per cent of practising managers had declared themselves interested in spirituality.[24] This was confirmed by an article entitled 'Shush the Guy in the Cubicle is Meditating'. In it Marci McDonald declared, 'More and more CEOs and high-level managers are coming out of the closet about their own spirituality.'[25] John Renesch (again in private conversation) agreed, but added that the interest was still largely a private one and there had not yet been much corporate expression of it. But he thought it would only be a matter of time before there was.

King *et al* report: 'Jerry Harvey [in a private conversation in 1996] recently observed that when he asks CEOs about their prayer life, they often become so engrossed in the conversation that they will offer to drive him to the airport to continue talking until the last minute.'[26]

Underpinning the growing SaW movement has been the burgeoning general interest in spirituality. According to McGeachy there are currently over 20,000 websites devoted to spirituality of one sort or another.

In the UK

The preceding paragraphs refer mainly to the progress of SaW in the United States, the country of its birth. But the movement is also well under way in the UK, in much of the rest of Europe, Australia and New Zealand, and in many other parts of the world.

As we have indicated in the previous chapter, one of the pioneers of SaW in the UK is Georgeanne Lamont. Her involvement in our subject goes back to 1989, which is an early enough date to suggest that SaW in Britain is at least in part an independent development. As far as we can tell, she had the field to herself then. At that time she was operating in the areas of education, local government and voluntary organizations, and this phase of her work was marked by the publication of *Values and Visions*, co-authored with Sally Burns – arguably Britain's first book on SaW – and eventually published by Hodder and Stoughton in 1995. The turning of her attention to business organizations *per se* was to come later. Georgeanne's splendid second book *The Spirited Business* has already been featured (especially in Chapter 13), as has her company Lamont Associates (see further below and in References).

Among the first organizations to take up SaW in the UK seem to have been colleges of Further and Higher Education. By the late 1990s they were promoting spirituality among their organizational aims, which included looking after the spiritual well-being of their students.

The earliest instance we can find of the subject featuring at a UK university is 1991 when the University of Lancaster ran a conference entitled 'Working with Spirituality in Organisations'. Later in the 1990s, Bath University ran an MBA course featuring spiritual values, and Peter Reason at Bath has written many papers on spirituality and research, and spirituality and learning. Leeds University's School of Healthcare Studies is currently launching a module that looks at the relevance of spirituality to employability and its importance in the professions. The University of Surrey, following its highly successful first 'International Conference on Organisational Spirituality' in 2002 (their second conference took place in July 2004 and they plan to continue these into the future) now offers a course on spirituality (see next chapter under ICOS). Our own lectures to various UK business schools, and in particular our work at Cranfield, were noted in the Introduction.

Earlier in this chapter we mentioned Judi Neal and the setting up of Chapters of the Association of Spirit at Work in the United States. In 2002 the first UK ASAW chapter was established in Greater Manchester. The monthly meetings provide an opportunity for business people to meet and discuss questions such as:

- What is spirituality and what relevance does it have in the workplace?
- How do we help to fulfil the lives of our employees?
- How can we find meaning and purpose in our work and lives?
- How can we release the passion, creativity, and energy in us and the people we work with?
- How can we lead our organizations from a perspective of love rather than fear?

Meetings include activities such as speakers, workshop exercises, business/ life stories, adventures, talking and sharing, book recommendations and discussions.[27]

Mention should also be made of MODEM (see also the Introduction), which has as its aim 'leading and enabling authentic dialogue between exponents of spirituality, theology and ministry and leadership, organisation and management'. MODEM has produced a number of books; its second, *Leading, Managing, Ministering*,[28] has some chapters that relate to SaW themes. MODEM's research project, 'the Hope of the Manager', has already been referred to (Chapter 10).

Management organizations in the UK, like their US counterparts, have recently shown a keen, if sometimes more cautious, interest in SaW. In April 2002 the Chartered Institute of Personnel and Development ran a consultation featuring Alan Briskin as a keynote speaker. (That same week Alan addressed a meeting of Cranfield MBA students.) The Institute of Directors have discussed SaW, and the Academy for Chief Executives, which is spiritually based, reaches about 300 CEOs.

Management journals in the UK have included articles on SaW. One of these is *People Management*, whose 20 February 2003 issue carried an article by Jon Watkins headed 'Spiritual Guidance: A Report on Spirituality in the Workplace'. It charts the progress of SaW in UK companies between 1998 and 2003. Its key message is that interest in SaW is growing but is coming mainly from employees. Employers tend to be wary. While 40 per cent of the latter would value the opportunity to discuss workplace spirituality, 52 per cent are experiencing tensions between the 'spiritual side of their values and their work'.

The previous quote comes from the 'The Management Report 2003', produced by the Roffey Park Institute in Sussex, who have conducted comprehensive research into SaW in the UK. This report also claims that 90 per cent of UK managers believe their organization has not 'attempted to discuss the issue with its employees', despite nearly three quarters of the workers being interested in 'learning to live the spiritual side of their values'. Watkins also quotes Simon Burton of the public house chain Greene King, who links spirituality to 'inspirational leadership', and Geraldine Brown of Domino Consultancy who believes that 'there are people at the top of organisations that really want to do something about [spirituality] but are afraid it will be perceived as forcing something on to their staff'.

Watkins says that many human resource professionals believe that 'firms attempting to address this matter with their employees could be playing with fire'. He quotes Richard Cree of the Institute of Directors who believes, 'it has to come from the employees'; and Clare McCartney, one of the co-authors of the Roffey report, who insists: 'Companies should definitely be discussing spirituality with their employees to find out if it is what they want and how important it is to them.' She adds, 'Employees want to know that companies are practicing what they preach when it comes to spirituality.' Watkins' own conclusion is that 'spirituality is becoming more prominent in UK workplaces [. . .] But the balance seems to be in favour of companies exercising a light touch.' He ends with a note of warning, again quoting from Cree: 'It is essential that companies don't force spirituality upon employees. There are still a hell of a lot of people who are not convinced by it.'[29] We hope our book will go some way towards allaying such concerns.

Some Roman Catholic abbeys have majored on spirituality and business. Since the late 1990s, Father Dermot Tredget at the Benedictine Abbey at Douai, near Reading, has been running successful courses for business leaders. These have focused on the lessons to be drawn from the sixth-century Rule of St Benedict for running businesses today. Our subject has also been taken up by at least two other abbeys, Worth Abbey and Ampleforth.

The work of Dermot Tredget, and the novelty value (to British news-papers) of a monk running highly relevant courses for business, have attracted quite a lot of media attention. Among the many articles featuring Dermot were a series of two in the *Financial Times*, and one in the (London) *Evening Standard*.[30] Gillian, in the Introduction, refers to other FT articles she had come across, and to several companies and indi-viduals who had taken up our subject.

As we mentioned in the Introduction, the year 2000 saw the inaugura-tion of the Spirituality in the Workplace Network, which meets quarterly at Douai Abbey. The mailing list grows apace and at each meeting new faces appear. (See Resources for further details.)

There are more stories than we can tell here from individuals that illus-trate the growing UK interest in SaW. Here is just one from Val Allen, a fellow member of the Spirituality in the Workplace Network. Val developed an interest in spirituality and, since she was also trained in transpersonal psychology, decided to conduct research into the linkage of the two.

Val Allen's story

When I started my research I was advised to expect difficulty with finding research participants. I was expecting the worst, especially writing from a transpersonal perspective with the word 'spirituality' in the title. To start the ball rolling, I sent an e-mail around my company, a career management group with divisions in much of South East England and some London boroughs. The e-mail asked people to express a general interest. I received 90 replies. These came from most areas of the company including senior and middle management, finance, careers practitioners and clerical staff. A further e-mail, sending details and asking people to make a commitment to taking part, received over 30 replies. Many of these were quite enthusiastic. Some people were not at all happy when I said that I was unable to include them.[31]

As in the USA, there has been a mushrooming of UK Consultancy firms offering resources and courses on workplace spirituality. Georgeanne Lamont's company, Lamont Associates, describe themselves as 'an organizational development company that provides in-house programmes, tools, mentoring and open courses to revolutionize company performance and create inspirational teams'. We featured one of the companies Lamont Associates has been working with, Broadway Tyres, in the last chapter. They are also offering training in spiritual principles to engineers at Xerox.

CorpTools UK, run by Phil Clothier, is a subsidiary of the Corporate Transformation Tools organization (CTT) founded by Richard Barrett. The transformation tools in question provide measurement of people and organizations to help understand values, culture, consciousness and motivation. There is emphasis on the need for nothing less than transformation, the start point of which is commitment from the organizational leaders themselves to transform in both mind and heart, to suspend beliefs and be open to new possibilities and new ways of being. CTT helps to structure conversations about the things that are truly important to people in their lives and in their business. CTT reports 'amazing results in terms of business success and personal fulfilment in both work and life'.

Ealing-based (West London) consultancy Corporate Heart aims to bring back the human spirit into workaday reality. It bases its spirituality on an ancient Buddhist view of 'value creation' (as documented by Makiguchi and Birnbaum[32]). Their approach to transforming behaviour features a 'Corporate Heart Wellness Map', which helps to implement long-lasting wellness throughout an organization. They use a pioneering 'wellness survey', a short workshop programme, and a communication cascade which sets up the dialogue and establishes the action needed to ensure that people at work are healthy and well. This is a practical and pragmatic approach underpinned by spiritual 'value creation' principles.

Peter Martin, who has spent the last 15 years working mostly on change issues in large organizations, is currently setting up the New Venture Centre. Its aim is to help create organizations with a more holistic approach to people and the planet. Says Peter, 'I expect New Venture Centre to become a useful resource, a community of practice, a link to service providers with compatible values, a route to funding.'

Purple Consulting specializes in creativity-based personal and organizational transformation. Its underlying belief is that each person and organization has a unique purpose in life and a unique contribution to make. The company generates creative learning environments in which individuals and teams 'activate' their purpose, and so find a natural motivation and ability to perform with excellence. The goal is business success in the service of the greater good.

We haven't the space to describe the work of any more consultancies, but many we haven't mentioned here (as well as those we have) are listed in the next chapter. And of course there are likely to be many, many more we haven't heard of.

Closely aligned to (and often coterminous with) the consultancy industry is the whole area of coaching, both individual and corporate – e.g. life coaching, executive coaching. Coaching is about unlocking a person's potential to maximize their performance. It's about helping people to learn rather than teaching them.[33] The following information came from some recently shared e-mail correspondence.

Richard Bentley, of the coaching consultancy Releasing Human Potential, reports:

> I went to the ICF [International Coach Federation] in Denver last week [November 2003] and wanted to share some of the impressions I gained about the state of the coaching industry.
>
> The two insights I took away were that coaching is definitely having a real impact across the world, particularly in the US, and that the coaching profession is maturing. (There were, by the way, 1,200 coaches at the conference.)
>
> There is no doubt, it seems to me, that coaching (both life coaching and in the corporate sector) is moving more strongly into the arena of spirituality and values, rather than just techniques or the 'quick fix' solution. There was a real sense of concern amongst those present, highlighted by a stunning keynote speech by Dr Paul Pearsall, that the world and its citizens may destroy themselves unless it develops a new set of values – the post-Enron effect. Paul Pearsall identified some of those desirable factors as Meaningful Work, Sustaining Intimacy, Adaptive Spirituality and Resilient Humour ...
>
> The key message I want to share with you is that coaching as a profession is not peaking, it is just starting! As the large corporates (big examples are IBM, Prudential and Diageo) roll out major coaching programmes, so the word is going to spread.

Further afield

The same flurry of e-mail correspondence produced the following perspective from Australia. Nicole Bailey from Melbourne reports that 'coaching is deemed to be the second fastest growing industry in Australia (after IT). It is an exciting time to be a coach and be at the beginning of something big.'

There are stories of SaW developments from many other parts of the world. The international SaW conferences were referred to earlier. Interest in Sweden is illustrated by the book *Funky Business*, authored by Swedish academics Kjell Nordstrom and Jonas Ridderstale.[34] The book looks at our 'weird, wild, wired e-conomy', and argues that spirituality is crucial to its success. There is also the inspirational European Baha'i Business Forum whose members are leading the way in terms of social entrepreneurship and corporate global responsibility.[35]

SaW is also spreading in Asia. Sander Tideman of Spirit in Business writes: 'The concept of Gross National Happiness (GNH) was proposed by the King of Bhutan because he understood that development indicators such as GNP and Per Capita Income[36] cannot properly reflect the general well-being of his nation [. . .] GNH – inspired by Buddhist values – aims to promote real progress and sustainability by measuring the quality of life, rather than the mere sum of production and consumption in the country.'[37] Tideman goes on to speak of a forthcoming seminar of the Centre of Bhutan Studies in Bhutan at which the GNH concept will be fully discussed, and says that follow-up meetings are planned in other parts of the world.

Spirit in Business (see also Chapter 9), a non-American-founded body, has a global brief and following. It held its first conference in Holland in October 1999 on the theme 'Enterprise and Development in the 21st Century: Compassion or Competition?' This was attended by some 400 people including the Dalai Lama. Its next conference in New York in 2002 attracted some 500. In that year the SiB World Institute was set up. SiB has chosen the Lassalle Institute, near Zug in Switzerland, as its European meeting place.

What does it all amount to?

The conclusion seems obvious: spirituality is well and truly on the business agenda as well as the wider public agenda. Yet, muse Renesch and DeFoore, 'Is this talk of "soul" and spirit at work a mere distraction or passing fad?'[38] Michal Levin voices a similar doubt: 'You wonder, are you seeing things as they truly are? Or as you want them to be?'[39] Is it all too good to be true? These are questions people in SaW frequently ask themselves.

Let's be deliberately cynical for a moment, and list the various reasons there might be for being pessimistic about SaW. First, there is the question of the number of businesses where SaW is apparently making headway, as against the majority of organizations which are run on the basis of contrary principles. Does not profit remain goal number one in the overwhelming majority of companies? When push comes to shove, don't economic considerations automatically and always take precedence over human ones?

Secondly, there's the question of consistency on the part of those companies that do claim to live by higher values. Take Nike, for example. In Chapter 11 we saw good reason to list Nike among the people- and planet-friendly companies. Yet Nike is high on the anti-capitalists' blacklist on account of its Far-Eastern sweatshops. Wal-Mart's subsidiary Asda is building up a good CSR record in the UK, deliberately stocks regionally generated products and even has a policy to appoint company chaplains in every one of its British stores. Yet, according to Anita Roddick, Wal-Mart is just about the worst company on God's earth. They have, however, in response to recent school shootings, agreed to stop selling bullets in their stores.

It would be relatively easy to build up to the conclusion that basically SaW has changed nothing. This leads Bill DeFoore to say, 'It is often unclear [...] whether we are speeding rapidly along a self-destruct course, or whether we are learning how to create healthier, more productive lifestyles and businesses.'[40] However, DeFoore goes on to remark, 'From a detached view, it becomes apparent that neither perspective is completely true nor completely false.' Business corporations, like individual human beings, are a mixture of good and bad. Our own introspection tells us that even though we earnestly and sincerely desire to do good, and sometimes succeed – on occasion magnificently – we also often let ourselves and others down. The fact that we feel bad about it afterwards at least indicates a genuine desire to behave well.

It is at this point that the Christian insights about failure and forgiveness are so relevant. The fact that forgiveness comes from an ultimate source means that we are always given a fresh chance. And since that ultimate source is also, in the idiom of David Bohm, the *generative* order, the energy for doing good can be constantly renewed in us and fresh opportunities are always being opened up to us. Openness to the divine (or however we wish to express higher power) is, then, the key to the success of SaW.

It all boils down to the question of our own individual and collective inner development as human beings. Without a fundamental spiritual transformation taking place in our own lives, any lasting transformation of the world economic order is out of the question. It won't happen.

Zohar expresses the positive alternative this way: 'As individuals we can act to raise our personal SQ – indeed, the further evolution of society depends upon enough individuals doing so.'[41] Levin makes the same basic point: 'It is a change in our perceptions that is needed to recognise and understand this new vibration in our consciousness.'[42] This is why spiritual praxis to reconnect with higher power is so crucial – see again the end of Chapter 7.

A historic moment?

In our best moments we sense the truth of Jaworski's contention: 'If individuals and organizations operate from a generative orientation, from possibility rather than resignation, we can *create* the future into which we are living.'[43]

It is in those best moments that we dare to believe the bold claims that many in SaW are making about our being poised on the threshold of a new era. Jaworski again: 'What is unfolding in the world is unique [. . .] this is an "open" moment of history.' His own experiences taught him how 'small discontinuities can suddenly and significantly transfer to the whole system' (cf. Sheldrake), and led him to conclude: 'We have enormous opportunities to create something new.'[44]

Zohar, Levin and McGeachy (to name but a few) share this belief:

- Intelligence has entered a new stage of evolution (Zohar and Marshall).[45]
- Human consciousness is changing. It is expanding to incorporate a sixth sense (Levin).[46]
- A trickle of people, which is steadily swelling, are reaching these levels [above the ego level] now, and the number is set to increase dramatically (Levin).[47]
- For many, ego will become a process largely based on the heart chakra values – a blessing for our relationships to each other and to our planet, and our passport to a future for our species (Levin).[48]
- Energetically we have moved on. The vibrations that the universe is facing are faster and faster, finer and finer. We have an unparalleled opportunity to embrace the whole of our nature – to realize our spiritual selves (Levin).[49]
- Never before has history offered a challenge of this order. Never before has there been a chance for so many to see it (Levin).[50]
- It would seem that Western consciousness has evolved to the point that it is ready to wholly and openly explore the practical application of spirituality in business and government (McGeachy).[51]

Here is DeFoore again:

> So what is being born? This is the exciting part [. . .] For those willing to look and listen for it there is a quiet revolution occurring in business that is becoming more powerful and gaining momentum. *In many a large corporation, its people are being valued as its greatest resource, which is setting many healthy transformation into motion.* The emergence of balance and wisdom is not newsworthy [. . .] thus the *quiet* revolution.[52] [. . .] It is happening, however, and each us of can be a part of it if we choose.[53]

Hopeful and realistic

The important thing is to balance this exalted hope with a clear-headed realism. Belonging to the latter is the realization that any advent of a new spiritual era won't come without a considerable struggle. 'We know from general systems theory', say Renesch and DeFoore, 'that all systems resist change and that big systems can be brutally resistant [. . .] The new bottom liners, therefore, will meet some serious opposition.'[54] Levin makes the same point: 'With the coming of spiritual intelligence the ego process in us all is changing, slowly but surely – and in the face of the inevitable backlash.'[55] McGeachy agrees: 'The process of transformation requires going upstream, against the great tide of public opinion.'[56] Being more spiritual ourselves and urging others to become so is a real 'hero's journey'.

Another possibility we should be prepared to face is that things will get a whole lot worse before they get better. We might have to experience a plunge into deep darkness and profound cosmic chaos before the new creation may be brought to birth. Perhaps the coming transformation is destined to be so vast as to be incapable of generation by any other means. Ruether provides a history of the view that new creation will only come after apocalypse.[57]

But we may be confident that in the end the spiritual cause, both in organizations and in wider society, will prevail. Judi Neal and colleagues state what will need to happen. 'When enough individuals make the shift to a new paradigm – and as more organizations do also – there is higher likelihood that society will transform as well.'[58] Levin looks hopefully to our younger people, who 'are able to tune in to the changes that are happening on earth with much greater ease than most adults'.[59] She also makes a more subtle point. Disagreeing with those who regret the modernist phase of our evolution and the left-hand brain developments that went with it, she argues: 'Where significant mental development is combined with deep emotional experience, spectacular progress can be made in spiritual understanding.'[60]

Being in the here and now

One of the marks of a spirited business, notes Georgeanne Lamont, is 'being in the here and now'.[61] This is a quality which all of us who hope for spiritual transformation, in ourselves and in our world, should seek to cultivate. Sullivan[62] reproduces this remarkable quote from Jeff Salz:

> If we're too focused on the summit we lose our footing and the joy of the process. In sustaining a career or spiritual path, there also has to be a constant focus on the moment, informed by a general direction, undertaken with the faith that the outcome will be positive [. . .] Savoring the intrinsic pleasures of each moment turns out to be the most effective method for dealing with the vicissitudes of long-term change.[63]

'Actually, all we have is the present,' says Levin.[64] 'Right now there's a call that all of us can hear. It is a persistent call. A call to grow up, almost an evolutionary demand to move towards spiritual maturity.'[65] 'Holding spiritual reality', she says, 'offers the opportunity to extend your awareness in the present, rather than dwell on the past or the future. The message is: understand and use to full advantage the opportunities offered by the present.'[66] She recommends 'resting in the arms of creation. Which brings bliss of its own'.[67]

We give the last word to SaW's favourite poet, Rainer Maria Rilke, who believes – as we do – that ultimately spirituality is about learning to live the questions and keep them alive.

> I want to beg you as much as I can to be patient
> Toward all that's unresolved in your heart,
> And to learn to love the questions themselves,
> Like locked rooms,
> Or like books that are written in a foreign tongue.
>
> Do not seek the answers that cannot be given you,
> Because you would not be able to live them,
> And the point is to live everything.
>
> Live the questions now,
> Perhaps you will then, gradually,
> Without noticing it,
> Live along some distant day,
> Into the answer.[68]

15

Resources

The Authors
Should anyone wish to contact us about any issues arising from this book, we would be delighted to hear from you. Please contact us in the first instance by e-mail: suejfhoward@hotmail.com or david@dwelbourn.freeserve.co.uk.

Conferences

Be The Change
Tel: 07050 160708
E-mail: info@bethechange.org.uk
www.bethechange.org.uk
Annual conferences organized to address the challenges of our times with a focus on 'whole systems' solutions.

ICOS
International Conference on Organisational Spirituality, University of Surrey, Guildford, Surrey GU2 7XH. Tel: 01483 689 760.

The organizers can be contacted via Livingspirit@surrey.ac.uk. More information can be found on their website at www.icosconference.com.

ICOS is organized by the University of Surrey's Human Potential Research Group, located within the Department of Educational Studies, which is part of the School of Arts. It's a non-profit project run by volunteers, with a team of experienced practitioners and academics working in the field of spiritual development and facilitation. It is also non-sectarian with no affiliations to any particular organization, business or school of thought.

The theme for 2004 was 'Living Spirit in Self and Society'. The 2002 theme was 'Living Spirit: New Dimensions in Work and Learning'. Overviews and summaries of the conference, including papers, can be found on the website.

Ridley Hall Foundation
Ridley Hall, Cambridge CB3 9HG. Tel: 01223 741074.
E-mail: rah41@cam.ac.uk
www.ridley.cam.ac.uk also www.fibq.org
The foundation is concerned with relating Christian faith to the world of work and

has been in existence since 1989. Richard Higginson, the Director, co-edits a journal, *Faith in Business Quarterly* (*FiBQ*), jointly with the Industrial Christian Fellowship. He is the author of several books including *Questions of Business Life: Exploring Workplace Issues from a Christian Perspective*, Spring Harvest, 2002. This includes chapters on all the business issues covered in the Foundation's programme of conferences since 1996.

The MODEM website provides links to most UK conferences on SaW (see under 'Networks' below).

The Spirit in Business (SiB) website (also see below) contains details of European and global conferences.

A variety of global and American conferences are detailed by the Association of Spirit at Work (ASAW) listed in 'Websites' section below.

Consultants

With one or two exceptions, we are unable to provide details about consultants' approaches due to lack of space. Please look at websites given, chapters where we describe their work (where indicated), or contact the consultants themselves for further details.

Azzur

Lorraine Flower, 192 Lent Rise Road, Burnham, Bucks SL1 7AH. Tel: 01628 662 645.
E-mail: lorraineflower@aol.com
www.azzur.co.uk

Cecara Consulting Ltd

Contact: Helen-Jane Nelson, Century House, Ashley Road, Hale, Cheshire WA15 9TG. Tel: 0161 929 1010.
E-mail: hj@cecara.com
www.cecara.com

Corporate Heart Ltd

Pauline Crawford, 120 Ealing Village, London W5 2EB. Tel: 020 8998 7032.
www.corporate-heart.co.uk
(See Chapter 14.)

CorpTools UK Ltd

(Process Tools, Cultural Transformation Tools and The Seven Levels of Consciousness)
Phil Clothier/Richard Barrett, 4 Cliff Avenue, Summerseat, Bury, Lancashire BL9 5NT. Tel: 01706 824 692.
E-mail: phil@corptools.com
www.corptools.com
(See Chapters 12 and 14.)

Developing Potential Ltd (DPL)

Contacts: Les Duggan/David Hemery (an ex-Olympic athlete), White Acre, Fyfield, Marlborough, Wiltshire SN8 1PX. Tel: 01249 815 200.
E-mail: lesdugganinfo@aol.com

Frameworks Coaching Process
www.frameworkscoach.com

Lamont Associates (formerly SpiritWorks)
Managing Director, Georgeanne Lamont and associate Graham Johnson, 3 Kinross Avenue, Ascot, Berkshire SL5 9EP. Tel: 01344 628329.
E-mail: Georgeanne@lamontassociates.com
www.lamontassociates.com
(See also Chapters 10, 13 and 14.)
Lamont Associates is an organizational development company 'enabling ordinary people to achieve extraordinary results'. Their mission is to inspire and encourage people to create soul-friendly work environments. Using a unique SpiritWorks process, they focus on delivering business results and revolutionized company performance by drawing on the spirit at work to release human potential and transform the workplace. Lamont Associates provides in-house programmes, tools, mentoring and transformational training courses which help organizations to create inspirational teams. They offer a monthly newsletter available to anyone who wishes to subscribe via the above contacts.

The Learning Corporation
Richard Fox, Parallel House, 32 London Road, Guildford, Surrey GU1 2AB. Tel: 01483 454 039.
E-mail: rjfox@tlc.eu.com
www.tlc.eu.com

Nick Williams, author of *The Work We Were Born to Do* (see Chapter 4)
Heart at Work, PO Box 2236, London W1A 5UA. Tel: 07000 781 922.
E-mail: hello@heartatwork.net
www.heartatwork.net
Offers a free monthly newsletter.

Organisational Re-thinking
63 Windsor Road, Pitstone, Buckinghamshire LU7 9GG. Tel: 01296 661 893.
E-mail: info@org-rethinking.com
www.org-rethinking.com

Performance Consultants Ltd (PCL)
Contact: John Whitmore, Southfield, Leigh, Kent TN11 8PJ. Tel: 01732 457700.
E-mail: enquire@performanceconsultants.co.uk
www.performanceconsultants.co.uk

Purple Consulting
Michael Schimmelschmidt/Pamela Emery, 66 Whitehall Park, London N19 3TN.
Tel: 020 7263 8689.
E-mail: purple.consulting@virgin.net
www.purpleconsulting.com
(See Chapter 14.)

Self Mastery International
UK contact Malcolm Piers-Taylor
mpt888@talk21.com
www.selfmasteryintl.com

SOAR – Spiritual Organisations and Reality
Tel: 01234 823 222 or 01582 831 073.
E-mail: alan@harpham.com or suejfhoward@hotmail.com
SOAR is, at the time of writing, a dormant company registered by a group of five consultants: Alan Harpham (Deputy Chairmen of MODEM and a Management Consultant in Coaching and Project Management), Toby Thompson (specialist in Networked Learning at Cranfield University School of Management), Karen Szulakowska (Executive and Leadership Coach), and the two authors of this book. SOAR intends to establish itself as a consultancy that can help individuals and organizations to discover their own spirituality, and work to enhance their spiritual well-being and performance.

Spiral Dynamics
UK contact: Christopher Cooke, Managing Director, 5 Deep Limited, 3 Dimple Wells Lane, Ossett, West Yorkshire WF5 8RN. Tel: 01924 270 786.
E-mail: enquiries@5deep.co.uk
www.5deep.co.uk
(See Chapter 12.)
Continuing and expanding the work of Dr Clare W. Graves for positive change in social systems, business management, the evolution of thinking, and real-world applications of Value Systems and Levels of Existence theory. (See also www.spiraldynamics.org.)

SustainAbility
20–22 Bedford Row, London WC1R 4EB. Tel: 020 7269 6900.
E-mail: info@sustainability.com
www.sustainability.com
SustainAbility are defining the triple bottom line (see Chapter 11) of sustainable development. They are the longest established international consultancy specializing in business strategy and sustainable development – environmental improvement, social equity and economic development.

Wildworks Consulting Ltd
Chaldene, Perks Lane, Prestwood, Great Missenden, Buckinghamshire HP16 0JG. Tel: 01494 864933.
E-mail: hilary@wildworks.co.uk

Wisborough
Chrissie McGinn and Richard Hewitt, Arunvale, Coldwaltham, Pulborough, West Sussex RH20 1LP. Tel: 01798 872266
E-mail: info@wisborough.com
www.wisborough.com

Christian workplace groups

CABE

Christian Association of Business Executives. Contact: John Lovatt, Lower Stone-house Farm, Brown Edge, Stoke-on-Trent ST6 8TF. Tel: 01782 505 354.
E-mail: john.lovatt@dial.pipex.com
CABE is a fellowship of Christians in business life sharing common concerns and offering each other mutual support. It seeks to promote the study and application of Christian moral principles in industry and business. It established the Institute of Business Ethics in 1986, and became an independent charity in 2000. CABE's current activities include regular lectures (available in published form) and papers on topics related to faith and work, including the annual Hugh Kay lecture. Further initiatives to explore Christian input to business practice are ongoing.

CIEBN

Christians International Europe Business Network, St Albans Branch, PO Box 721, St Albans, Herts AL1 5XT. Tel: 01727 762 355.
E-mail: info@ciebnstalbans.org
An evangelistic organization assisting Christians to fulfil their calling in the workplace.

Connected Community Learning

E-mail: petern@allbelievers.org
www.e-quip.org.uk
'Equipping God's people for work in his service' via e-learning. CCL are offering networked learning, i.e. learning with a community of others on-line, and providing a variety of Christian discipleship courses relevant to being a Christian in the workplace.

ICF

Industrial Christian Fellowship. Contact: Ann Wright, St Matthew's House, 100 George Street, Croydon CR0 1PE. Tel: 020 8681 5496.
E-mail: wright@btinternet.com
www.icf-online.org
Formed to proclaim Christ's presence with industrial workers and to link Christians in fighting for social justice. ICF now provides information about current activities in UK faith and work initiatives – through regular newsletters, publications, theological study materials and its website. Its membership network provides fellowship opportunities for people in any workplace situation who are concerned about applying spiritual values and their faith.

Industrial Mission Association

Contact: Crispin White.
E-mail: crispin.white@eccr.org.uk
The professional association of UK industrial chaplains and their associates, the IMA is organized into nine regional groups, and has a monthly publication – *IMAgenda*. The contact for *IMAgenda* is Heather Pencavel who can provide details about several recent articles on SaW – hpencavel@ukonline.co.uk. The IMA holds a biennial national conference.

LICC

London Institute for Contemporary Christianity, St Peter's Church, Vere Street, London W1G 0DQ. Tel: 020 7399 9555.
E-mail: mail@licc.org.uk
www.licc.org.uk
LICC was founded to support Christians in making a difference in their everyday lives. They operate as an influential resource group, equipping Christians to engage biblically and relevantly with the issues they face in contemporary society. Offers a particularly useful guide 'Supporting Christians at Work' for pastors.

Ridley Hall Foundation
(See under Conferences.)

St Paul's Institute
Canon Edmund Newell, Director, 3b Amen Court, London EC4M 7BU. Tel: 07977 911 020.
E-mail: institute@stpaulscathedral.org.uk
www.stpaulscathedral.org.uk (then click on St Paul's Institute)
Established in 2002 by St Paul's Cathedral to provide a forum for education and debate on issues to do with faith and ethics. Particularly interested in issues in relation to the City of London and its role in the global economy.

TBN
Transformational Business Network, Nelson House, 271 Kingston Road, Wimbledon, London SW19 3NW. Tel: 0845 330 5142.
E-mail: info@tbnetwork.org
www.tbnetwork.org.
Using business skills to bring spiritual and physical transformation to the world.

Courses/Training

There may be many courses other than those we have listed running in the UK; these are simply the ones we are aware of. We apologize in advance for any omissions, which we would be interested to hear about.

Douai Abbey
Upper Woolhampton, Reading, Berkshire RG7 5TQ. Tel: 0118 971 5300.
E-mail: pastoral@douaiabbey.org.uk
www.douaiabbey.org.uk (Look under '2. For You'; and then '2.3 Talks, Courses, Workshops'.)
As part of the Pastoral Programme Fr Dermot Tredget has developed a series of six Retreat/Workshops entitled 'Spirituality in the Workplace' designed for people in leadership positions. These workshops are always oversubscribed and have attracted media attention. Consequently, Fr Dermot has lectured in a variety of places, including at the Chartered Institute of Personnel Development's annual conference. He has advised various management consultants and led a retreat for the Academy of Chief Executives.
    Douai also offers regular retreats on contemplative prayer and spirituality in

business. (Other Roman Catholic Abbeys also offer similar e.g. Worth Abbey, www.worth.org.uk and Ampleforth, www.ampleforth.org.uk/abbey/.) Douai also hosts the Spirituality in Workplace Network group, listed under 'Networks' below.

International Coach Federation
www.coachfederation.org
This is a non-profit, professional organization of personal and business coaches. It offers training and accreditation, and holds an annual conference. (See Chapter 14.)

Roffey Park Institute
Forest Road, Horsham, West Sussex RH12 4TD. Tel: 01293 851 644.
E-mail: info@roffeypark.com
www.roffeypark.com
Roffey offer a variety of personal development programmes and has conducted comprehensive research into SaW in the UK (as referred to on page 186). Information about research findings can be obtained from Nigel Springett – Nigel.Springett@btinternet.com.

The Trinity Forum
European Office: Barr Hall, 31 Barr Hall Road, Portaferry, BT22 1RQ, Northern Ireland. Tel: 028 4272 9020.
E-mail: Maureen.Edmondson@ttf.org
www.thetrinityforum.org
The Trinity Forum (TTF) describes itself as 'a Christ-centred leadership academy without walls, open to people of all beliefs and none'. It helps leaders in business, academe and politics engage in key issues of their personal and public lives in the context of faith. TTF offers a variety of programmes and publications that provide leaders with an opportunity for personal reflection and self-appraisal, and encourages cultural renewal by encouraging leaders to apply what they learn within their spheres of influence. The TTF started in the USA and spread to Europe; while rooted in Christianity it promotes interfaith dialogue.

Universities that have demonstrated interest in SaW include Cranfield, Bath, Lancaster (see under 'Journals'), Leeds and Surrey.

Cranfield School of Management
Cranfield, Beds MK43 0AL. Tel: 01234 751122. Enquire through the Praxis Centre, whose stated aim is achieving organizational success through people: www.cranfield.ac.uk/som/groups/praxis. E-mail: m.k.mills@cranfield.ac.uk; or Professor Andrew Kakabadse in the faculty group People and Organisations, e-mail: a.p.kakabadse@cranfield.ac.uk; or Dr Pauline Weight in the Strategic Management group, e-mail: p.weight@cranfield.ac.uk.

At the **University of Bath**, Professor Peter Reason has written a number of papers incorporating spirituality. Bath also offers an MSc in Responsibility and Business Practice. See the Centre for Action Research in Professional Practice at www.bath.ac.uk/carpp/carpp.htm. Tel: 01225 826826. It offers many insights into Co-operative/Collaborative Inquiry as a form of research and practice.

University of Leeds
www.leeds.ac.uk
The School of Healthcare Studies is offering an elective about spirituality and the caring professions (HECS 3052), and includes spirituality in other courses.

University of Surrey are offering a post-graduation Certificate in Spiritual Development and Facilitation. This is facilitated by the Human Potential Research Group, School of Arts, Department of Educational Studies, University of Surrey, Guildford, Surrey GU2 7XH. Tel: 01483 689 751.
E-mail: j.gregory@surrey.ac.uk
See www.surrey.ac.uk/education
A groundbreaking one year part-time course exploring the nature, facilitation and application of spiritual development in personal and work contexts.

Waverley Learning
Waverley Abbey House, Waverley Lane, Farnham, Surrey GU9 8EP. Tel: 01252 784 733.
E-mail: learning@waverley.uk.com
www.waverley.uk.com
Offers executive, management and personal development programmes and retreats in areas such as leadership, communication and change, run from a Christian perspective. Linked with Crusade for World Revival www.cwr.org.uk, whose aim is applying God's word to everyday life and relationships.

Interfaith Groups/Resources

Alternatives
St James Church, 197 Piccadilly, London W1J 9LL. Tel: 020 7287 6711.
E-mail: alternatives@ukonline.co.uk
www.alternatives.org.uk
Alternatives is a non-profit making organization, founded in 1982, and based in the heart of London. It seeks to inspire new visions for living through holistic education and connection to the sacred dimension of life. Offers a programme of talks and workshops honouring all spiritual traditions and welcoming people from all cultural backgrounds.

Brahma Kumaris World Spiritual University (BKWSU)
Global Co-operation House, 65 Pound Lane, London NW10 2HH. Tel: 020 8727 3350.
E-mail: london@bkwsu.com
www.bkwsu.org.uk
Dadi Janki was one of the ten Keepers of Wisdom, an eminent group of world spiritual leaders convened to advise the Earth Summit in Brazil (1992) on the fundamental spiritual dilemmas underpinning world-wide environment issues. She was also a founding member of the BKWSU which focuses on understanding the self, its inner resources and strengths, and developing attributes of leadership and the highest level of personal integrity. As an international Non-Governmental Organization in consultative status with the Economic and Social Council of the United

Nations (UN) and UNICEF, the University has organized three major international projects during the last decade. These include 'The Million Minutes of Peace' (1986) and 'Global Co-operation for a Better World' (1988–91). The most recent project is 'Sharing Our Values for a Better World' (launched in 1995), dedicated to the 50th anniversary of the UN. Operating world-wide, the University's 3000 centres offer free courses, lectures and seminars on human, moral and spiritual values; meditation; positive thinking; self management and stress management.

European Baha'i Business Forum

35 avenue Jean Jaures, 73000 Chambery, France. Tel: 33 (0)4 79 96 22 72.
General Secretary: George Starcher.
E-mail: george.starcher@ebbf.org
www.ebbf.org.
Founded in 1990, EBBF is a professional network of business men and women (some of the Baha'i faith, others not) from over 50 countries. It promotes sustainable, socially responsible and ethical practices in management. It is partner to a wide variety of organizations, from international to small businesses and hosts an annual event in Holland to highlight the need for businesses to work together across generations, borders, sectors and beliefs to bring results.

FIL

Faith in London, E-mail: info@faithinlondon.org.
In 2003 FIL produced a package of resource materials under the title *Faith Communities Toolkit*, for use by the employment agency Jobcentreplus. Copies may be obtained by e-mailing a request for the British Social Attitudes Survey, of which the Toolkit forms a part.

Graham Wilson

Tel: 07785 222 380.
E-mail: gw@grahamwilson.org
www.grahamwilson.org / www.thefutureofwork.org / www.inter-faith.net /
www.inter-faithforum.net
Graham works as a non-executive director and coach with senior managers who want their organization to succeed, while they and all their colleagues look forward to work and go home fulfilled. A psychotherapist and inter-faith minister, his books are published in more than a dozen languages and he is in demand as a motivational speaker specializing in people and business, corporate governance and the future of work.

The New Seminary UK

Administrative Office: Elms Court, Chapel Way, Botley, Oxford OX2 9LP. Tel: 01865 244 835.
E-mail: newseminary@community.co.uk
An organization which trains interfaith ministers and spiritual counsellors. The new seminary believes there is one God and many paths leading to the same Source. It promotes an ethic of respect, reconciliation, forgiveness and fellowship between peoples of all faiths and none, supporting peacemaking and the remembrance of our fundamental human unity.

Journals (including special issues on SaW)

Business Spirit Journal
www.bizspirit.com
On-line magazine with articles on many topics by leaders in the field.

Journal of Management Inquiry (JMI)
See www.sagepub.com (click on Journals, then see Index of Journals under J).
JMI publishes the latest original research and practice written by top management scholars and professionals from a wide variety of areas within the management, business and organization fields.

Journal for Management, Spirituality and Religion
www.jmsr.com
A new journal (first edition due 2004) linked to the new MSR interest group in the US Academy of Management (see under 'Learning and Research'). The journal aims to serve scholars of business studies and religious studies, and to provide a forum for the cross-fertilization of both camps.

Journal of Managerial Psychology
Published by Emerald www.emeraldinsight.com
This journal is international in scope and brings together key findings in psychology to allow for greater understanding and development of people at all levels of organizational life. Volume 17, Number 3, 2002 is a special issue on Spirituality, leadership, work and organizations. Guest Editor: Nada Korac-Kakabadse.

Journal of Organizational Change Management
Published by Emerald www.emeraldinsight.com
This journal is unique in its ability to set the management and organizational change and development agenda by analysing new approaches and research theories.

Journal of Spirituality, Leadership and Management (JSLM)
www.slam.net.au
Produced by the Spirituality, Leadership and Management (SLaM) Network Limited, which was established in 2000 following two successful Australian conferences. The magazine aims to foster the integration of spirituality, leadership and management in organizations and communities and in our relationship with the natural world through networking, education and research. It brings together consultants, academics, teachers, researchers and people from every level of work in corporations, institutions, business, government and local communities in an active learning, collaborative network. SLaM Network Ltd. has no religious affiliations.

Management Learning
Formerly entitled *Management Education and Development Journal*, Volume 22, part 3 (1991) was a special issue offering articles which emerged from a conference entitled 'Working with Spirituality in Organizations'. Management Learning is produced by **Lancaster University** – see list of journals recommended by the

Department of Management Learning (DML) at www.lums.lancs.ac.uk/pages/
Departments/DML/resources/journals. DML also offer a Master's degree in Management Learning.

New Renaissance Magazine
www.newren.org.uk
This is a quarterly magazine serving as a forum for progressive discussion on the
future of society. Since 1990 it has been bringing a holistic perspective to the
economic, environmental, political, social, spiritual and cultural concerns of today.
Aiming to inspire a creative burst of energy which will help humanity surmount its
present global crisis, New Renaissance is a comprehensive source of 'alternative'
news and commentary.

People Management
www.ipd.co.uk
Produced on behalf of the Chartered Institute of Personnel and Development, this
magazine keeps abreast of a variety of topical human resource issues.

Spirit at Work Newsletter
Quarterly newsletter from the Association of Spirit at Work (see ASAW under
'Websites' section).

Spirit in Work
A new journal/magazine due for publication in 2004 initially by MODEM (see
under 'Networks'). The journal will focus on MODEM's mission, with particular
emphasis on SaW. Contact via MODEM – www.modem.uk.com.

Learning and Research

Academy of Management
www.aomonline.org
The Academy (AOM) is a leading professional association for scholars dedicated to
creating and disseminating knowledge about management and organizations. The Management Spirituality and Religion stream (MSR) was set up recently. See
www.aom.pace.edu/msr. 'The primary purpose of the special interest group is to
encourage professional scholarship in the relationship between management,
spirituality and religion. The domain of this special interest group is the study of the
relationship and relevance of spirituality and religion in management and organizations.'

Center for Creative Leadership (CCL)
www.ccl.org
The CCL is the world's largest institute devoted to leadership research and
education. Its mission is to advance the understanding, practice and development
of leadership for the benefit of society world-wide. They offer a range of programmes and products.

Dialogue

See www.david-bohm.net to find out more about David Bohm's contribution to dialogue – the site has excellent links to websites about dialogue.
www.dialogos-inc.com is the website for Bill Isaacs whose approach we mentioned in Chapter 5. (Also see Peter Senge below.)

Institute for Noetic Sciences
www.ions.org
A leader in the field of consciousness and human potential research and education for more than twenty-five years. A membership organization with great publications and meetings.

Meg Wheatley
See articles at her site: www.margaretwheatley.com.

Peter Senge and the theory and practice of the learning organization
www.infed.org
Peter Senge's vision of a learning organization has been deeply influential. This well-researched encyclopaedic site discusses Senge's contribution and contains some excellent links, particularly to dialogue. (See also SoL under 'Networks'.)

Networks

Whilst there are many networks already in existence, we encourage anyone who wishes to set up a new network in their local area. For help with this task in the first instance (and particularly for details of existing contacts in your area) please talk to Alan Harpham, tel: 01234 823 222. E-mail: alanh@modem.uk.com.

Association for Spirit at Work (ASAW) Greater Manchester Chapter (UK)
St James Church Centre, St James Avenue, Woolfold, Bury BL8 1TD.
Regular meetings with a variety of different speakers, organized by Phil Clothier. Tel: 01706 824 692. E-mail: phil@corptools.com. Meetings are usually listed on MODEM's website www.modem.uk.com. (See under 'Websites' for main USA ASAW site.)

MODEM
Managerial and Organisational Disciplines for the Enhancement of Ministry
Registered Office: CTBI, Bastille Court, 2 Paris Gardens, London SE1 8ND.
www.modem.uk.com
Contact Alan Harpham (Deputy Chairman), tel: 01234 823 222, e-mail: alanh@modem.uk.com, or Peter Bates (Treasurer and Membership Secretary), tel: 01273 493172, e-mail: peterb@modem.uk.com, for further details.
MODEM is a national, ecumenical charity set up to encourage better understanding between leadership, management and ministry. Its mission is to lead and enable 'authentic dialogue between exponents of spirituality, theology and ministry and leadership, organisation and management'. It has produced three books, the most recent being *Creative Church Leadership*, which was published in March 2004. It welcomes new members to join its ongoing dialogue.

MODEM East Midlands Branch (MODEM-EM)

MODEM-EM was set up in October 1997 by the Revd Dr Norman Todd, a MODEM trustee and member of the management committee. A series of bi-monthly meetings are held on a Friday lunchtime 12 noon – 2.30 p.m. at 1 Broadway, The Lace Market, Nottingham. Contact via e-mail: julia.piech @wholtd.fsbusiness.co.uk.

MODEM Liverpool

At time of going to press a new group is being formed in Liverpool. Contact: harry@rhema.uk.com for further details.

SlaM Network

www.slam.net.au
(See under 'Journals, JSLM', above.)

Spirit in Business (SiB)

www.spiritinbusiness.org
(See Chapter 9.)

SiB's Mission is to connect leaders in a global community of inquiry, learning and action, to release the creative and visionary power of individuals and organizations for the benefit of the whole. SiB acts at three main levels:

1. The individual dimension – supporting leaders towards authenticity, integrity, passion and well-being.
2. The micro dimension – unleashing purpose, vision and love in business, winning the hearts and minds of stakeholders allowing greater performance.
3. The macro dimension – promoting the moral, ethical and human basis of capitalism, becoming aware and responsible for effects on the whole economy.

All of these link the inner capital of human beings (values, passions, beliefs) to outer capital (actions and interactions with the business environment).

Over 3,000 business leaders have joined SiB as champions and promoters across all cultures and beliefs. SiB facilitate successful conferences world-wide (Amsterdam 1999, New York, Zurich 2002, Bangkok, Sao Paulo, San Francisco 2003, Australia 2005), plus a number of parallel events, executive retreats, leadership journeys, publications, news and media initiatives. A significant contribution is the integrated Spirit in Business Knowledge Platform (as described in Chapter 9).

Specific projects include:

1. the feminine perspective in business;
2. a metrics index allowing ranking, auditing, and growing awareness of values and spirit;
3. a leadership development programme empowering organizations to unleash the highest possible creativity and commitment from their people;
4. financial incentives for business leadership to transform their companies into agents of world benefit.

Spirit in Business – Europe

Brinklaan 151, 1404 GE Bussum, The Netherlands. Tel: +31-35-6951920, Fax: +31-35-6935254.
E-mail: sgtideman@csi.com

Spirit in Business – USA

PO Box 228, Greenfield, MA 01302. Tel: 413-586-8950
E-mail: spiritinbusiness@gmx.net

Spirituality in the Workplace

Douai Abbey, Upper Woolhampton, Reading, Berkshire RG7 5TQ. Tel: 0118 971 5333.
E-mail: pastoral@douaiabbey.org.uk
(See also website for Douai Abbey, www.douaiabbey.org.uk.)
Co-founded by Father Dermot Tredget and David Welbourn in 2000, this network of people, of all faiths and none, meets informally at quarterly intervals at Douai. The agenda usually consists of a presentation by one of the members on a SaW-related subject, discussion, a practical spiritual exercise, and news-sharing. For further information or joining details, contact David on 01483 825 541, e-mail david@dwelbourn.freeserve.co.uk.

Society for Organizational Learning (SoL)

www.solonline.org/aboutsol/who/
SoL is a learning community composed of organizations, individuals, and local SoL communities around the world. It was formed in 1997 to continue the work of MIT's Center for Organizational Learning (1991–97). Peter Senge is the founding Chairman of SoL. Members are committed to developing the capacity to address issues such as: the social and economic divide; the system seeing itself; redefining growth; variety and inclusiveness; attracting talented people and realizing their potential; the role of the corporation.

Other Organizations

Organizations that have been referred to in this book, or that are simply extremely useful, and not listed elsewhere.

American Leadership Forum

www.alfnational.org
ALF was founded in 1980 by Joseph Jaworski to offer a new leadership model for addressing the complex problems in society.

Business in the Community (BITC)

137 Shepherdess Walk, London N1 7RQ. Tel: 0870 600 2482.
E-mail: information@bitc.org.uk
www.bitc.org.uk
BITC is a movement of businesses committed to continually improving their positive impact on society. Over 700 top UK companies are members.

Centre for Tomorrow's Company

19 Buckingham Street, London WC2N 6EF. Tel: 020 7930 5150.

E-mail: info@tomorrowscompany.com

www.tomorrowscompany.com

The Centre's director is Mark Goyder – mark@tomorrowscompany.com.

The brainchild of the RSA (see below), it started with a lecture by Professor Charles Handy at the RSA, called 'What is a company for?' It is now an influential think-tank. It aims to create a future for business which makes sense to staff, shareholders and society. It works with business members and partners to accomplish four main objectives, to: act as a leading and influential networking hub for organizations; identify and explore the future of sustainable success; undertake and publish agenda-setting research; and promote the adoption of new ideas and concepts.

Corporate Social Responsibility Europe

www.csreurope.org

CSR Europe is a non-profit organization that promotes corporate social responsibility. Its mission is to help companies achieve profitability, sustainable growth and human progress by placing corporate social responsibility in the mainstream of business practice.

If you are interested in becoming a member of CSR Europe please contact Karla Slechtova, membership and account management coordinator. Tel +32 2 541 1621.

E-mail: ks@csreurope.org

Ecumenical Committee for Corporate Responsibility

www.eccr.org.uk

UK chair Barbara Hayes' e-mail: Barbara.hayes@talk21.com

ECCR is an ecumenical organization incorporating Christian denominations, churches, religious communities and orders, and individuals. Based in the industrial mission movement, it raises the profile of corporate responsibility by acting to ensure companies adopt world-wide operational standards for environmental and ethical practices and that churches follow socially responsible investment policies. Its main focus is on international businesses, which it studies using its own Benchmarks for Measuring Business Performance assessment tool. It has links with sister organizations world-wide.

The Fetzer Institute

www.fetzer.org

The Fetzer Institute supports research, education, and service programmes aiming to foster the integration of the inner life of mind and spirit and the outer life of action in the world. The Institute was established by an endowment from John E. Fetzer (1901–91), whose vision inspired its guiding purpose – to awaken into and serve spirit for the transformation of self and society, based on the principles of wholeness of reality, freedom of spirit, and unconditional love.

The Grubb Institute of Behavioural Studies

Based in Islington, London. Tel: 020 7278 8061.

E-mail: info@grubb.org.uk

www.grubb.org.uk

The Grubb Institute was set up in 1969 to contribute to the well-being and wholeness of society by providing space for clients to find purpose, and discover the leadership and management which makes their institution 'fit for purpose'. They use a collaborative research-oriented approach to explore the dynamics of human systems from a human sciences and Christian theological framework.

Institute of Business Ethics (IBE)

24 Greencoat Place, London SW1P 1BE. Tel: 020 7798 6040.
E-mail: info@ibe.org.uk
www.ibe.org.uk

IBE was established in 1986 to encourage high standards of corporate and business behaviour and the sharing of best practice, and to be the leader in knowledge and practice of corporate business ethics. It raises company awareness and helps businesses to build relationships of trust with customers, employees, suppliers, owners and the communities in which they work. It has a high profile role in speaking up on national and international business conduct, offers advice, practical help, research data and informed opinion to organizations and the media, as well as training, public events, and publications to help people understand and solve ethical dilemmas within the corporate context.

The New Economics Foundation (NEF)

3 Jonathan Street, London SE11 5NH. Tel: 020 7820 6300.
E-mail: info@neweconomics.org
www.neweconomics.org

NEF was founded in 1986 by the leaders of The Other Economic Summit (TOES) which forced issues such as international debt on to the agenda of the G7 and G8 summits. It is one of the UK's most creative independent think-tanks, combining analysis, research, advocacy, policy debate, training and practical (often locally designed) action. It aims to construct a new economy centred on people and the environment and promotes innovative solutions that challenge mainstream thinking on economic, sustainability and social issues. It also creates new ways of measuring progress towards increased well-being in these areas. NEF works with all sections of society in the UK and internationally – civil society, government, individuals, businesses and academia.

New Venture Centre

E-mail: petermartin@NewVentreCentre.net
www.newventurecentre.net
(See Chapter 14.)

Royal Society of Arts (RSA – originally the Royal Society for the Encouragement of Arts, Manufactures and Commerce, which spawned the Great Exhibition of 1851) and SAGE: Sustainability Action Group Exchange

Main contact: Anita Beardsley, SAGE Project Manager, RSA at Bristol, Rooms 25 and 28, St Matthias Campus, UWE, Oldbury Court Road, Fishponds, Bristol BS16 2JP. Tel: 0117 344 4445.
E-mail: anita.beardsley@rsa.org.uk
www.sage-rsa.org.uk

The RSA has been working for sustainability and good environmental practice throughout its existence and has a number of environmental award schemes. Its website stimulates its 22,000 RSA Fellows to champion sustainable practices in their workplaces and communities, and to discuss sustainable development via SAGE.

SAGE aims to encourage positive action at local level (using the slogan 'Think Global – Act Local'). It embraces three broad objectives: effective protection of the environment, prudent use of natural resources, and social progress that recognizes the needs of everyone, particularly future generations. SAGE is combined with the RSA's powerful resource www.EnvironmentAwards.net, which provides a searchable on-line database of over 300 environmental awards and grants, as well as a new section devoted purely to Sustainable Resource Management.

Spiritual Unfoldment Society
www.martinrutte.com/spiritbank.html
This society began at the World Bank under the guidance of Richard Barrett. The website links to Richard's friend, Martin Rutte, who contributed to a popular SaW book entitled *Chicken Soup for the Soul*. Martin's site has a good selection of useful links.

University of Creation Spirituality
www.creationspirituality.com
Matthew Fox is the founder and president of the University of Creation Spirituality (UCS) located in California. UCS is committed to bringing spirit to education and professions and offers a range of educational programmes.

The Work Foundation (formerly part of the Industrial Society which restructured; another part became 'Industrial Society Learning and Development', owned by the Capita Group plc)
Peter Runge House, 3 Carlton House Terrace, London SW1Y 5DG. Tel: 0870 165 6700.
E-mail: contactcentre@theworkfoundation.com
www.theworkfoundation.com
The Work Foundation, established in 2002, is a charity with an 85-year-long history based on Christian values. It works with employers to improve the productivity and quality of working life in the UK. *Working Capital*, The Work Foundation's launch report, forms the basis of its work. It states that British employers must address the growing disaffection of their employees. A copy of this report can be obtained from the website.

Psychology/Psychotherapy

UK Council for Psychotherapy, Humanistic and Integrative Psychotherapy Section
www.psychotherapy.org.uk
Offers a useful overview of different psychotherapeutic approaches and lists the main professional bodies including: **CCPE – Centre for Counselling and Psychotherapy Education**, www.ccpe.org.uk (who offer a helpful initial assessment of individual needs); and **GAPS – Guild of Analytical Psychology and Spirituality** – www.gaps.co.uk, plus many other interesting organizations.

Re-Vision
97 Brondesbury Road, London NW6 6RY. Tel: 020 8357 8881.
E-mail: info@re-vision.org.uk
www.re-vision.org.uk
A counselling and psychotherapy training centre with a Transpersonal and Integrative perspective based on the principles of Psychosynthesis. It offers new pathways to self-development and professional training with a primary focus on the care of the soul.

Process Tools

Appreciative Inquiry (AI)
Banaga, G, 'A Spiritual Path to Organizational Renewal: The Christian Spiritual Dimension of AI', in Hammond, S. and Royal C. (eds), *Lessons from the field: Applying Appreciative Inquiry*. Practical Press Inc, 1998.
Cooperrider, David L., and Srivastva, S. (eds), *Appreciative Management and Leadership: The Power of Positive Thought and Action in Organizations*. Jossey-Bass, San Francisco, 1990. (Searching on Cooperrider in www.amazon.co.uk reveals an amazing number of books on AI – take your pick!)
Hammond, Sue A., *The Thin Book of Appreciative Inquiry*. 2nd edn. Thin Book Publishing, 1998.

Future Search Conferences
These 'conferences' are particularly appropriate for community issues. You bring stakeholders together, focus on a theme and work on solving the problem together. A book which goes into the practice and pitfalls in detail is *Discovering Common Ground* by Marvin Weisboard and thirty-five international co-authors (Berrett-Koehler, 1992).

Real-time strategic change – Robert W. Jacobs' book of this title (Berrett-Koehler, 1994) advocates a fundamental redesign of the way organizations change. This approach involves large group meetings enabling hundreds of people to collaborate in creating their collective future.

Spirituality at Work Conversations
A great place to start to explore spirit and work in the context of all traditions is www.spiritualityatwork.com. The site offers SaW conversation starter exercises from Whitney Roberson's *Spirituality at Work: A Handbook for Conversation Convenors and Facilitators*. David Welbourn has produced Whitney Roberson-style conversation notes to supplement her collection for use in UK companies. These are available from david@dwelbourn.freeserve.co.uk.

Storytelling
Business Storytellers (www.bizstorytellers.org) provide information on the importance of stories, guidelines, and resources, including excellent book recommendations, as well as notes from storytellers on varied workplace topics. If you are interested in storytelling check this site out.

Also see www.storydynamics.com, who offer a newsletter, and the Metaphor Project www.metaphorproject.org.

Open Space Technology
www.openspaceworld.org
Originated by Harrison Owen, Open Space Technology is one way to enable ordinary people, in any kind of organization, to create inspired meetings and events. Participants create and manage their own agenda of parallel working sessions around a central theme of strategic importance. With groups of five to 1000, working in one-day workshops, three-day conferences or the regular weekly staff meeting, the common result is a powerful, effective connecting and strengthening of what's already happening in the organization: planning and action, learning and doing, passion and responsibility, participation and performance.

Websites

Academy for Chief Executives
www.chiefexecutive.com
The Academy for Chief Executives provides a confidential learning environment for Chief Executives and Managing Directors from all sectors of industry, commerce and the 'not for profit' sector. Its purpose is to nurture an environment which inspires leaders to achieve their extraordinary potential.

Alliance for Work/Life Progress
www.awlp.org
This is a membership organization for those who work in business, academia or the public sector to promote a healthier balance between work and life.

Association for Spirit at Work
www.spiritatwork.org
This is a 'must visit' site – if you only visit one site, make sure it is this one! Founded by Judi Neal, at the University of New Haven, in Connecticut, USA, this site has provided information on spirit at work since 1996. It has a huge variety of connections including articles, books, conferences and special events world-wide, courses, research and offers a network to connect with professionals in the field. Its mission is 'to make a difference in the world by expanding the role of businesses, groups and organizations in transforming society'.

Business Ethics
www.business-ethics.com
See also www.eben.org for the European Business Ethics Network. Also www.meaning.org for the Foundation for Ethics and Meaning. We have already referred to the Institute of Business Ethics above (www.ibe.org.uk).

Business for Social Responsibility
www.bsr.org

Helps companies integrate commercial success with ethical values, people, communities and the environment. See also www.csreurope.org above.

Center for Spirituality and Work
www.spiritualityatwork.org
Contains a variety of ideas and links.

Center for Visionary Leadership
www.visionarylead.org
Offers new models for integrating spirituality and politics. It has co-sponsored conferences on spirit and work.

Chaordic Alliance
www.chaordic.org
Founded by Dee Hock, creator of VISA, this site seeks to create visionary business through sharing research, ideas and resources. (The word 'chaordic' combines 'chaos' and 'order'.) The site has great articles and links.

Forgiveness
www.forgivenessNet.co.uk
Stories, articles, insights and religious scriptures about the meaning and power of forgiveness, human and divine.

Greenleaf Center for Servant Leadership
www.greenleaf.org
Based on the work of Robert Greenleaf, who is often cited as the guiding elder of the current SaW movement. The site offers networking, resources and information about Servant Leadership.

Heartland Institute
www.heartlandinstitute.com
Has sponsored several conferences on SaW and now promotes thought-leader gatherings.

Institute for Management Excellence
www.itstime.com
Lives up to its name in that it has excellent links to spirituality-in-the-workplace websites and resources, including www.workplacespirituality.info and www.worldbusiness.com. One of the first sites to post listings related to SaW.

John Templeton Foundation
www.templeton.org
The mission is to pursue new insights at the boundary between theology and science through a rigorous, open-minded and empirically focused research methodology, drawing together talented representatives from a wide spectrum of fields of expertise. Research focuses on topical areas which have spiritual and theological significance ranging across the disciplines from cosmology to healthcare. Subscribe to two free newsletters: Works of Love, and Milestones. An exciting website!

Spiritual Exercises of St Ignatius of Loyola
www.ccel.org/i/ignatius/exercises
As translated from his autobiography. (See Chapter 7.)

Transforming Practices
www.transformingpractices.com
Contains articles, book excerpts, interviews, and exercises about how to integrate spiritual practices into the legal profession.

Via3 Ltd
www.via3.net
E-mail: enquiries@via3.net
This online network provides information, ideas and support for ethical businesses, non-profit organizations and charities. It has a strong CSR emphasis and has links with several like-minded bodies, such as New Economics Foundation. It publishes a newsletter.

Work and Soul
www.workandsoul.com
Contains inspirational resources link.

The World Business Academy
www.worldbusiness.org
Founded on the understanding that business must adopt a new tradition of responsibility for the whole and define its interests within the wider perspective of society in order to create a positive and sustainable future. The Academy's goal is to enable members to explore, clarify and integrate the new paradigm into their lives, businesses and the world to rekindle the human spirit in business.

Websites www.beliefnet.com, www.spiritualityhealth.com and www.about.com offer brief links to all religions, as well as articles and columns about practical spirituality.

Spiritual refreshment

Findhorn Foundation
www.findhorn.org
The Findhorn Foundation, located in Scotland, is the educational and organizational cornerstone of the world-famous Findhorn Community, founded in 1962. It is a major international centre of spiritual education and personal transformation offering many ways for people to visit, live or work. It is associated with the United Nations (UN) as a Non-Governmental Organization and is represented at regular briefing sessions at UN Headquarters.

The Retreat Association
Central Hall, 256 Bermondsey Street, London SE1 3UJ. Tel: 0845 456 1429.
E-mail: info@retreats.org.uk
www.retreats.org.uk

Can provide a variety of publications and resources about retreats including *Retreats 2004*, an annual journal giving information about retreat houses in the UK and their programmes for the current year.

Other diverse resources

Administry
62 Farm Road, Rowley Regis, Birmingham B65 8ET. Tel: 0845 128 5177.
E-mail: mail@administry.co.uk
www.administry.co.uk
Publisher in 2000 of Adminisheet 70, *Identifying Gifts and Potential: Making the Most of People's Strengths,* by Jill Garrett.

Enneagram
www.enneagram.org.uk
This is a personality profile tool, similar to the Myers Briggs Type Indicator (MBTI), but takes the spiritual dimension into account. The Enneagram's 'Strategy Board' uses nine types which offer a map of the spiritual journeys we make – where we are, where we have been, and where we might go to. It can show us routes towards our natural spiritual gifts.

Spiritual Intelligence Assessment Instrument
www.consciouspursuits.com
Conscious Pursuits Inc are developing an assessment instrument intended for individual and corporate use. It uses faith-neutral language and is designed to give feedback in 21 spiritual intelligence (SQ) fields.

Teleconference classes
www.newstorytel.com
Provides educational classes on healthy and sustainable living led by experts by means of teleconference calls.

Tom Heuerman's Pamphlets
www.amorenaturalway.com
Provides interesting on-line pamphlets about life, change, leadership and organizations.

Values in Healthcare
E-mail: values@jankifoundation.org
A spiritual approach. See Janki Foundation for Global Healthcare.

Further reading (not listed in reference section)

Although already listed in our references section, we highly recommend Pat Sullivan's book *Work with Meaning, Work with Joy* (Sheed and Ward, 2003) which has an extensive resources section, listing many resources that we have not had space to include here. We have extracted some recommendations from her book in this section, along with some further books of our own choosing, but this is only a representative sample.

The Art of Happiness at Work, by the Dalai Lama and Howard Cutler (Hodder Mobius, 2003).
Explores issues such as work and identity, making money, the Buddhist concept of 'right livelihood', and transforming dissatisfaction at work. The Dalai Lama's wisdom and sensitivity emerge.

Effective Strategic Leadership, by John Adair (Pan Books, 2003).
To be a strategic life-leader means that one develops a vision and direction for one's life. This book explores what makes a person effective as a strategic leader.

Getting to a Better Future: A Matter of Conscious Choosing, by John Renesch and Anita Roddick (New Business Books, San Francisco, 2000). An optimistic book from two realists who have been working with spiritual principles in business for many years.

Handbook of Workplace Spirituality and Organizational Performance, edited by Robert Giacalone and Carole L. Jurkiewicz (M. E. Sharpe Publishers, 2003).
This is a comprehensive, interdisciplinary, and action-oriented book and highlights the work of leading scholars who connect spirituality to mainstream organizational research.

Heart at Work: Stories and Strategies for Building Self-Esteem and Reawakening the Soul at Work, edited by Jack Canfield and Jacqueline Miller (McGraw-Hill, New York, 1996), and *Chicken Soup for the Soul at Work: 101 Stories of Compassion and Creativity in the Workplace,* edited by Jack Canfield, Mark Victor Hansen, Maida Rogerson, Martin Rutte and Tim Clauss (Health Communications, Deerfield Beach, FL, 1996). These books are useful even in firms where the word 'spirituality' seems anathema. They also provide insights into workplace issues for clergy, therapists and vocational counsellors.

Holy Work: Be Love, Be Blessed, Be a Blessing, by Marsha Sinetar (Crossroad, New York, 1998). By the author of *Do What you Love the Money Will Follow,* which is credited with transforming the vocational consulting field and popularizing the concept of right livelihood.

How to Get a Job You'll Love: A Practical Guide to Unlocking Your Talents and Finding Your Ideal Career, by John Lees (Higher Education, 2003).
This book takes a refreshing look at career planning. It teaches you how to think outside the box, tap into your hidden talents and identify what type of career you really want.

Love the Work You're With: Find the Job You Always Wanted Without Leaving the One You Have, by Richard C. Whitely (Henry Holt, New York, 2001). Well researched and easily readable tools for transforming your work – even if your organization does not change.

Practicing the Power of Now: Meditations and Exercises and Core Teachings for Living the Liberated Life, by Eckhart Tolle (New World Library, 2003).

A collection of simple meditations and exercises helps readers heighten their consciousness of the present and live in the moment more completely.

The Call by David Spangler (Riverhead Books, New York, 1992). How divine love is interpreted through the various traditions; our need to listen carefully so we can know who we are and what we are called to do.

The Dignity of Difference: How to Avoid the Clash of Civilizations, by Jonathan Sacks (Continuum International Publishing, 2003).
Rabbi Jonathan Sacks presents the first major statement by a Jewish leader on the ethics of globalization and sheds fresh light on global challenges. Sacks argues that we must learn to make space for difference, since the unity of the Creator is expressed in the diversity of creation.

The Gatehouse: A Book about Business, A Story about Life, by Craig Elkins (Beaver's Pond Press, 2003). See www.gatehousealliance.com for details.

The Power of Purpose: Creating Meaning in your Life and Work by Richard J. Leider (Berrett-Koehler, San Francisco, 1997). An often-quoted book on how to use your talents purposively in a mission greater than yourself. For individual and group use.

The Seven-Day Weekend – The Wisdom Revolution: Finding the Work/Life Balance, by Richard Semler (Century, 2003). Semler is the author of *Maverick*, a bestselling book detailing how he overturned control-based management. *Maverick* became a must-read for MBA students everywhere, and this follow-up book shows how a deep belief in the capacity, intelligence and desire for fulfilment of his fellow human beings has led to continuing, sustainable and enjoyable business success.

The Soul Search: a Spiritual Journey to Intimacy with God, by Gary Collins (STL, 1998). New spiritualities and Christian spirituality contrasted. Collins discusses why many people are interested in spirituality and not religion. He encourages readers to be tolerant enough to reconsider Christian spirituality.

Weaving Complexity and Business: Engaging the Soul at Work, by Roger Lewin and Birute Regine (Texere Publishing, 2001).
This is the paperback edition of *The Soul at Work: Unleashing the Power of Complexity Science for Business Success*. Lewin is a science writer, Regine a psychologist. This book explores how complexity offers a mental and practical framework to come to terms with today's profound changes. It provides business leaders with a deeper understanding of the organizational dynamics of today's fast-paced, changing business environment.

APPENDICES

1

The Story of Our Universe

(This story is usually told in 'old science' style, i.e. without reference to meaning, purpose or direction. Here we attempt to tell the story from a spiritual point of view, while at the same time using recent scientific insights. The account is partly based on Russell Stannard's little book on science and religion, *Doing Away with God?* [1])

Our universe began its creative unfolding with the Big Bang some 15 billion years ago. With that almighty explosion time and space began. All that would come to be was potentially present in that original fireball. The blast was just the right strength to get evolution under way. Had it been the tiniest fraction more violent, matter would have dispersed too quickly to condense and form galaxies and stars. Had it been the tiniest fraction less violent the matter of the universe would have collapsed back on itself.

The early universe contained only the lightest elements – hydrogen and helium. It required 'ovens' to transform a portion of them into the heavier elements needed to build rocks and rivers and the bodies of living creatures. It found them in the stars. By burning at precisely the right temperature, these ovens enabled the nuclei of the two light elements to fuse with one another and so produce the heavier elements, notably carbon – on which all life depends.

The next challenge was to get these newly-formed elements locked in the middle of stars out into space. Stars are so big that they have huge gravity, and to prevent them collapsing in on themselves the particles at their centres need to rush around sufficiently furiously to keep the neighbouring particles at a distance. Stars, though, eventually grow old. The particles at their centres slow down and can no longer keep the stars from imploding. As this happens, the matter of each star becomes so dense that things get totally out of control. The result is a huge explosion. The star has become a supernova. The matter of the exploded star gets hurled out into space, making it available for further development.

The ejected material gathers together to form new stars – like our Sun – and the debris surrounding them coalesces to form planets. Benefiting from a rare combination of favourable conditions, evolution was able to proceed further on at least one of them – our Earth. From inanimate chemicals, primitive life-forms gradually appeared. The universal tendency of matter to become both more complex and more conscious, coupled with natural selection, succeeded at length in producing life-forms with sufficiently intricate brains to become conscious. In time these were succeeded by self-conscious beings, ourselves. It has taken evolution on Earth 4.5 billion years to progress this far. And now our species seems poised to cross a new threshold – into super-consciousness.

In the course of this long unfolding, many crises have occurred. There have been major destructions and, at the level of life, major extinctions. But each threat has served as a challenge to give birth to something new and more advanced. So while from our human point of view the universe's methods appear very wasteful, the net result has always been further progress onwards and upwards.

2

God Within

(The following is a much-abbreviated version of part of a lecture given by David at Ridley Hall, Cambridge, in June 2001. It is an attempt to show that the idea of 'God within' forms part of orthodox Christian teaching about God.)

St Paul and the New Testament

Paul frequently speaks of Christians as members of the Body of Christ and as being 'in Christ'. Many New Testament scholars believe that for Paul 'the Body' is more than just a vivid metaphor. Rather, it is a mystical reality. Christians are actually 'in' Christ; we share in his christhood. Christhood is therefore something in us, and insofar as Jesus' christhood is divine, then we as 'body of Christ' possess the divine in us.

Paul's teaching on the body is not the only instance in the New Testament of the idea of divinity within. One thinks of texts such as 'in him we live and move and have our being', 'abide in me as I abide in you' and the idea of meeting Christ himself in the hungry, the thirsty etc.[2] In 2 Peter 1.4 Christians are described as 'participants in the divine nature'. This is not a verse that gets preached on much in the Christian West, but for the Christian East it is very much a favourite text.

Eastern Christianity

Eastern Christians (the various 'orthodox' traditions) take the verse from 2 Peter quite literally. The ideas of human deification and 'God within' are favourite ones in the early Church:

- For Clement of Alexandria, Christian perfection consists in the knowledge of the good and assimilation to God.
- Athanasius speaks often of the deification to which created beings are called.
- Basil writes, 'Man is a creature who has received a commandment to become God.'

- Cyril teaches that we participate in Christ's divinity and are indeed penetrated by divinity.
- Symeon, called 'the New Theologian', has a favourite image of God – light – and declares, 'I have often seen the light and sometimes it has appeared to me within myself'.

Readers may be unfamiliar with the names here mentioned, but these – like those referred to below – are all key figures in the history of Christianity.

Western Christian mysticism

You might suppose that all this stands in marked contrast to the theology and spirituality of Western Christianity. Not so! There has been a strand in Western Christianity which has reflected these conceptions.

- Hildegard of Bingen sees God not just in human beings but in every creature.
- Mechtild of Magdeburg reports that in one of her 'soul dialogues' God said to her, 'I who am divine am truly in you [. . .] I am in you and you are in me. We could not be any closer; we two are fused into one.'
- Meister Eckhart declares, 'God created all things in such a way that they are not outside himself.'
- Julian of Norwich sees 'no difference between God and our substance but as if it were all God'.

We could go on producing examples in the same vein, such as the reference in the Rule of Benedict to the effect that in receiving guests one receives Christ; or the belief of George Fox, founder of the Society of Friends, that the divine spark and image are found in everyone. In our own day there is Matthew Fox and the creation spirituality movement.

There are therefore strong traditions within Christianity which emphasize the idea of God within.

3

The New Age and SaW

In his book *What is the New Age Still Saying to the Churches?* Christian writer John Drane speaks of the New Age as 'a growing movement towards a do-it-yourself spirituality which exhibits a robust disregard for religious establishments of all kinds, yet at the same time is rooted in traditions from the past, though expressed in ways that have immediate relevance to the felt needs of the day'.[3]

Some of the more common New Age themes as noted by Drane are:

- There is a *life force*, *energy field* or *consciousness* that animates the whole of existence. All things – from humans, to animals, plants, rocks and stars – are 'bound together into one great system by this energy force that is common to them all. In fact, this energy field is the only ultimate reality there is, which means that finding true meaning and fulfilment in life is a matter of recognizing and accepting one's place in the great cosmic scheme of things'.[4]

- There are available to us *influences from beyond the present world or from higher planes*. These 'entities' are thought to possess greater wisdom than we do and can see things from a wider perspective, and therefore have a special role in alerting us to the real meaning of our lives.
- *We create our own reality*. Many New Agers believe we have no limitations apart from those we place on ourselves, and that we *choose* to be who we are.
- There is a *higher self*, or *the superconscious, oversoul, God-self*, or *Christ-consciousness*. It is through our higher self that we choose to be who we are.[5]
- *Reincarnation* is also commonly accepted among New Agers, which is to be expected in a movement profoundly attracted to the Eastern religions.
- *Environmental concern* is also prominent, often coupled with widespread acceptance of Lovelock's Gaia hypothesis (see our Chapter 6) – except that many New Agers, unlike Lovelock himself, see Gaia as a spiritual entity, around which there has been a revival of Earth Mother Goddess worship and other aspects of neo-paganism.[6]

Drane points out the moral dangers that can stem from the idea that 'we create, or choose, our own reality'. For it can follow, on that view, that those who are disadvantaged or victims of abuse etc. have chosen their situation; in which case we can disregard their needs and pass by on the other side, and at the same time congratulate ourselves for choosing to be rich and successful.

The New Age writer Gary Zukav has an alternative explanation: the karmic need of the disadvantaged may be for a situation in which they can be recipients of compassion. If that is the case, then those who are more fortunate have a moral duty of love towards such people. This reference to Zukav highlights the need to study (alongside someone like Drane, who writes about the New Age from outside its ranks) someone who speaks from the inside. Zukav's book *The Seat of the Soul*[7] fits the bill admirably, providing a coherent philosophy embracing most of the New Age themes highlighted above.

It is unfortunate that in his treatment of the New Age as it relates to business John Drane emphasizes only its more bizarre or morally questionable aspects. He refers mainly to books and practices that are at the wacky end of the New Age spectrum.

It is difficult to say what proportion of people in SaW are following, or have followed – as some no doubt have at one stage or another – a distinctly New Age path. Our impression though is that most of the people we have met or read about, or whose books we have studied, would have little sympathy for the more extreme or bizarre aspects of New Age belief.

Many SaW writers, and writers quoted by them, either make no reference at all to the New Age or show ambivalence towards it. Some make distinctly hostile remarks about it. The following quotes between them probably reflect the balance of SaW opinion:

- Michal Levin: 'Spirituality does not equate with superstition. Crystals, incense, chants, gurus, tarot cards, even alternative therapies may all be offered up as new forms of spirituality. Some may play no useful role other than increasing our superstition quotient, and making us vulnerable to those who wield power by playing with the forces of fear. Some may bring us closer to the deeper mysteries which perhaps an inner instinctual or even intuitive sense suggests. But at the same time they may affront our intelligence, or do little to build our sense of well-being in and for the world.'[8]
- Levin again: 'There is a great temptation to fall into what is sometimes called "spiritual shopping". Never really following through with one course of ideas because another, that promises better or quicker results, appears.'[9]
- Sullivan: 'A spiritual journey is more than a trip.'[10]

Our remarks about SaW writers also apply to SaW practitioners. The 'spiritual' CEOs David met on sabbatical rarely referred to the New Age. One who did said he wished to have nothing to do with 'New Age hocus-pocus'. However, it would appear that many who are unwilling to have the actual label 'New Age' attached to them have in fact taken on board aspects of New Age thinking. It is difficult to draw firm conclusions about the degree to which the New Age has influenced SaW.

Notes

Introduction

1 1802–85, French poet, novelist and playwright.
2 Some in the movement speak of 'spirituality at work', others prefer 'spirit at work'. Our slight preference is for the latter phrase. We shall use throughout the book the abbreviation 'SaW', which will satisfy both camps! Other commonly used phrases are 'spirit(uality) in the workplace', 'spirit(uality) in business'. They can all be regarded as synonymous.
3 Howard, 2000.
4 Welbourn, 2000.
5 It will be noted that in this sentence the word spirit appears twice and each time is spelt with a small 's'. We have thought long and hard about whether and when 'spirit' should be capitalized. In Chapter 3 we shall be discussing the suggestion that big 'S' should be used when the subject is a transcendent spiritual reality (Reality?), e.g. the divine Spirit, and little 's' when speaking of lowlier realities, e.g. the human spirit. But quite often we shall be wanting to discuss both aspects at the same time, and then the choice becomes problematical. In the SaW literature there is no consistency in this matter: usage varies from writer to writer, with the majority preferring small 's'. This is the usage we have decided to follow, except in quotations when of course we adhere to the usage of the writer being quoted. A similar problem arises in connection with 'self' and 'Self'. Again, except when specifically discussing Jung's teaching about the Self (see Chapter 4), we shall adopt lower case.

Chapter 1   Global Issues and Workplace Sensibilities

1 In Renesch and DeFoore, 1996, p. 273.
2 See Egan and Wilson, 2002, pp. 49–50.
3 The Industrial Society has been restructured; see Chapter 15 under Other Organizations, Work Foundation.
4 Wheatley, 2002, p. 123.
5 Sullivan, 2003, p. xxi.
6 In Renesch and DeFoore, 1996, p. 272.
7 In Renesch and DeFoore, 1996, p. 45.
8 In Renesch and DeFoore, 1996, pp. 192–3.
9 Helliwell, 2000, quoted in McGeachy, 2001, pp. 78–9.
10 In Biberman and Whitty, 2000, p. 283.
11 Korac-Kakabadse in the *Journal of Managerial Psychology*, Special issue on 'Spirituality, Leadership, Work and Organizations', 2002, pp. 151–2.
12 See www.deepermind.com/maslow.htm.

13 Zohar and Marshall, 2001, Chapter 2.
14 Zohar, 1997, p. 67.
15 Zohar, 1997, p. 69.
16 Wheatley, 2002, p. 127.
17 Welbourn, 2000, p. 37.
18 Moore, 1992, p. 187.
19 In Renesch and DeFoore, 1996, p. 250.
20 In Biberman and Whitty, 2000, p. 285.
21 McGeachy, 2001, p. 11.

Chapter 2 Disconnection and Reconnection: The New Paradigm

1 In Renesch and DeFoore, 1996, p. 192.
2 Zohar, 1997, p. 8.
3 Whyte, 1999, p. 4.
4 Kuhn, 1996.
5 Wilber, 2001b.
6 Wilber, 2001b, p. 8.
7 Wilber, 2001a.
8 Russell, 2000.
9 Capra, 1982.
10 Davies, 1990.
11 Davies, 1993.
12 Davies and Gribbin, 1991.
13 Sheldrake, 1991.
14 Sheldrake, 1985.
15 Sheldrake, 1988.
16 Grof, 2000.
17 These are administered under tightly controlled conditions.
18 Adams, 1998a.
19 Briskin, 1998.
20 In Adams, 1998a, pp. ix–xiii.
21 In Adams, 1998a, pp. 28–9, 33–4, 38.

Chapter 3 What is Spirituality?

1 Fox, 1991, pp. 11–12.
2 Block, 1993, p. 48.
3 Turner, 1999, pp. 41–2.
4 See Welbourn, 2000.
5 Moxley, 2000, p. 24.
6 Owen, 1987, pp. 2, 6.
7 Tredget, 2000, pp. 4–8.
8 P. Sheldrake, 1995, p. 58.
9 Turner, 1999, pp. 41–2.
10 Joseph, 2002, p. 35.
11 Ó Murchú, 1997, p. 61.
12 Rowan, 1993, p. 9.
13 Maslow, 1970, p. 273.
14 Joseph, 2002, p. 208.
15 Briskin, 1998, p. 37.
16 Whyte, 1999, pp. 12, 14.
17 Moore, 1992, pp. 233–63.

18 Briskin, 1998, p. 18.
19 Howard, 2000, p. 76.
20 Whyte, 1999, pp. 13–14.
21 Scott Peck, 1993, p. 234.
22 Jung, cited in Jaworski, 1998, p. 191.
23 Moxley, 2000, p. 23.
24 Gibbons, 1999, pp. 14–15.
25 Moxley, 2000, p. 8.
26 Lips-Wiersma and Mills, 2002, p. 183.
27 Mitroff and Denton, 1999a, p. 84.
28 Lips-Wiersma and Mills, p. 183.
29 Mitroff and Denton, 1999a.
30 Joseph, 2000, pp. 3–5.
31 Moxley, 2000, pp. 22–4.
32 Mitroff and Denton, 1999a, p. 83. As our later discussion of higher power indicates, we understand 'being connected with . . . the entire universe' to include the divine or generative power which underpins the universe, which many of us call 'God'.

Chapter 4   Connecting with Self

1 Second-century saint and theologian.
2 Rilke, 2001.
3 King and Nicol, 2000, p. 138.
4 Senge, 1995, p. 220.
5 Adapted from Whyte, 1999, p. 18.
6 Sullivan, 2003, p. 25.
7 Campbell, 1968.
8 Moore, 1992.
9 Moore, 1992, p. 229.
10 King and Nicol, 2000, p. 139.
11 Peppers and Briskin, 2000, p. 57.
12 Briggs and Myers, 1995.
13 Storr, 1995.
14 Hayman, 1999.
15 Pearson, 1998.
16 Peppers and Briskin, 2000.
17 Moore, 1992, p. 133.
18 Scott Peck, 1993, p. 25.
19 Whyte, 1999, p. 45.
20 Whyte, 1999, p. 20.
21 Williamson, 1996, pp. 190–1.
22 Peppers and Briskin, 2000, p. 70.
23 Smith, 1987, p. 46.
24 Williams, 1999, p. 206.
25 Williams, 1999, p. 200.
26 Smith, 1987, p. 27.
27 Romans 7.19.
28 Morgan, 1986, p. 255.
29 Moore, 1992, pp. 259–60.
30 Wilber, 2001a.
31 Rowan, 1993, p. 107.
32 Rowan, 1993, p. 111.
33 Rowan, 1993, p. 119.
34 Rowan, 1993, p. 112.

35 Heron, 1988.
36 Wilber, 2001a, p. 199.
37 Wilber, 2001a, p. 142.
38 Rowan, 1993, p. 116.
39 Rowan, 1993, p. 119.
40 Gardner, 1993.
41 Goleman, 1996.
42 Goleman, 1998, p. 317.
43 Tischler, Biberman and McCeage, 2002, p. 212.
44 As a cautionary note, the branding of both our emotions and our spirituality as an 'intelli-
    gence' has troubled some. There have been criticisms of both the EQ and SQ approaches.
45 Emmons, 2000.
46 Levin, 2001.
47 McGeachy, 2001.
48 Zohar and Marshall, 2001.
49 Zohar and Marshall, 2001, pp. 3–4.
50 Holland, 1997.
51 Zohar and Marshall, 2001, p. 8.
52 Extracted from Tischler *et al*, 2001, p. 211.
53 Zohar and Marshall, 2001, p. 35.
54 Jaworski, 1998, p. xi.
55 Adair, 2000.
56 Knight, 1995.
57 N. Williams, 1999.
58 N. Williams, 1999, p. 22.
59 Buckingham and Clifton, 2002.
60 Wheatley, 1999, p. 167.
61 Buber, quoted by Jaworksi, 1996, p. 133.
62 This term is explained in Chapter 5.

Chapter 5   Connecting with Others

1   Needleman, 2001, p. 4.
2   Reason, 1998a, p. 425.
3   Cited in Owen, 1987, pp. 88–9.
4   Moxley, 2000, p. 33.
5   Reason, 1998a, p. 419.
6   Wheatley, 2002, p. 119.
7   Fetzer Institute, 2001.
8   Hurley, 2001, p. 36.
9   See Peppers and Briskin, 2000, pp. 174–6.
10 Senge, 1996, p. 15.
11 Needleman, 2001, p. 4.
12 Hurley, 2001, p. 35.
13 Williams, 1999, p. 200.
14 Williams, 1999, p. 203.
15 Hurley, 2001, p. 37, from a dialogue with Alan Briskin.
16 Isaacs, 1999, p. 159.
17 Hurley, 2001, p. 40.
18 Hurley, 2001, p. 41.
19 Bohm, 1995, p. ix .
20 Isaacs, 1999, p. 39.
21 Extracted from Zohar, 1997, p. 46.
22 Jaworski, 1998, pp. 80–1, from a taped conversation with Bohm.

23 Musson and Cohen, 1999, p. 34.
24 Isaacs, 1994, pp. 359–60.
25 Isaacs, 1999, p. 6.
26 Wheatley, 2002, pp. 32–3.
27 Reason, 1998a, p. 421.
28 Dixon, 1998, p. 51.
29 Dixon, 1998, p. 53.
30 Quoted by Potter, 1996, p. 266.
31 Marcic, 1997.
32 Williams, 1999, p. 220.
33 Cited in Williams, 1999, p. 227.
34 Wheatley, 2002, p. 22.

Chapter 6   Connecting with Nature

1 Macy, 1991, p. 14.
2 See www.earthsummit2002.org.
3 See again the description of Wilber's levels of spiritual awareness above, p. 54.
4 Skynner and Cleese, 1993, pp. 289–93.
5 Jaworski, 1998, pp. 51–2.
6 Jaworski, 1998, p. 55.
7 Fox, 1988, pp. 32–3.
8 R. Sheldrake, 1990, pp. 180–9.
9 R. Sheldrake, 1990, p. xii.
10 R. Sheldrake, 1990, p. xiii.
11 We are all scientists now – whether professional scientists or not – to the extent that we have embraced a scientific worldview.
12 R. Sheldrake, 1990, p. 58.
13 R. Sheldrake, 1990, p. 181.
14 R. Sheldrake, 1990, p. 180.
15 Fox, 1994, p. 192.
16 Fox, 1994, p. 194.
17 Lovelock, 2000a, 2000b.
18 Ruether, 1993, Chapters 6, 7.
19 Wilber, 2001a.
20 Moore, 1992, p. 186.
21 Moore, 1992, pp. 267–8.
22 Moore, 1992, p. 270.
23 Moore, 1992, p. 271.
24 Moore, 1992, p. 186.
25 Schumacher, 1980, p. 121.
26 Fox, 1994, pp. 27–8.
27 Stephens and Isen, 1998, p. 219.
28 Owen, 1998, pp. 246, 257.
29 R. Sheldrake, 1990, pp. 10–12.
30 Ruether, 1993, pp. 15–26.
31 Ruether, 1993, Chapter 2.
32 Fox, 1994, pp. 5, 24, 62.
33 Swimme and Berry, 1992, p. 1.
34 Fox, 1994, p. 9.
35 Fox, 1994, p. 63.
36 Fox, 1994, p. 65.
37 Fox, 1994, p. 69.
38 Fox, 1994, p. 298.

39 Ruether, 1993, pp. 40–7.
40 Swimme and Berry, 1992.
41 Ruether, 1993, Chapter 4.
42 Fox, 1994, p. 59.
43 Rilke is much-quoted in the SaW literature. He is described by Thomas Moore (1992, p. 75) as 'the poet of [the] philosophy of transforming the everyday into the sacred, the visible into the invisible'. Moore goes on to quote one of Rilke's letters of 1925, where the poet states: 'Our task is to stamp this provisional, perishing earth into ourselves so deeply, so painfully and passionately, that it may rise again "invisibly" in us.'
44 Fox, 1994, p. 61.
45 Fox, 1994, p. 128.
46 The Tao is the basic principle underlying the whole way the universe works.
47 *Tao Te Ching*, tr. Mitchell, 1999, Section 39.
48 In the SaW literature, in order to be inclusive of the non-Christian religions, the convention BCE (Before the Common Era), and CE (Common Era) are used instead of BC and AD.
49 Fox, 1994, p. 6.
50 Fox, 1994, p. 105.
51 Fox, 1994, p. 75.
52 Fox, 1994, p. 3.
53 Fox, 1987, p. 35.
54 Fox, 1994, p. 22.
55 Fox, 1994, p. 9.
56 *Bhagavad Gita*, tr. Mascaro, p. 62.
57 *Bhagavad Gita*, tr. Mascaro, pp. 58–9, 62–3.
58 *Bhagavad Gita*, tr. Mascaro, p. 58.
59 Hobday, 1992, p. 20.
60 *Bhagavad Gita*, tr. Mascaro, p. 66.
61 Jaworski, 1998, p. 144.
62 *Tao Te Ching*, 1999, Sections 9, 24.
63 Pieper, 1965, p. 44.
64 Fox, 1994, p. 72.
65 Fox, 1994, p. 4.
66 Lawrence, 1968, p. 258.

Chapter 7 Connecting with Higher Power

1 Rowan, 1993, p. 2.
2 Fox, 1994, p. 64.
3 Fox, 1994, p. 64.
4 Fox, 1994, p. 111.
5 Fox, 1994, p. 68.
6 Fox, 1994, p. 123.
7 Fox, 1994, p. 124.
8 Fox, 1994, p. 301.
9 See note 48 in Chapter 6.
10 Ruether, 1993, pp. 240–5.
11 Ruether, 1993, p. 245.
12 Teilhard de Chardin, 1964.
13 King, 1997.
14 Ruether, 1993, pp. 246–7.
15 Rowan, 1993, p. 3.
16 James, 1974.
17 Butts, 2000, p. 38.
18 Rowan, 1993.

19 Grof, 1979, pp. 155–6.
20 Quoted in Rowan, 1993, p. 7.
21 Fabry, 1980, p. 81.
22 Hay, 1990.
23 Anthony *et al*, 1987, p. 188.
24 Hay, 1990, p. 50, cited in Rowan, 1993, p. 21.
25 Maslow, 1973, p. 185.
26 Wren-Lewis, 1991, p. 6.
27 Cited in Rowan, 1993, p. 24. No reference given.
28 Introduced in Chapter 4.
29 See Chapter 6.
30 Wilber, 2001a, p. 192.
31 Rowan, 1993, p. 16.
32 Wilber, 2001a, p. 191.
33 Wilber, 2001a, p. 197.
34 Rowan, 1993, p. 26.
35 See Chapter 5.
36 From Senge's introduction to Jaworski's *Synchronicity*, 1996, p. 6.
37 Zohar, 1997, p. 197.
38 John 1.1. The *logos* in Greek philosophy was the organizing principle behind the whole universe (cf. the *tao* in Taoism).
39 Chopra, 2000, p. 11.
40 Jaworski, 1998, p. ix.
41 In Jaworski, 1998, pp. 12ff. Emphasis in original.
42 Jaworski, 1998, p. 126.
43 Wilber, 2001a, p. 136.
44 Zohar and Marshall, 2001, p. 177.
45 Zohar and Marshall, 2001, p. 178.
46 Zohar and Marshall, 2001, p. 178.
47 Zohar and Marshall, 2001, p. 178.
48 Zohar and Marshall, 2001, pp. 178–9.
49 Zohar and Marshall, 2001, p. 180.
50 Wheatley, 2002, p. 8.
51 Jung, 1973, p. 30.
52 Fox, 1983.
53 Levin, 2001, pp. 326–35.
54 Levin, 2001, p. 326.
55 Levin, 2001, p. 328.
56 Levin, 2001, p. 332.
57 Zohar, 1997, p. 3.
58 McGeachy, 2001, p. 146.
59 In Renesch and DeFoore, 1996, pp. 287–8.
60 Moore, 1992, p. 47.
61 Moore, 1992, p. 144.
62 Delbecq, in *Journal of Management Inquiry*, September 2001, pp. 221–6.
63 Harrison, 1998, p. 115.
64 Harrison, 1998, pp. 115–16.
65 Ruether, 1993, pp. 115–16.
66 e.g. Murphy and Donovan, 1996.
67 Heaton, 2000, p. 321.
68 Kabat-Zinn, 1994.
69 See Kriger and Hanson, 2000, p. 343.
70 de Mello, 1984.
71 Sogyal Rinpoche, 1998.

72 Witten, 1999.
73 Rowan, 1993, pp. 80–5.
74 Zohar and Marshall, 2001, p. 196.
75 Zohar and Marshall, 2001, p. 184.
76 Sullivan, 2003, p. xxiv, citing Fox, 2001.
77 Sullivan, 2003, p. 9.
78 Sullivan, 2003, p. 10.
79 Sullivan, 2003, p. xxiv. See also our Resources chapter.
80 Sullivan, 2003, p. 81.
81 See Sullivan, 2003, p. 75.
82 In Biberman and Whitty, p. 185.
83 Chopra, 2000.
84 Jaworski, 1996, pp. 129–30.
85 Peppers and Briskin, 2000.
86 In Biberman and Whitty, 2000, p. 364.
87 Fox, 1994, especially Chapter 7.
88 Fox, 1994, p. 266.
89 Fox, 1994, pp. 292–3, 313–14.
90 Guss, 2000, pp. 365–6.
91 Levin, 2001, especially Chapters 4 and 5.
92 In his guest chapter (20) in Nixon, 2000.
93 Capra, 1983, Chapter 10.
94 Sullivan, 2003, pp. xiv, 79.
95 Sullivan, 2003, pp. 80–1.

Chapter 8 Religion and Spirituality: Our Journey in Faith

1 Sullivan, 2003, pp. xix –xx.
2 In Biberman and Whitty, p. 56.
3 In Biberman and Whitty, p. 113.
4 McGeachy, 2001, p. 60.
5 McGeachy, 2001, p. 61.
6 Slee, 2003, p. 95.
7 H. Smith, 1991.
8 Monism is a philosophy which denies any distinction between God and the world or, as in the case of Buddhism, denies there is a specifically divine reality.
9 Thich Nhat Hanh, 1998.
10 Sogyal Rinpoche, 1998.
11 Sullivan, 2003.
12 See Welbourn, 2000.
13 Quoted on the credits page of *The Heart of the Buddha's Teaching*.
14 In Renesch and DeFoore, 1996, pp. 36–7.
15 Quoted in Zohar and Marshall, 2001, p. 10.
16 Maitland, 1995, p. 50.
17 Ó Murchú, 1997, pp. 2–4.
18 Fox, 1983.
19 Fox, 1988.
20 Fox, 1988, pp. 47–67.
21 Fox, 1994.
22 Kriger and Hanson, 2000, pp. 332–44.
23 Kriger and Hanson, 2000, p. 340.
24 Moore, 1992, pp. 180–1.
25 Moore, 1992, p. 183.
26 Moore, 1992, p. 181.

27 Wheatley, 2002, p. 119.
28 Chopra, 2000.
29 Chopra, 1994.
30 Fields *et al* in Whitmeyer, 1994; cited by Gibbons, 2000, pp 123–4.
31 Sullivan, 2003, p. 62.
32 See Boje, 2000, pp. 77–91.
33 Richmond, 2000.
34 Whitmeyer, 1994, cited by Gibbons, 2000, p. 117.
35 McGeachy, 2001, p. 42.
36 See Levin, 2001, pp. 237–9.
37 O'Connor, 1971.
38 McGeachy, 2001, p. 111.
39 The subtitle of one of his more recent books; Fox, 2003.
40 Berg, 2003, p. 52.
41 Berg, 2003, pp. 58–60.
42 Sullivan, 2003, p. 4.
43 Brueggemann, 2001.
44 There are many examples of this in Lamont, 2002.
45 Haessly, 1996, p. 110.
46 Haessly, 1998, pp. 113, 115. A good introduction to Christian feminist theology is Slee, 2003.
47 McGeachy, 2001, p. 25.
48 Sullivan, 2003, pp. 64–5.
49 Sullivan, 2003, p. 83.
50 Sullivan, 2003, p. 46.
51 Sullivan, 2003, p. 96.
52 See Mark 10.42–5; John 13.3–15.
53 In Adams, 1998, Chapter 5.
54 It may be argued, however, that Wilber's conception of 'finally stepping off the ladder altogether' represents a compromise of that principle. We recall a similar criticism by Ruether of part of Teilhard's philosophy (see above, p. 84). It has to be admitted that Christianity has not always consistently adhered to its officially held belief in 'the resurrection of the body'.
55 However, we should not forget that (a) the majority of workers no longer work with matter/material (agriculture, manufacturing) but in services with ideas and concepts, and (b) the 'new science' regards matter as 'packets of energy'. Perhaps therefore the distinction between matter and non-matter is not ultimately sustainable. See Davies and Gribbin, 1991.
56 In a telephone interview with Pat Sullivan, reported in Sullivan, 2003, pp. 71–2.
57 Bayrak, 1985. Cited by Kriger and Hanson, 2000, p. 340.
58 In Biberman and Whitty, 2000, p. 340.
59 Pir Vilayat Inayat Khan, 2000.
60 Pir Vilayat Inayat Khan, 2000, p. 129.
61 Pir Vilayat Inayat Khan, 2000, p. 130.
62 Pir Vilayat Inayat Khan, 2000, p. 132.
63 Pir Vilayat Inayat Khan, 2000, p. 132.
64 Quoted in Renesch and DeFoore, 1996, p. 83.
65 Wheatley, 2002, p. 107.
66 Sullivan, 2003, p. 58.
67 Sullivan, 2003, p. 59.
68 Our colleague Alan Harpham reports once hearing Bear Grills (the youngest Englishman ever to climb Mount Everest) say that 'you do not conquer a mountain like Everest; if you are lucky it lets you both climb it and return safely to sea level'.
69 In Renesch and DeFoore, 1996, p. 325.
70 Sullivan, 2003, p. 83.
71 Arrien, 1993.

Chapter 9   Becoming an Authentic Leader

1 We have no references for these quotes – one was from a sermon, the other from a charity magazine.
2 Cited in Kippenberger, 2002, p. 6.
3 Drucker, 1996, cited in Kippenberger, 2002, p. 9.
4 Buckingham and Coffman, 1999.
5 In Kippenberger, 2002, p. 56.
6 Wagner-Marsh and Conley, 2000, p. 204.
7 Quoted in Kippenberger, 2002, p. 10.
8 Heuerman, Web pamphlet 47. See Chapter 15, under Other Diverse Resources for details.
9 Mintzberg, 1976, quoted in Korac-Kakabadse *et al*, 2002, p. 83.
10 Korac-Kakabadse *et al*, 2002, p. 168.
11 Delbecq, 2000, pp. 117–28.
12 Marshall, 2000.
13 Turner, 1999, pp. 41–2.
14 Moxley, 2000, p. 10.
15 Rieser, 1995, p. 50.
16 Rieser, 1995, p. 52.
17 Block, 1993, p. 6.
18 Covey, 1992.
19 Senge, in Adams, 1998b, p. 158.
20 Greenleaf, quoted in Spears, 1995, p. 57.
21 Jaworski, 1998, p. 44.
22 Wheatley, 1999, p. 165.
23 Zohar, 1997, pp. 146, 153–4. See also Marcic, 1997.
24 Wheatley, 1999, p. 39.

Chapter 10   Spirituality and Learning: Being in Community

1 Dixon, 1998, p. 13.
2 Gibbons, 1999, p. 62.
3 Vaill, 1998b, p. 188.
4 Vaill, 1998b, p. 150.
5 Vaill, 1998a, p. 29.
6 Vaill, 1998a, p. 42. (Vaill derives this concept from the German existentialist philosopher Heidegger.)
7 Senge, 1990.
8 Easterby-Smith, 1997.
9 Porth, McCall and Bausch, 2000, p. 251.
10 Bartlett and Ghoshal, 1995, pp. 132–42.
11 Gratton, 2000, pp. 12–16.
12 Cunningham, in Burgoyne and Reynolds, 1997, p. 180.
13 Vaill, 1998b, p. 199.
14 Porth, McCall and Bausch, 2000, pp. 252–3.
15 Woodhall and Winstanley, 1998.
16 Burgoyne and Reynolds, 1997.
17 Wilmott, citing Watson, in Burgoyne and Reynolds, 1997, p. 173.
18 Both 2002.
19 Wilmott, in Burgoyne and Reynolds, 1997, p. 162.
20 Burgoyne and Reynolds, 1997, p. 179.
21 Burgoyne and Reynolds, 1997, p. 12.
22 Mezirow, 1991, p. 155.
23 Mezirow, 1991, p. 11.

24 Mezirow, 1991, p. 35.
25 Buckley and Perkins, in Adams, 1998a, p. 73.
26 Freire, cited in Mezirow, 1991, pp. xvi–xvii.
27 Bateson, 1973, p. 250.
28 Hawkins, 1991, pp. 172–87.
29 Owen, 1987, p. 5.
30 Porth *et al.*, 2000, p. 252.
31 In Reason, 1998b, p. 42.
32 Knowles, 1980, cited in Bell and Taylor, 2002, p. 5.
33 Reid, 1986, p. 20, cited in Bell and Taylor, 2002, p. 3.
34 Chia, 1997, p. 82.
35 Chia, 1997, p. 85.
36 Chia, 1997, p. 85.
37 Chia, 1997, p. 86.
38 Chia, 1997, p. 85.
39 In Adams, 1998a, p. 140.
40 Adams, 1998a, p. 145.
41 Ackerman Anderson, in Adams, 1998a, p. 151.
42 Csikzentmihalyi, 1998.
43 Lievegoed, 1991, p. 124.
44 Chia, 1997, pp. 78, 85.
45 As told by Williams, 1999, pp. 84–5.
46 For the SpiritWorks website, see p. 198.
47 Levine, 1994, p. 71.
48 Senge, 1994, p. 299.
49 Senge, 1994, p. 354.
50 Senge, 1994, p. 355.
51 See www.modem.uk.com.
52 See under Pettifer, 2000, in the Reference section for further details.
53 Senge, 1994, p. 514.
54 Gratton, 2000, p. 54.

Chapter 11   Doing Well by the Planet?

1 In Biberman and Whitty, 2000, p. 111.
2 In Biberman and Whitty, p. 191.
3 For example, Richard Leakey. See Leakey and Lewin, 1992, p. 353.
4 McGeachy, 2001, pp. 19–20.
5 Adams, 1998a, p. 3.
6 In Jaworski, 1998, pp. 4–5.
7 Jaworski, 1998, p. 165.
8 Adams, 1998a, pp. 3, 5.
9 Adams, 1998a, p. 48.
10 Adams, 1998a, pp. 88, 105.
11 Adams, 1998a, p. 167, 173.
12 Adams, 1998a, pp. 283, 287.
13 Korten, 1995 and Korten, 2000.
14 Soros, 1998.
15 Schumacher, 1974.
16 Egan and Wilson, 2002.
17 Hawken and Lovins, 1999.
18 Having not read this volume ourselves yet, we are drawing on a review of it by Paul Darley in the Spring 2002 issue of *Faith in Business Quarterly*.
19 Details about the Centre are found in Chapter 15.

20 January 2003 issue.
21 Heslam, 2004, p. 132.
22 See Renesch and DeFoore, 1996, p. 1.
23 McGeachy, 2001, p. 116.
24 In Biberman and Whitty, 2000, p. 307.
25 Wheatley, 2002, p. 106.
26 Waddock, 2000, p. 306.
27 In Biberman and Whitty, 2000, p. 64.
28 Biberman and Whitty, 2000, pp. 61–2.
29 Fox, 1994, p. 221.
30 Fox, 1994, p. 148.
31 Swimme and Berry, 1992, p. 242.
32 Berry, 1988, p. 34.
33 Berry, 1988, p. 78.
34 See www.stakeholderforum.org.
35 Vol. 1, Nos 3 and 4, 1997.
36 In Biberman and Whitty, 2000, p. 318.
37 In Biberman and Whitty, 2000, p. 306.
38 Capra, 1995.
39 In Biberman and Whitty, pp. 226–7.
40 In Renesch and DeFoore, 1996.
41 In Renesch and DeFoore, 1996, p. 78.
42 Fox, 1994, p. 200.
43 Fox, 1994, p. 230.
44 Cook, 2003, p. 44.
45 In Renesch and DeFoore, 1996, pp. 327–8.
46 See Jaworski, 1998.
47 Reported in McGeachy, 2001, p. 120.
48 Collins and Porras, 1994.
49 Cited in Egan and Wilson, 2002, p. 150.
50 In his Foreword to Renesch and DeFoore, pp. vi–vii.
51 *Business Ethics*, Nov/Dec 1993; cited in Biberman and Whitty, 2000, p. 208.
52 Extracted from the company's Annual Report 2003, which includes several other similar examples.
53 Zohar and Marshall, 2001, pp. 261–2.
54 Skelton, *Spirituality in the Workplace.*
55 Ephesians 6.12.
56 See www.fairtrade.org.uk, www.tradejusticemovement.org.uk and www.jubilee2000uk.org.
57 Levin, 2001.
58 Levin, 2001, pp. 206–7.
59 Levin, 2001, pp. 209–10.
60 Levin, 2001, p. 210.
61 Levin, 2001, p. 343.
62 Levin, 2001, p. 135.

Chapter 12 Unlocking Corporate Transformation: The Work of Spirit in the World of Business

1 Fetzer Institute, 2001, p. 9.
2 Morgan, 1986, p. 138.
3 Zohar, 1997, p. 1.
4 Moxley, 2000, p. 39. We have slightly amended the columns in Table 6.
5 Joseph, 2002, p. 202.
6 Joseph, 2002, p. 221.

 7 Gibbons, 2000, pp. 117–18.
 8 Wilber, 2001a.
 9 Mitroff and Denton, 1999b.
10 The principles of AA embody the idea that addicts, though needing to exert their willpower, are unable to cure their addiction just by their own efforts but are totally reliant on 'higher power'. See Mitroff and Denton, 1999b, p. 102. Mitroff and Denton also outline the Twelve Steps of AA, p. 100. See also www.alcoholics-anonymous.org.
11 Joseph, 2002, p. 209.
12 Mitroff and Denton, 1999b, pp. 175–6.
13 Moxley, 2000, p. 19.
14 Moxley, 2000, p. 19, citing Collins and Porras, 1994.
15 McGeachy, 2001, p. 74.
16 Gibbons, 2000, p. 127.
17 Levin, 2001, p. 109.
18 In Biberman and Whitty, 2000, p. 10.
19 See www.spiritworks.ltd.uk.
20 See www.spiraldynamics.com, or Beck and Cowan, 1996. Also www.5deep.com.
21 www.corptools.com. See Chapter 15, under Consultants, Corp Tools UK Ltd.
22 Barrett, 1998, p. 175.
23 Sullivan, 2003, pp. 45–9.
24 Allen and Kraft in Adams, 1998a, p. 49.
25 Fox, 1991, pp. 18–21.
26 Sullivan, 2003, p. 86.
27 Sullivan, 2003, pp. 50–1.

13 Spirit-led Companies

 1 Wagner-Marsh and Conley, in Biberman and Whitty, 2000, p. 203.
 2 Matthew 7.16.
 3 Biberman and Whitty, 2000.
 4 Lamont, 2002. See also SpiritWorks in Chapter 15, and www.spiritworks.ltd.uk.
 5 This update comes from the SpiritWorks Newsletter, October 2003.
 6 Galatians 5.22–3. The 'fruits' there listed are: love, joy, peace, patience, kindness, generosity, faithfulness, gentleness and self-control.
 7 Joseph, 2002.
 8 See above, pp. 160–1.
 9 Milliman *et al*, 2000.
10 For more on the role of storytelling in reinforcing company culture, see Owen, 1987.
11 Milliman *et al*, 2000, pp. 268–74.
12 Chappell, 1993.
13 DePree, 1992.
14 Melrose, 1995.
15 Hess, 1995.
16 Roddick, 1991.
17 Cohen and Greenfield, 1997. The story of Ben and Jerry's is told in Mitroff and Denton (1999b), who produce many quotes from Cohen and Greenfield's book.
18 Burack, 2000, p. 105
19 Wagner-Marsh and Conley, 2000, p. 106.
20 Mitroff and Denton, 1999b.
21 Campbell, 1968.
22 Burack, 2000, pp. 96–7.
23 Burack, 2000, p. 107.
24 Hogan, 2000, p. 59.
25 Cavanagh, 2000, p. 159.

26 Marcic, 2000, p. 195.
27 Marcic, 2000, pp. 195–6.
28 Marcic, 2000, p. 196.
29 Marcic, 2000, p. 197.
30 Marcic, 2000, p. 199.
31 Burack, 2000, p. 97; Milliman *et al.*, 2000, p. 264.
32 Hogan, 2000, pp. 59–60.
33 Cavanagh, 2000, pp. 159–60.
34 Wagner-Marsh and Conley, 2000, p. 203.
35 Wagner-Marsh and Conley, 2000, p. 205.
36 Wagner-Marsh and Conley, 2000, p. 208.
37 Wagner-Marsh and Conley, 2000, p. 206.
38 Wagner-Marsh and Conley, 2000, p. 209.
39 Wagner-Marsh and Conley, 2000, p. 211.
40 Alkhafagi, 2000, pp. 167, 171.
41 Conger, 1994, quoted by King *et al*, 2000, p. 284.
42 Mitroff and Denton, 1999b, pp. 91–3.
43 Schumacher, 1974, p. 202.

Chapter 14   The Progress and Future of Spirit at Work

 1 Okri, 1999, pp. 14–15.
 2 Sullivan, 2003, p. 115.
 3 This is the result of typing in just the words 'spirituality' and 'business'.
 4 According to Spirituality at Work (see Resources under Spirituality at Work Conversations), in January 2004 SaW publications numbered 219 in the UK and 16,040 in the USA; according to SAW (see next paragraph) those figures were respectively 334 and a staggering 75,423.
 5 Sullivan, 2003, p. xvii.
 6 See Resources.
 7 Judi Neal and the Spirit at Work network she founded have for many years been a comprehensive resource for all aspects of SaW, not just for the USA but for the whole worldwide movement. See Resources.
 8 Hogan, 2000, p. 55 footnote 1.
 9 Cavanagh, 2000, p. 150.
10 Barrett, 1996, p. 32.
11 Levey, 1996, p. 71.
12 Levey, 1996, p. 72.
13 King *et al*, 2000, p. 286.
14 King *et al*, 2000, pp. 288–90.
15 Cavanagh, 2000, p. 162.
16 Delbecq, 2000, p. 176.
17 On the role of the Jesuit Universities, see Konz and Ryan, 2000, pp. 233–44.
18 Neal *et al*, 2000, p. 24.
19 Neal *et al*, 2000, p. 24.
20 Cavanagh, 2000, p. 151.
21 Cavanagh, 2000, p. 152.
22 For details of this article, see under *Wall Street Journal* in our References section.
23 Cavanagh, 2000, p. 157.
24 Welbourn, 2000.
25 McDonald, 1999.
26 King *et al*, 2000, p. 284.
27 For e-mail and/or website addresses of this and all the other organizations, groups and consultancies mentioned from now on in this chapter, see Resources.

28 MODEM, 1999.
29 Watkins' article is reproduced in *IMAgenda*, December 2003 issue.
30 In 2002.
31 From private e-mail correspondence.
32 Makiguchi and Birnbaum, 1989.
33 Chapter 10, p. 131, mentions two useful books which explore this area more fully. See the References section for full details.
34 From SpiritWorks Newsletter, November 2003.
35 SpiritWorks Newsletter, November 2003.
36 See again Chapter 11.
37 E-mail correspondence, November 2003.
38 Renesch and DeFoore, 1996, p. 9.
39 Levin, 2001, p. 264.
40 DeFoore,1996, p. 286.
41 Zohar and Marshall, 2001, p. 16.
42 Levin, 2001, p. 34.
43 Jaworski, 1998, p. 182.
44 Jaworski, 1998, pp. 161–2.
45 Zohar and Marshall, 2001, p. 21.
46 Levin, 2001, p. 33.
47 Levin, 2001, p. 147.
48 Levin, 2001, p. 149.
49 Levin, 2001, p. 246.
50 Levin, 2001, p. 247.
51 McGeachy, 2001, p. 120.
52 Emphases in the original.
53 DeFoore, 1996, pp. 292–3.
54 Renesch and DeFoore, 1996, p. 3.
55 Levin, 2001, p. 149.
56 McGeachy, 2001, p. 77.
57 Ruether, 1993, Chapters 3 and 4.
58 Neal *et al*, 2000, p. 13.
59 Levin, 2001, p. 231.
60 Levin, 2001, p. 104.
61 Lamont, 2002, pp. 9–10.
62 Sullivan, 2003, p. 31.
63 Salz, 2000, p. 23.
64 Levin, 2001, p. 346.
65 Levin, 2001, p. 42.
66 Levin, 2001, p. 347.
67 Levin, 2001, p. 350.
68 Rilke's poem 'Live the Questions'. Rilke, 2001.

Appendices

1 Stannard, 1993.
2 Acts 17.28; John 15.4; Matthew 25.31–46.
3 Drane, 1999, p. x.
4 Drane, 1999, p. 59.
5 Drane, 1999, pp. 99–100.
6 Drane, 1999, pp. 146–9.
7 Zukav, 1990.
8 Levin, 2001, p. 4.
9 Levin, 2001, p. 296.
10 Sullivan, 2003, p. 13.

References

Ackerman Anderson, L. (1998), 'The Flow State: a New View of Organizations and Managing', in Adams, J. (ed.), *Transforming Work*, 2nd edn, Miles River Press (1st edn 1984).

Adair, J. (2002), *How to Find Your Vocation: A Guide to Discovering the Work You Love*, Canterbury Press (1st edn 2000).

Adams, J. (ed.) (1998a), *Transforming Work*, 2nd edn, Miles River Press (1st edn 1984).

Adams, J. (ed.) (1998b), *Transforming Leadership*, 2nd edn, Miles River Press.

Alkhafagi, A. (2000), 'What Does Spirituality Mean for Me?', in Biberman, J., and Whitty, M. (eds), *Work and Spirit: A Reader of New Spiritual Paradigms for Organizations*, University of Scranton Press, Scranton.

Allen, R., and Kraft, C. (1998), 'Transformations that Last: A Cultural Approach', in Adams, J. (ed.), *Transforming Work*, 2nd edn, Miles River Press (1st edn 1984).

Anthony, R., Ecker, B., and Wilber, K. (eds) (1997), *Spiritual Choices*, Paragon House, New York.

Arrien, A. (1993), *The Four-fold Way: Walking the Path of the Warrior, Teacher, Healer and Visionary*, HarperCollins, San Francisco.

Arrien, A. (1996), 'Shape-Shifting the Work Experience', in Renesch, J., and DeFoore, W. (eds), *The New Bottom Line: Bringing Heart and Soul to Business*, New Leaders Press/Sterling and Stone, San Francisco.

Barrett, R. (1998), *Liberating the Corporate Soul: Building a Visionary Organization*, Butterworth-Heinemann.

Bartlett, C. A., and Ghoshal, S. (1995), 'Changing the Role of Top Management: Beyond Systems to People', *Harvard Business Review*, May–June 1995.

Bateson, G. (1985), *Steps to an Ecology of Mind*, Ballantine, New York (1st edn Granada, 1973).

Bayrak, T. (1985), *The Most Beautiful Names*, Threshold Books, Putney, VT.

Beck, D., and Cowan, C. (1996), *Spiral Dynamics: Mastering Values, Leadership and Change*, Blackwell.

Bell, E., and Taylor, S. (2002), 'Knowing as a Way of Being: the Spiritual Dimension of Management Education'. Paper for the 1st International Conference on Organizational Spirituality: Living Spirit – New Dimensions in Work and Learning, University of Surrey, UK, July 22–24, 2002.

Bennis, W. (1994), *On Becoming a Leader*, 2nd edn, Perseus.

Berg, Y. (2003), *The Power of the Kabbalah*, Hodder and Stoughton (1st edn 2001).

Berry, T. (1998), *The Dream of the Earth*, Sierra Club, San Francisco.

The Bhagavad Gita, tr. J. Mascaro (1962), Penguin.

Biberman, J., and Whitty, M. (eds) (2000), *Work and Spirit: A Reader of New Spiritual Paradigms for Organizations*, University of Scranton Press, Scranton.

Biberman, J., Whitty, M., and Robbins, L. (2000), 'Lessons from Oz: Balance and Wholeness in Organizations', in Biberman, J., and Whitty, M. (eds), *Work and Spirit: A Reader of New Spiritual Paradigms for Organizations*, University of Scranton Press, Scranton.

Block, P. (1993), *Stewardship: Choosing Service over Self-Interest*, Berrett-Koehler, San Francisco.

Bohm, D. (1995), *Wholeness and the Implicate Order*, Routledge (1st edn 1980).

Boje, D. (2000), 'Festivalism at Work: Towards Ahimsa in Production and Consumption', in Biberman, J. and Whitty, M. (eds), *Work and Spirit: A Reader of New Spiritual Paradigms for Organizations*, University of Scranton Press, Scranton.

Briggs, I. with Myers, P. B. (1995), *Gifts Differing*, Davies-Black, Palo Alto, CA.

Briskin, A. (1998), *The Stirring of Soul in the Workplace*, Berrett-Koehler, San Francisco (1st edn Jossey-Bass, 1996).

Brueggemann, W. (2001), *The Prophetic Imagination*, 2nd edn, Fortress Press, Minneapolis.

Buber, M., tr. W. Kaufmann (1970), *I and Thou*, Charles Scribner's Sons, New York.

Buckingham, M., and Clifton, D. (2002), *Now Discover Your Strengths: How to Develop Your Talents and Those of the People You Manage*, Free Press.

Buckingham, M., and Coffman, C. (1999), *First Break All the Rules: What the World's Greatest Managers Do Differently*, Simon and Schuster.

Buckley, K., and Perkins, D. (1998), 'Managing the Complexity of Organizational Transformation', in Adams, J. (ed.), *Transforming Work*, 2nd edn, Miles River Press (1st edn 1984).

Burack, E. (2000), 'Spirituality in the Workplace', in Biberman, J., and Whitty, M. (eds), *Work and Spirit: A Reader of New Spiritual Paradigms for Organizations*, University of Scranton Press, Scranton.

Burgoyne, J., and Reynolds, M. (1997), *Management Learning: Integrating Perspectives in Theory and Practice*, Sage.

Butts, D. (2000), 'Spirituality at Work: An Overview', in Biberman, J., and Whitty, M. (eds), *Work and Spirit: A Reader of New Spiritual Paradigms for Organizations*, University of Scranton Press, Scranton.

Campbell, J. (1968), *The Hero with a Thousand Faces*, Princeton University Press, Princeton, NJ (1st edn 1949).

Capra, F. (1982), *The Tao of Physics*, Flamingo (1st edn 1976).

Capra, F. (1983), *The Turning Point*, Flamingo (1st edn 1982).

Capra, F. (1995), *The Web of Life*, Anchor Doubleday, New York.

Caridas, E. (1996), 'Participative Work and the Human Spirit', in Renesch, J., and DeFoore, W. (eds), *The New Bottom Line: Bringing Heart and Soul to Business*, New Leaders Press/Sterling and Stone, San Francisco.

Cavanagh, G. (2000), 'Spirituality for Managers', in Biberman, J., and Whitty, M. (eds), *Work and Spirit: A Reader of New Spiritual Paradigms for Organizations*, University of Scranton Press, Scranton.

Chappell, T. (1993), *The Soul of a Business: Managing for Profit and the Common Good*, Bantam Books, New York.

Chia, R. (1997), 'Process Philosophy and Management Learning: Cultivating "Foresight" in Management', in Burgoyne J., and Reynolds, M., *Management Learning: Integrating Perspectives in Theory and Practice*, Sage.

Chopra, D. (1996), *The Seven Spiritual Laws of Success: A Practical Guide to the Fulfillment of Your Dreams*, Bantam Press.

Chopra, D. (2000), *How to Know God*, Rider.

Cohen, B., and Greenfield, J. (1997), *Ben & Jerry's Double Dip: Lead with your Values and Make Money Too*, Simon and Schuster, New York.

Collins, J., and Porras, J. (1994), *Built to Last: Successful Habits of Visionary Companies*, Harper Business, New York.

Conger, J. (1994), *Spirit at Work: Discovering the Spirituality in Leadership*, Jossey-Bass, San Francisco.

Cook, S. (2003), 'Who Cares Wins', in *Management Today*, January issue, pp. 40–7.

Covey, S. (1992), *The 7 Habits of Highly Effective People*, Simon and Schuster (1st edn 1989).

Csikszentmihalyi, M. (1998), *Finding Flow: The Psychology of Engagement with Everyday Life*, Basic Books.

Cunningham, I. (1994), *The Wisdom of Strategic Learning*, McGraw-Hill.

Darley, P. (2002), 'Book Review: Natural Capitalism – the Next Industrial Revolution', *Faith in Business Quarterly*, Vol. 6 No. 1.

Davies, P. (1990), *God and the New Physics*, Penguin (1st edn 1983).

Davies, P., and Gribbin, J. (1991), *The Matter Myth: Towards 21st-Century Science*, Viking (1st edn Century, 1990).

Davies, P. (1993), *The Mind of God*, Penguin (1st edn 1992).

De Bivort, L. (1998), 'Fast-tracking the Transformation of Organizations', in Adams, J. (ed.), *Transforming Work*, 2nd edn, Miles River Press (1st edn 1984).

DeFoore, W. (1996), 'The Self-Healing Spirit of Commerce', in Renesch, J., and DeFoore, W. (eds), *The New Bottom Line: Bringing Heart and Soul to Business*, New Leaders Press/Sterling and Stone, San Francisco.

de Geus, Arie, (1999), *The Living Company: Growth, Learning and Longevity in Business*, Nicholas Brealey.

Delbecq, A. (2000), 'Spirituality for Business Leadership: Reporting on a Pilot Course for MBAs and CEOs', *Journal of Management Inquiry*, Vol. 9, No. 2.

Delbecq, A. (2001), '"Evil" Manifested in Destructive Individual Behavior: A Senior Leadership Challenge', *Journal of Management Inquiry*, Vol. 10, No. 3.

de Mello, A. (1984), *Sadhana: A Way to God – Christian Exercises in Eastern Form*, Doubleday (1st edn 1978).

DePree, M. (1992), *Leadership Jazz*, Dell, New York.

Dixon, N. (1998), *Dialogue at Work: Making Talk Developmental for People and Organizations*, Lemos and Crane.

Drane, J. (1999), *What is the New Age Still Saying to the Churches?*, Marshall Pickering.

Drucker, P. (1996), 'Foreword' to Hesselbein, F., Goldsmith, M., and Beckhard, R. (eds), *The Leader of the Future*, Jossey-Bass, San Francisco.

Easterby-Smith, M. (1997), 'Disciplines of Organizational Learning: Contributions and Critiques', *Human Relations*, Vol. 50, Issue 9.

Egan, J., and Wilson, D. (2002), *Private Business – Public Battleground: The Case for 21st Century Stakeholder Companies*, Palgrave.

Emmons, R. A. (2000), 'Is Spirituality an Intelligence? Motivation, Cognition and the Psychology of Ultimate Concerns', *The International Journal for the Psychology of Religion*, Vol. 10, No. 1., cited in Tischler, L., Biberman, J. and McKeage, R., 'Linking Emotional Intelligence, Spirituality and Workplace Performance', *Journal of Managerial Psychology*, Vol. 17, No. 3 (special edition on Spirituality, Leadership, Work and Organisations).

Fabry, J. (1980), 'Use of the Transpersonal in Logotherapy', in Boorstein, S. (ed.), *Transpersonal Psychotherapy*, Science and Behaviour, Palo Alto, CA.

Fetzer Institute (2001), *Centered on the Edge: Mapping a Field of Collective Intelligence and Spiritual Wisdom*, Morgan Press (see www.CenteredOnTheEdge.org or www.Fetzer.org/resources/CenteredOnTheEdge).

Fox, M. (1983), *Original Blessing*, Bear, Santa Fe.

Fox, M. (ed.) (1987), *Hildegard of Bingen's Books*, Bear, Santa Fe.

Fox, M. (1988), *The Coming of the Cosmic Christ*, HarperSanFrancisco.

Fox, M. (1991), *Creation Spirituality: Liberating Gifts for the People of the Earth*, HarperCollins.

Fox, M. (1994), *The Reinvention of Work: A New Vision of Livelihood for our Time*, HarperSanFrancisco.

Fox, M. (2003), *Creativity: Where the Divine and the Human Meet*, Tarcher (1st edn 2002).

Gardner, H. (1993), *Multiple Intelligences*, HarperCollins (Basic Books), New York.

George, W. (1996), 'Foreword' to Renesch, J., and DeFoore, W. (eds), *The New Bottom Line: Bringing Heart and Soul to Business*, New Leaders Press/Sterling and Stone, San Francisco.

Gibbons, P. (1999), 'Spirituality at Work: A Pre-theoretical Overview'. Dissertation for the MSc in Organisational Behaviour, Birkbeck College, University of London. Unpublished but available from paulgibbo@aol.com.

Gibbons, P. (2000), 'Spirituality at Work: Definitions, Measures, Assumptions and Validity Claims', in Biberman, J., and Whitty, M. (eds), *Work and Spirit: A Reader of New Spiritual Paradigms for Organizations*, Scranton University Press, Scranton.

Gilley, K. (1996), 'Conscious Leadership: Bringing Life to Social Responsibility', in Renesch, J. and DeFoore, W. (eds), *The New Bottom Line: Bringing Heart and Soul to Business*, New Leaders Press/Sterling and Stone, San Francisco.

Goleman, D. (1996), *Emotional Intelligence: Why It Can Matter More Than IQ*, Bloomsbury.

Goleman, D. (1998), *Working with the Emotional Intelligence*, Bantam Books.

Gratton, L. (2000), *Living Strategy: Putting People at the Heart of Corporate Purpose*, Financial Times/Prentice Hall (Pearson Education).

Greenleaf, R. (1977), *Servant Leadership: A Journey into the Nature of Legitimate Power and Greatness*, Paulist Press, New York.

Grof, S. (1979), *Realms of the Human Unconscious*, Souvenir Press.

Grof, S. (2000), *Psychology of the Future: Lessons from Modern Consciousness Research*, State University of New York.

Guillory, W. (1997), *The Living Organization: Spirituality in the Workplace*, Innovations International, Salt Lake City, Utah.

Guss, E. (2000), 'On Finding an Integrated Path', in Biberman, J., and Whitty, M. (eds), *Work and Spirit: A Reader of New Spiritual Paradigms for Organizations*, University of Scranton Press, Scranton.

Haessly, J. (1996), 'Transformation and the World of Commerce', in Renesch, J., and DeFoore, W. (eds), *The New Bottom Line: Bringing Heart and Soul to Business*, New Leaders Press/Sterling and Stone, San Francisco.

Harrison, R. (1998), 'Leadership and Strategy for a New Age', in Adams, D. (ed.), *Transforming Work*, (2nd edn), Miles River Press (1st edn 1984).

Hauser, L. (1996), 'The Intangible Dimension: Can You Afford to Neglect It?', in Renesch, J., and DeFoore, W. (eds), *The New Bottom Line: Bringing Heart and Soul to Business*, New Leaders Press/Sterling and Stone, San Francisco.

Hawken, P., Lovins A., and Lovins, H. (1999), *Natural Capitalism: the Next Industrial Revolution*, Earthscan.

Hawkins, P. (1991), 'The Spiritual Dimension of the Learning Organisation', *Management Education and Development Journal* (now re-titled *Management Learning*), Vol. 22, part 3.

Hay, D. (1990), *Religious Experience Today: Studying the Facts*, Mowbray.

Hayman, R. (1999), *A Life of Jung*, Bloomsbury.

Heaton, D. (2000), 'Holistic Health for Holistic Management', in Biberman, J., and Whitty, M. (eds), *Work and Spirit: A Reader of New Spiritual Paradigms for Organizations*. University of Scranton Press, Scranton.

Heermann, B. (1996), 'The Spirit of Team' in Renesch, J., and DeFoore, W. (eds), *The New Bottom Line: Bringing Heart and Soul to Business*, New Leaders Press/Sterling and Stone, San Francisco.

Helliwell, T. (2000), *Take Your Soul to Work*, Adams Media Business.

Heron, J. (1988), *Cosmic Psychology*, Endymion Press.

Heron, J. (1992), *Feeling and Personhood: Psychology in Another Key*, Sage.

Heslam, P. (ed.) (2004), *Globalization and the Good*, SPCK.

Hess, E. (1995), 'Character in the Marketplace', in Eberly, D. (ed.), *The Content of America's Character: Recovering Civic Virtue*, Madison Books.

Hesselbein, F., Goldsmith, M., and Beckhard, R. (eds) (1996), *The Leader of the Future*, Jossey-Bass, San Francisco.

Heuerman, T., Web pamphlet 47 (see Resources for details).

Hobday, J. (1992), 'Neither Late Nor Working', *Creation Spirituality*, May/June issue.

Hogan, L. (2000), 'A Framework for the Practical Application of Spirituality at Work', in Biberman, J., and Whitty, M. (eds), *Work and Spirit: A Reader of New Spiritual Paradigms for Organizations*, University of Scranton Press, Scranton.

Holland, J. L. (1997), *Making Vocational Choices*, 3rd edn, Psychological Assessment Resources, Florida.

Howard, S. (2000), 'Spirituality and its Links to Learning in the Workplace'. Unpublished Dissertation for Master's in Management Learning (MAML 17), Lancaster University. Available from Sue at suejfhoward@hotmail.com.

Hurley, T. (2001), 'The Cauldron and the Crystal: Awakening to the Truth of Our Experience', from an interview with Alan Briskin, in Fetzer Institute, *Centered on the Edge: Mapping a Field of Collective Intelligence and Spiritual Wisdom*, Morgan Press (see www.CenteredOnTheEdge.org or www.Fetzer.org/resources/CenteredOnTheEdge).

Isaacs, W. (1994), 'Dialogue', in Senge, P., Roberts, C., Ross, R., Smith, B., and Kleiner, A., *The Fifth Discipline Fieldbook: Strategies and Tools for Building and Learning Organization*, Nicholas Brealey.

Isaacs, W. (1999), *Dialogue and the Art of Thinking Together*, Doubleday, Random House.

James, W. (1974), *The Varieties of Religious Experience*, Collins, London (1st edn 1901).

Janni, N. (2000), 'Uniting Body, Heart, Mind and Spirit', Guest Chapter 20 in Nixon, B., *Global Forces*, Management Books.

Japanese Science Council (2000), 'Towards a Comprehensive Solution to Problems in Education and the Environment'.

Jaworski, J. (1998), *Synchronicity: The Inner Path of Leadership*, Berrett-Koehler, San Francisco.

Joseph, M. (2000), 'Spirituality in the Workplace – What are we talking about?', *Faith in Business Quarterly*, Vol. 4, No. 3.

Joseph, M. (2002), 'Leaders and Spirituality: A Case Study'. Unpublished PhD Dissertation, University of Surrey.

Journal of Managerial Psychology (2002) (special issue on Spirituality, Leadership, Work and Organizations), Vol. 17, No. 3.

Jung, C. G. (1973), 'Two Essays in Analytical Psychology', *Collected Works Vol. 7*, Routledge and Kegan Paul.

Kabat-Zinn, J. (1994), *Wherever You Go, There You Are: Mindfulness Meditation in Everyday Life*, Hyperion, New York.

Kiefer, C., and Senge, P. (1998), 'Metanoic Organizations', in Adams, D. (ed.), *Transforming Work*, 2nd edn, Miles River Press (1st edn 1984).

King, S., Biberman, J., Robbins, L., and Nicol, D. (2000), 'Integrating Spirituality into Management Education in Academia and Organizations: Origins, a Conceptual Framework, and Current Practices', in Biberman, J., and Whitty, M. (eds), *Work and Spirit: A Reader of New Spiritual Paradigms for Organizations*, University of Scranton Press, Scranton.

King, S., and Nicol, D. (2000), 'Organizational Enhancement through Recognition of Individual Spirituality: Reflections of Jaques and Jung', in Biberman, J., and Whitty, M. (eds), *Work and Spirit: A Reader of New Spiritual Paradigms for Organizations*, University of Scranton Press, Scranton.

King, U. (1997), *Christ in All Things*, SCM Press.

Kippenberger, T. (2002), *Leadership Express*, Capstone Publishing.

Knight, S. (1995), *NLP at Work: The Difference that Makes a Difference in Business*, Nicholas Brealey.

Knowles, M. (1980), *The Modern Practice of Adult Education*, Follett, Chicago.

Konz, G., and Ryan, F. (2000), 'Maintaining an Organizational Spirituality: No Easy Task', in Biberman, J., and Whitty, M. (eds), *Work and Spirit: A Reader of New Spiritual Paradigms for Organizations*, University of Scranton Press, Scranton.

Korac-Kakabadse, N. (2002), Guest Editorial, in *Journal of Managerial Psychology* (special issue on Spirituality, Leadership, Work and Organisations), Vol. 17, No. 3.

Korac-Kakabadse, N., Kouzmin, A., and Kakabadse, A. (2002), 'Spirituality and Leadership Praxis', in *Journal of Managerial Psychology* (special issue on Spirituality, Leadership, Work and Organisations), Vol. 17, No. 3.

Korten, D. (1995), *When Corporations Rule the World*, Kumarian Press, West Hartford, CT, and Berrett-Koehler, San Francisco.

Korten, D. (2000), *The Post-Corporate World: Life after Capitalism*, Kumarian Press, West Hartford, CT, and Berrett-Koehler, San Francisco.

Kriger, M., and Hanson, B. (2000), 'A Values-Based Paradigm for Creating Truly Healthy Organizations', in Biberman, J., and Whitty, M. (eds), *Work and Spirit: A Reader of New Spiritual Paradigms for Organizations*, University of Scranton Press, Scranton.

Kuhn, T. (1996), *The Structure of Scientific Revolutions*, University of Chicago Press (1st edn 1962).

Lamont, G., and Burns, S. (1995), *Values and Visions*, Hodder and Stoughton.

Lamont, G. (2002), *The Spirited Business: Success Stories of Soul-friendly Companies*, Hodder and Stoughton.

Lawrence, D. H. (1968), 'Morality and the Novel', in McDonald (ed.), *Phoenix: The Posthumous Papers of D. H. Lawrence*, Viking Press, New York (1st edn 1928).

Leakey, R., and Lewin, R. (1992), *Origins Reconsidered*, Doubleday, New York.

Levey, J. (1996), 'Consciousness, Caring, and Commerce: Sustainable Values for the Global Marketplace', in Renesch, J., and DeFoore, W. (eds), *The New Bottom Line: Bringing Heart and Soul to Business*, New Leaders Press/Sterling and Stone, San Francisco.

Levin, M. (2001), *Spiritual Intelligence: Awakening the Power of Your Spirituality and Intuition*, Coronet Books (1st edn 2000).

Levine, L. (1994), 'Listening with Spirit and the Art of Team Dialogue, *Journal of Organizational Change Management*, Vol. 7, No. 1, pp. 61–3.

Lievegoed, B. (1991), *Managing the Developing Organisation: Tapping the Spirit of Europe*, Blackwell.

Lips-Wiersma, M., and Mills, C. (2002), 'Coming out of the Closet: Negotiating Spiritual Expression in the Workplace', *Journal of Managerial Psychology* (special issue on Spirituality, Leadership, Work and Organizations), Vol. 17, No. 3.

Lovelock, J. (2000a), *Gaia: A New Look at Life on Earth*, Oxford University Press (1st edn 1979).

Lovelock, J. (2000b), *The Ages of Gaia: A Biography of our Living Earth*, Oxford University Press (1st edn 1988).

McDonald, M. (1999), 'Shush the Guy in the Cubicle is Meditating', *Business and Technology*, 5th March issue.

McGeachy, C. (2001), *Spiritual Intelligence in the Workplace*, Veritas.

McKnight, R. (1998), 'Spirituality in the Workplace', in Adams, J. (ed.), *Transforming Work*, 2nd edn, Miles River Press (1st edn 1984).

Macy, J. (1991), *World as Lover, World as Self*, Parallax Press, Berkeley.

Maitland, S. (1995), *A Big Enough God?*, Mowbray.

Makiguchi, T., and Birnbaum, A. (1989), *Education for Creative Living: Ideas and Proposals of Tsunesaburo Makiguch*, Iowa State University Press, Ames.

Marcic, D. (1997), *Leading with the Wisdom of Love: Uncovering Virtue in People and Organizations*, Jossey-Bass, San Francisco.

Marcic, D. (2000), 'Hospitable to the Human Spirit: An Imperative for Organizations', in Biberman, J., and Whitty, M. (eds), *Work and Spirit: A Reader of New Spiritual Paradigms for Organizations*, University of Scranton Press, Scranton.

Marshall, R. (2000), *God @ Work*, Destiny Image Publishers, PA.

Maslow, A. H. (1970), *Motivation and Personality*, Harper and Row.

Maslow, A. H. (1973), *The Further Reaches of Human Nature*, Penguin.

Melrose, K. (1995), *Making the Grass Greener on Your Side: A CEO's Journey to Leading and Serving*, Berrett-Koehler, San Francisco.

Mezirow, J. (1991), *Transformative Dimensions of Adult Learning*, Jossey-Bass, San Francisco.

Milliman, J., Ferguson, J., Trickett, D., and Condemi, B. (2000), 'Spirit and Community at Southwest Airlines: An Investigation of a Spiritual Values-based Model', in Biberman, J., and Whitty, M. (eds), *Work and Spirit: A Reader of New Spiritual Paradigms for Organizations*, University of Scranton Press, Scranton.

Mintzberg, H. (1976), 'Planning on the Left Side and Managing on the Right', *Harvard Business Review*, Vol. 54, No. 4.

Mitroff I., and Denton E. (1999a), 'A Study of Spirituality in the Workplace', *Sloan Management Review*, Vol. 40, Issue 4, pp. 78–84.

Mitroff, I., and Denton E. (1999b), *A Spiritual Audit of Corporate America: A Hard Look at Spirituality, Religion and Values in the Workplace*, Jossey-Bass, San Francisco.

MODEM (1999): Nelson, J. (ed.), *Leading, Managing, Ministering: Challenging Questions for Church and Society*. Canterbury Press, Norwich.

Moore, T. (1992), *Care of the Soul*, Piatkus.

Morgan, G. (1986), *Images of Organization*, Sage, Newbury Park, CA.

Moxley, R. (2000), *Leadership and Spirit: Breathing New Vitality and Energy into Individuals and Organizations*, Centre for Creative Leadership/Jossey-Bass, San Francisco.

Murphy, M., and Donovan, S. (1996), *The Physical and Psychological Effects of Meditation: A Review of Contemporary Research with a Comprehensive Bibliography 1931–1996*, 2nd edn, Institute of Noetic Sciences, Salsalito, CA.

Musson, G., and Cohen, C. (1999), 'Understanding Language Processes: A Neglected Skill in the Management Curriculum', *Management Learning*, March issue.

Neal, J., Bergmann Lichtenstein, B., and Banner, D. (2000), 'Spiritual Perspectives on Organizational and Societal Transformation', in Biberman, J., and Whitty, M. (eds), *Work and Spirit: A Reader of New Spiritual Paradigms for Organizations*, University of Scranton Press, Scranton.

Needleman, J. (2001), 'The Group as Art Form', from an interview with Alan Briskin, in Fetzer Institute, *Centered on the Edge: Mapping a Field of Collective Intelligence and Spiritual Wisdom*, Morgan Press (see www.CenteredOnTheEdge.org or www.Fetzer.org/resources/CenteredOnTheEdge).

Nixon, B. (2000), *Global Forces*, Management Books.

Nordstrom, K., and Ridderstale, J. (2001), *Funky Business*, Financial Times/Prentice Hall.

O'Connor, E. (1971), *The Eighth Day of Creation*, Word Books, Waco, TX.

Okri, B. (1999), *Mental Fight*, Phoenix House.

Ó Murchú, D. (1997), *Reclaiming Spirituality*, Gateway.

Owen, H. (1987), *Spirit: Transformation and Development in Organizations*, Abbott, Potomac, MD.

Owen, H. (1998), 'Facilitating Organizational Transformation: the Uses of Myth and Ritual', in Adams, J. (ed.), *Transforming Work*, 2nd edn, Miles River Press (1st edn 1984).

Pearson, C. (1998), *The Hero Within: Six Archetypes We Live By*, HarperCollins.

Peppers, C., and Briskin, A. (2000), *Bringing Your Soul to Work*, Berrett-Koehler, San Francisco.

Pettifer, B. (ed.) (2000), 'Spiritual Energy in Management'. The summary report of the MODEM research project 'The Hope of Managers', available from www.modem.uk.com.

Pieper, J. (1965), *Leisure the Basis of Culture*, Fontana (1st edn Faber and Faber).

Pir Vilayat Inayat Khan (2000), *Thinking Like the Universe: The Sufi Path of Awakening*. Thorsons/HarperCollins (1st edn 1999).

Porth, S., McCall, J., and Bausch, T. (2000), 'Spiritual Themes of the "Learning Organization"', in Biberman, J., and Whitty, M., *Work and Spirit: A Reader in New Spiritual Paradigms for Organizations*, University of Scranton Press, Scranton.

Potter, D. (1996), 'Journey into the Soul of an Organization', in Renesch J., and DeFoore, W. (eds), *The New Bottom Line: Bringing Heart and Soul to Business*, New Leaders Press/Sterling and Stone, San Francisco.

Randall, R., and Southgate, J. (1980), *Co-operative and Community Group Dynamics . . . or your meetings needn't be so appalling*, Barefoot Books.

Rankin, M. (1996), 'Spiritual Entrepreneuring', in Renesch, J., and DeFoore, W. (eds), *The New Bottom Line: Bringing Heart and Soul to Business*, New Leaders Press/Sterling and Stone, San Francisco.

Reason, P. (1998a), 'Co-operative Inquiry as a Discipline of Professional Practice', *Journal of Interprofessional Care*, Vol. 12 No. 4.

Reason, P. (1998b), 'Participatory World', *Resurgence*, No. 186.

Reid, L. A. (1986), *Ways of Understanding and Education*, Heinmann.

Renesch, J., and DeFoore, W. (eds) (1996), *The New Bottom Line: Bringing Heart and Soul to Business*, New Leaders Press/Sterling and Stone, San Francisco.

Richmond, L. (2000), *Work as a Spiritual Practice*, Bantam Doubleday Dell.

Rieser, C. (1995), 'Claiming Servant-Leadership as Your Heritage', in Spears, L. (ed.) *Reflections on Leadership: How Robert K. Greenleaf's Theory of Servant-Leadership Influenced Today's Top Management Thinkers*, Wiley, New York.

Rilke, R. M., tr. S. Mitchell (2001), *Letters to a Young Poet*, Random House.

Roddick, A. (1991), *Body and Soul*, Crown, New York.

Roddick, A. (1996), 'Finding Spirit through Service', in Renesch, J., and DeFoore, W. (eds), *The New Bottom Line: Bringing Heart and Soul to Business*, New Leaders Press/Sterling and Stone, San Francisco.

Rosile, G. (2000), 'Managing with Ahimsa and Horse Sense: A Convergence of Body, Mind and Spirit', in Biberman, J., and Whitty, M. (eds), *Work and Spirit: A Reader in New Spiritual Paradigms for Organizations*, University of Scranton Press, Scranton.

Rowan, J. (1993), *The Transpersonal: Psychotherapy and Counselling*, Routledge.

Ruether, R. R. (1993), *Gaia and God: An Ecofeminist Theology of Earth Healing*, SCM Press.

Russell, P. (2000), *From Science to God*, Peter Russell.

Salz, J. (2000), *The Way of Adventure: Transforming Your Life with Spirit and Vision*, John Wiley.

Schumacher, E. F. (1974), *Small is Beautiful: A Study of Economics as if People Mattered*, Abacus (1st edn Blond and Briggs, 1973).

Schumacher, E. F. (1980), *Good Work*, Abacus.

Scott Peck, M. (1993), *Further Along the Road Less Traveled: The Unending Journey towards Spiritual Growth*, Simon and Schuster.

Senge, P. (1990), *The Fifth Discipline: The Art and Practice of the Learning Organization*, Century Business.

Senge, P., with Kleiner, A., Roberts, C., Ross, R., and Smith, B. (1994), *The Fifth Discipline Fieldbook: Strategies and Tools for Building a Learning Organization*, Nicholas Brealey.

Senge, P. (1995), 'Robert Greenleaf's Legacy: A New Foundation for Twenty First Century Institutions', in Spears, L. (ed.), *Reflections on Leadership: How Robert K. Greenleaf's Theory of Servant-Leadership Influenced Today's Top Management Thinkers*, Wiley, New York.

Senge, P. (1996), Guest Introduction, in Jaworski, J., *Synchronicity: The Inner Path of Leadership*, Berrett-Koehler, San Francisco.

Sheldrake, P. (1995), *Spirituality and History: Questions of Interpretation and Method*, SPCK (1st edn 1991).

Sheldrake, R. (1985), *A New Science of Life: The Hypothesis of Formative Causation*, Anthony Blond (1st edn 1981).

Sheldrake, R. (1988), *The Presence of the Past*, Collins.

Sheldrake, R. (1991), *The Rebirth of Nature: The Greening of Science and God*, Rider (1st edn 1990).

Skelton, H., *Spirituality in the Workplace*, www.omegactr.com/source/spirwork.htm.

Skynner, R., and Cleese, J. (1993), *Life and How to Survive It*, Vermillion.

Slee, N. (2003), *Faith and Feminism: An Introduction to Christian Feminist Theology*, Darton, Longman and Todd.

Smith, C. (1987), *Spiritual Life as Taught by Meister Eckhart*, Darton, Longman and Todd.

Smith, H. (1991), *The World's Religions*, HarperSanFrancisco.

Sogyal Rinpoche (1998), *The Tibetan Book of Living and Dying*, Rider (1st edn 1992).

Soros, G. (1998), *The Crisis of Global Capitalism: Open Society Endangered*, Little, Brown.

Spears, L. (ed.) (1995), *Reflections on Leadership: How Robert K. Greenleaf's Theory of Servant-Leadership Influenced Today's Top Management Thinkers*, Wiley, New York.

Stacey, R. (1996), *Strategic Management and Organisational Dynamics*, 2nd edn, Pitman.

'The Stakeholder Economy', Parts 1 and 2, (1997), *Faith in Business Quarterly*, Vol. 1, Nos 3 and 4.

Stannard, R. (1993), *Doing Away with God?: Creation and the Big Bang*, Marshall Pickering.

Stephens, C., and Isen, S. (1998), 'Myth, Transformation and the Change Agent', in Adams, J. (ed.), *Transforming Work*, 2nd edn, Miles River Press (1st edn 1984).

Storr, A. (1995), *Jung*, Fontana (Modern Masters series).

Sullivan, P. (2003), *Work with Meaning, Work with Joy: Bringing Your Spirit to Any Job*, Sheed and Ward.

Swimme, B., and Berry, T. (1992), *The Universe Story: From the Primordial Flaring Forth to the Ecozoic Era*, HarperSanFrancisco.

Tao Te Ching: An Illustrated Journey (1999), tr. Mitchell, S., 1988, Frances Lincoln.

Teilhard de Chardin, P. (1964), *Le Milieu Divin*. Fontana.

Thich Nhat Hanh (1998), *The Heart of the Buddha's Teaching*, Rider.

Tischler, L., Biberman, J., and McKeage, R. (2002), 'Linking Emotional Intelligence, Spirituality and Workplace Performance', *Journal of Managerial Psychology* (Special Edition on Spirituality, Leadership, Work and Organisations), Vol. 17, No. 3.

Torbert, W. R. (1991), *The Power of Balance: Transforming Self, Society, and Scientific Inquiry*, Sage, Newbury Park, CA.

Tredget, D. (2000), 'Beyond the Obvious', *Faith in Business Quarterly*, Vol. 4, No. 1.

Turner, J. (1999), 'Spirituality in the Workplace', *CA* (Canadian Institute of Chartered Accountants) *Magazine*, Vol. 132, Issue 10.

Vaill, P. (1998a), 'Process Wisdom for a New Age', in Adams, D. (ed.), *Transforming Work*, 2nd edn, Miles River Press (1st edn 1984).

Vaill, P. (1998b), *Spirited Leading and Learning: Process Wisdom for a New Age*, Jossey-Bass, San Francisco.

Waddock, S. (2000), 'Linking Community and Spirit: A Commentary and Some Propositions', in Biberman, J., and Whitty, M. (eds), *Work and Spirit: A Reader of New Spiritual Paradigms for Organizations*, University of Scranton Press, Scranton.

Wagner-Marsh, F., and Conley, J. (2000), 'The Fourth Wave: The Spiritually Based Firm', in Biberman, J., and Whitty, M. (eds), *Work and Spirit: A Reader of New Spiritual Paradigms for Organizations*, University of Scranton Press, Scranton.

Wall Street Journal, 'After Their Checkup for the Body, Some Get One for the Soul', July 1998.

Watkins, J. (2003), 'Spiritual Guidance: A Report on Spirituality in the Workplace', in *People Management* (20 February issue).

Welbourn, D. (2000), 'A Spiritual Pilgrimage to Corporate America'. Unpublished report of a sabbatical study. Available from david@dwelbourn.freeserve.co.uk.

Wheatley, M. (1999), *Leadership and the New Science: Learning About Organization from an Orderly Universe*, Berrett-Koehler, San Francisco (1st edn 1992).

Wheatley, M. (2002), *Turning to One Another: Simple Conversations to Restore Hope to the Future*, Berrett-Koehler, San Francisco.

Whitmeyer, C. (ed.) (1994), *Mindfulness and Meaningful Work*, Parallax Press, Berkeley.

Whitmore, J. (2002), *Coaching for Performance: Growing People, Performance and Purpose*, 3rd edn, Nicholas Brealey.

Whyte, D. (1999), *The Heart Aroused: Poetry and the Preservation of the Soul at Work*, The Industrial Society.

Wilber, K. (2001a), *A Brief History of Everything*, Gateway (1st edn Shambhala, Boston, 1996).

Wilber, K. (2001b), *The Marriage of Sense and Soul*, Gateway (1st edn Random House, 1998).

Williams, N. (1999), *The Work We Were Born To Do: Find the Work you Love, Love the Work you Do*, Element.

Williams, P., and Davis, D. (2002), *The Therapist as Life Coach: Transforming Your Practice*, W.W. Norton.

Williamson, M. (1996), *A Return to Love*, Thorsons/HarperCollins (1st edn 1992).

Wilmott, H. (1997), 'Critical Management Learning', in Burgoyne, J., and Reynolds, M., *Management Learning: Integrating Perspectives in Theory and Practice*, Sage.

Witten, D., with Akong Tulku Rinpoche (1998), *Enlightened Management: Bringing Buddhist Principles to Work*, Rider (USA edn Park Street Press, 1999).

Woodhall, J., and Winstanley, D. (1998), *Management Development, Strategy and Practice*, Blackwell.

Wren-Lewis, J. (1991), 'A Reluctant Mystic', *Self and Society*, Vol. 19, No. 2.

Zohar, D. (1997), *Rewiring the Corporate Brain: Using the New Science to Rethink How We Structure and Lead Organizations*, Berrett-Koehler, San Francisco.

Zohar, D., and Marshall, I. (2001), *SQ: Spiritual Intelligence, The Ultimate Intelligence*, Bloomsbury (1st edn 2000).

Zukav, G. (1990), *The Seat of the Soul*, Rider.